Degree Course Descriptions

edited by
Ken Reynolds

Degree Course Descriptions

This 2015 edition published by Cambridge Occupational Analysts Ltd
Sparham, Norwich, NR9 5PR

Editorial and Publishing Team

Editor Ken Reynolds
Cover Design Made by PFD
Design and typesetting Simon Foster and Paul Rankin

© Cambridge Occupational Analysts 2015

British Library Cataloguing in Publication Data
A catalogue record for this book is available from the British Library.

ISBN 978-1-906711-20-7

Typeset by Cambridge Occupational Analysts Ltd, Sparham, Norwich NR9 5PR
Printed and bound in Great Britain by Clays Ltd, Bungay, Suffolk NR35 1ED

Contents

Introduction

The illustrious author of one of the Degree Course Descriptions in this book offers the following advice to aspiring students of his subject:

Explore, enquire, experiment and enjoy!

These words apply just as much to every other subject covered. How do you find the right course in higher education? How do you know where to study? There is no single truth; no simple answer. There are over 37,000 potential courses in more than 370 UK universities and colleges. It is down to you to find the most suitable course to meet your personal needs.

The Degree Course Descriptions offered should prove a valuable resource as you research your higher education goals. The articles are written in most cases by leading university professors and lecturers, and have been selected to cover the major degree course fields. They are regularly updated and checked for accuracy. The intention is to give a broad overview of each subject area rather than to promote courses at any particular institution.

Here's another top tip from one of our contributors: "Lecturers tend to focus their teaching on their research interests - the best lectures are given by enthusiasts, and active researchers are great enthusiasts!"

In addition to the Degree Course Descriptions, we offer a series of general articles on higher education and a selection of pieces covering specific issues:

General articles

- Online information and advice
- Budgeting
- Choosing a course
- Self-Select
- Admissions tests
- The UCAS tariff

Specific issues

- Applying for Art and Design courses
- Gap Year considerations
- Medicine dissected

Beyond the UK – degree courses in other countries

- Study programmes taught in English across Europe
- Undergraduate study in the United States
- Studying in Canada
- Study options in Australia and New Zealand

Disclaimer

While we have made every effort to ensure that the content of Degree Course Descriptions is accurate and up to date, we recognise that educational information is always changing and that broad descriptions cannot hope to cover every detail of every degree programme. We do not, therefore, accept any liability for errors, omissions or apparently misleading statements.

We welcome comments and suggestions for improvement. Please email any observations to: info@coa.co.uk

---

Online Information and Advice

Original article by Jasper Selwyn, formerly Head of Careers, Marlborough College

Introduction

Applying for admission to higher education is very much an online process nowadays. The essential starting point for almost all provision in the United Kingdom is the Universities and Colleges Admissions Service (UCAS) website at: **www.ucas.com**

The equivalent for students in the Republic of Ireland is the Central Applications Office (CAO) website at: **www.cao.ie**

Either website will give you several options. From the UCAS home page, for example, clicking on 'How it all works' at the top of the page will open up several pages of detailed information on how to research appropriate courses and course providers, how to complete your application and how to submit it at the right time. You will almost certainly want to spend a lot of time in the 'Search for courses' section, in which you say where you normally live and enter a course title to obtain details of all higher education institutions (HEIs) offering relevant undergraduate degrees. Clicking on 'view all relevant courses' for any HEI starts a process leading to a summary of entry requirements, fees and finances and all the codes needed to make an application. You can also link directly to the HEI's own website to research more detailed information.

HEI websites are all organised differently but generally include:

- News about the institution

- Descriptions of facilities

- Lists of courses, which may get as detailed as individual lecture notes if you go on digging

- Names of lecturers, with email addresses. Click on one and you can send an email straight away

- Information about accommodation, the surrounding area and so on

Working online allows you to proceed at your own pace, gradually making sense of a vast amount of information and extracting just what you need to meet your own requirements. The UCAS website alone has details of some 37,000 courses at more than 370 HEIs. UCAS placed 495,600 people into higher education in the 2013 cycle, an increase of 30,700 (6.6%) on 2012 entry and the highest number ever recorded. With a 73.2% acceptance rate, university entry remains competitive, making it important that you present yourself as a strong, well-informed applicant.

You can look up the advice you need at any time, wherever you are, via the UCAS website. A single click from the homepage gives access to UCAS' Twitter, LinkedIn, YouTube and Facebook pages, where you can watch short videos and read real-time answers from expert advisers.

To see the full range of services on offer visit UCAS Connect at **www.ucasconnect.com**

Having researched all the relevant information, you can apply online and subsequently track your application to see how it is progressing.

You can start doing this after UCAS has sent you a Welcome email, logging in anytime with the Personal ID contained in your email, along with the username and password you applied with. UCAS will email you whenever there's an update to your application.

Finding a focus

If you are struggling to decide which course and institution might suit you, you could start by making use of *Centigrade Online*.

Centigrade Online analyses your interests, study subjects and qualifications before inviting you to explore up to eight strongly matched course areas. Once you have answered the questionnaire, publishers COA will send you a detailed bound report with your best-matched selections. Centigrade costs £30 in the UK or £35 overseas for a full-colour printed personal report of approximately 48 pages. The service is also available with an emailed report for just £20.

Further Information

Woody's Webwatch - independent tips on post-18 options from a committed teacher
www.facebook.com/woodyswebwatch

Centigrade Online
www.centigradeonline.co.uk

The Student Room - online community of secondary school, sixth form and university students
www.thestudentroom.co.uk

Unistats - an official site to help you compare subjects at different HEIs in the UK
http://unistats.direct.gov.uk

Qualifax – the national learners' database in Ireland
www.qualifax.ie

Budgeting

How much will it cost you to be a student in higher education? The answer depends to a large extent on what you study, where you live and how extravagant a lifestyle you aspire to.

There are two major financial elements to consider when planning your studies in the UK: course tuition fees and living costs. Tuition fees can be extremely complex to calculate, depending on whether you have 'home' or 'overseas' status, where you live in the United Kingdom and where you intend to study. For example, an English student starting at an English university in 2014 will have to pay tuition fees of up to £9,000 per year. An eligible Scottish student starting a similar course in Scotland will pay nothing, while a Welsh student can get a grant of £5,315 towards fees of £9,000 anywhere in the UK and will pay only up to £3,685 per year. A non-EU overseas student in England will usually have to pay the full economic rate. Cambridge, for example, currently quotes £15,063 per year for an arts degree, £16,800 for mathematics, £22,923 for engineering, and £36,459 for medicine. On top of this, there are college fees which can range from £5,500 to £6,500 per year, and the University warns that all fees are likely to increase in subsequent years. You may be able to reduce the impact of tuition fees by obtaining a grant, scholarship or bursary. Most higher education institutions (HEIs) provide details of possible financial support via each course entry profile on the UCAS website. Failing any other form of support, you may be able to secure a loan to cover your tuition fees for the duration of your course.

As for living costs, we identify the key components and illustrate how you can plan to manage your finances when living as a student.

Accommodation

Unless you are lucky enough to be offered free accommodation at home, or with friends or relations, you will find that getting a roof over your head will make the greatest demands on your non-fee finances, usually taking away at least half and sometimes as much as three-quarters of your budget.

It is essential to find a suitable place to live, especially during the first twelve months. Everything else revolves around your feeling secure and comfortable - your attitude to student life, your ability to focus on studying successfully, your opportunities to make new friendships and so on. Will you, for example, be able to walk to your study centre or will you have to make a long and possibly expensive journey every day? Do you want to be surrounded by other students or do you crave peace and quiet?

Before you accept a place, contact the accommodation office at your chosen university or college to check out the service on offer. Is there official accommodation in a hall of residence? Will you get a priority place if you need to travel a long way to start your course? Are meals provided? Would you be expected to share a room? Can you inspect the accommodation before you sign any agreement? Does the accommodation office have a list of approved premises in the private sector?

Here are some key points to consider:

- *Cost.* Ask especially how many weeks you have to pay for. Is it term-time only (in which case you would have to go home or find somewhere else to live during the vacations) or do you have to take out a full ten- or twelve-month rental agreement?

- *Catering.* How many meals are supplied a day, if any? Are meals provided at weekends or Monday to Friday only? Do you have access to a kitchen to prepare your own meals?

- *Space.* How big are the rooms? Do you have to share? Is there an en-suite bathroom?

- *Transport and travel.* Will you be on-campus or many miles away? What sort of transport is available and how much does it cost?

- *Local services.* Would you have easy access to a bank, shops and leisure facilities?

- *Insurance.* Is there a comprehensive policy covering all students in a hall of residence? How secure are the doors and windows? Is crime a serious problem?

The average rent for a room in purpose-built student accommodation has gone up by 25% over the past three years to just under £124 a week, according to the latest figures from the National Union of Students (NUS). That is guaranteed to take up most of the maximum available student maintenance loan of £5,740 (£8,009 in London) if you come from England, with slightly different figures applying for other UK countries.

There is, however, considerable variation in the weekly rents charged by different provider types. In purpose-built accommodation, for example, the average weekly rent is £118.49 in university-owned halls of residence, £119.83 in privately owned halls of residence linked to universities through a 'nomination' agreement but £140.07 in halls operated by private suppliers without institutional links.

Rents also vary depending on where in the country you are studying and on the category of accommodation you choose. Predictably, London is the area with the most expensive rents overall, averaging £157.48 a week. This is largely attributable to the increasing number of expensive privately run student studio flats in the capital, some of which cost more than £300 a week. The east of England has the second-highest rents for purpose-built student accommodation overall at £134.18 a week and Northern Ireland the cheapest at £83.01.

En-suite self-catered rooms, the most common type of accommodation accounting for 55% of the purpose-built market, cost an average of £121.71 per week for a single room, compared with an average of £97.48 for a single room with shared bathroom facilities. Shared non en-suite cluster flats have historically been at the more affordable end of student accommodation options, but this cheaper type of offering is shrinking as a proportion of the market and is not evenly spread among all universities. The number of bed spaces in catered accommodation is also declining, with students at institutions where this is available paying an average of £139.99 a week for a full-board single room or £165.36 for full-board en-suite.

Food

Unless it's already included in your accommodation costs, food will be your second major expense. Unlike property rents, the cost of food is fairly similar all over the UK. London students tend, however, to spend more on food, perhaps because there are so many tempting restaurants and other places to eat!

Expect to spend around £50 each week making sure that you are reasonably well fed.

Going out

You may intend to devote all of your time to your studies but most students feel that socialising is an important part of their life at university or college. This is a serious lifestyle decision for each individual and it could cost you anything from nothing to over £100 per week, depending on how gregarious you are, whether you have a taste for expensive concerts or theatres and how determined you are generally to have a good time.

Books, photocopying and stationery

Books can be exceptionally expensive but you don't necessarily have to buy a new copy of every book mentioned by your tutors. Check to see how well stocked the library is in your subject area and find out whether there is a good second-hand bookshop. You will almost certainly have to photocopy some material and you will have to make sure that you have adequate supplies of paper.

You may need to allow around £6 a week to cover these items.

Computer and other equipment

You may already own a computer and decide to bring it with you. If not, you could easily spend £1,000 on a new machine! Do you really need it or does your university or college offer 24-hour IT facilities?

You may be required to purchase materials and equipment for some courses, especially in areas such as science and design.

Telephone

It seems that no student can live in the 21st century without a mobile phone! How much it costs depends entirely on what sort of contract you sign up to. Many companies are keen to capture a slice of the student market and may offer a free phone plus other goodies if you take out a 24-month contract costing around £23 to £38 per month. On the other hand, you might happily settle for a simple Pay-as-you-go phone or make free calls on your computer via Skype.

Clothing

Even if you don't rush out every week to buy the latest fashions, you will need to allow a certain amount of money for new clothes. The average is around £15 per week but some students spend a great deal more.

Basics

You'll need to put some cash aside to wash your clothes and to keep yourself clean. You'll also have to pay for electricity and gas unless you are paying a fully inclusive charge in a hall of residence.

Travel

You may live on campus and walk or cycle everywhere but you could find yourself spending a small fortune if, say, you are living in a London suburb and have to commute every day to lectures in the centre of town.

It is generally not a good idea to drive your own car and we make no allowance for this in our calculations.

Plan your own budget!

Look at the figures in our rather modest student budget and then make your own projections about what it might cost you to be a student at your chosen university or college. We have left two columns blank for you to work out your own weekly and yearly expenses. Our calculations assume that you will need your accommodation for the full 52 weeks of the year but you may stay for, say, nine months or less and could make savings accordingly. You may want to repeat the exercise several times in order to get an idea of the real difference in costs between, say, London, Sunderland and Plymouth.

Item	Cost per week	Cost per year	Your weekly estimate	Your yearly estimate
Rent	£100	£5,200		
Food	£50	£2,600		
Electricity /Gas	£5	£260		
Clothes	£15	£780		
Telephone	£10	£520		
Basics - laundry and toiletries	£6	£312		
Travel	£5	£260		
Going out	£8	£416		
Books, equipment etc	£6	£312		
Total	£205	£10,660		

Remember that our figures don't allow for other expenditure such as insurance, TV licence, buying presents for friends and family, treating yourself to an occasional luxury or taking a weekend or more away from your studies from time to time.

Put everything together and you'll quickly see why you need to be budgeting for non-fee expenses of around £10,000 to £12,000 a year outside London and some £12,000 to £15,000 in London. Please let us know if your own calculations are very different from ours.

You can try to offset some of the expense by getting a job, working for up to 20 hours a week during term time and full-time during the vacations. Your university or college should be able to give you further information on employment options in the area. Depending on how many hours you work in total and how well you are paid, you may be able to cover a large amount of the living costs outlined in this article.

Tuition fee loans may be available to help pay the cost of your tuition fees. They are paid directly to your university or college by the government.

Living cost loans - also called maintenance loans - are also available for eligible full-time students to help pay for such living costs as food, travel, accommodation and so on.

In England and Wales, you don't have to start repaying your tuition fee and living cost loans until you are earning more than £21,000 a year. The equivalent figure in Scotland and Northern Ireland is £16,910.

Repayment is at a rate of 9% of your income over £21,000. If, for example, your salary is £25,000 a year, you pay 9% of £4,000 (£6.92 a week).

Interest in England and Wales is currently charged at the rate of inflation (based on the Retail Price Index or RPI) plus 3% from the date you take out the loan. Your repayments will be deducted automatically each month from your pay.

Be prepared!

The key message is to plan your finances carefully in advance. If you have thought about your budget and worked out how to cover the inevitable expense of eating and sleeping, you can focus on your studies without fretting too much about money.

Suggested Reading

Cut the Cost of Uni: Tips and Advice to make Uni Affordable
- Gwenda Thomas, Trotman, 2012

Brightside Student Calculator
- log on to: **www.studentcalculator.org**

Further Information

Student Finance (England)
www.gov.uk/student-finance/loans-and-grants

Student Awards Agency for Scotland
www.saas.gov.uk

Wales
www.studentfinancewales.co.uk

Northern Ireland
www.studentfinanceni.co.uk

Other EU countries
www.gov.uk/student-finance/who-qualifies

Non-EU international students (UK Council for International Student Affairs)
www.ukcisa.org.uk

Choosing a Higher Education Course in the UK

Original article by Jasper Selwyn, formerly Head of Careers, Marlborough College

Choosing a Higher Education Course:

You face a bewildering range of possibilities: over 37,000 different degree course options, covering 750 different subjects, at some 370 institutions in the UCAS scheme; courses with the same title can approach the subject in widely different ways; and you can only pick five to put on your form. You need to end up doing a course that motivates you and is suitable for your future career, at a place where you enjoy living. The entry requirements need to be within your reach. If you use an interests and ability questionnaire such as *Centigrade*, it will start the task for you by listing a range of different subject titles within some general areas which seem to match your interests, and identifying some specific courses. But you have to choose within that list, and you may want to move outside it. So how do you go about making your choice?

Three Ways to Choose Your Subject:

- **Forward from your school or college subjects:** If there is a subject you are enjoying and doing well at, you may wish to continue with it in Higher Education. But remember that the style of the course may be very different: in Modern Languages, for example, there could be more emphasis on studying literature. You may also be able to specialise in one area of a subject, such as Contemporary Literature, Economic History or Cell Biology.

- **Backwards from a career goal:** For the majority of careers, any Higher Education course is appropriate, and you are best advised to study something which will really interest you, so that you get a good qualification. For some, such as Law and Business, you can take a professional course at postgraduate level if you have not done the relevant first degree. You do not need any specific subject to become an accountant, a journalist or a marketing manager. Medicine and related careers, engineering, architecture, surveying, scientific research and translating are, however, examples of areas which do usually require a particular Higher Education course.

- **Leaping into the Unknown:** There are a vast number of subjects you can study in Higher Education which are not available at your school or college. If you have done *Centigrade* it may have come up with some, and it would be a pity to reject them just because you have not come across them before. Make sure that you find out as much as you can about them - sometimes what they actually involve turns out to be different from what you had assumed. Read the *Degree Course Descriptions* and do some background reading.

Types of Course:

- **Single Subject:** You may want to concentrate on the subject of your dreams, but often you will have the opportunity to do modules in other subjects as well, maybe unrelated to your main choice. Normally you will be expected to follow a broad course in the first year, but after that you will be allowed progressively to specialise. In the final year you are likely to complete a project on an area of your own choice.

- **Joint:** Many degree courses allow you to study two subjects. You may do both equally (X *and* Y), or you may spend more time on one of them (X *with* Y). You may be able to pick up a few modules in other subjects as well. The two main subjects may be formally linked (e.g. Business Studies with a Language) or they may be taught quite independently. A joint degree has the same number of modules in it as a single-subject one, so should not involve more hours, but having to switch continually between the disciplines may be intellectually challenging. You will not be able to explore a subject in as much depth if you are doing it as part of a joint course.

- **Combined:** There are some courses available which give great flexibility, allowing you to start with up to four subjects, and then discard some, and maybe take up new ones, as you move on. This is excellent if you have a wide range of interests, or feel you can't decide about a subject until you have tried it out. A combined course may also allow you to approach a particular theme from the viewpoints of different disciplines: for example Geography, Anthropology and Economics would all support an interest in International Development.

- **Sandwich:** Some people like to see how what they are learning relates to a career area, and employers value people with relevant work experience. A sandwich course builds in work placements alongside your study, so it normally lasts an extra year. A *thick* sandwich involves a full year of work, usually after the second year of study. A *thin* sandwich gives you several shorter periods of work (typically, three or four months each). Often your course tutors help you find a work placement, and almost always you are visited while working, and asked to write a report. You may well do a project in your final year based on a problem you have encountered in your work place. If you solve it, and save the company some money, obviously your prospects for a longer-term job after you graduate will be good!

- **Study Abroad:** The European Union operates a programme called Erasmus+ to encourage students to spend time in other European countries. Many courses (but not all) are linked to this programme, so that you can spend between four months and a year studying abroad. What you do counts toward your degree, you are given financial help if the cost of living in the other country is higher, and you will have tuition in the foreign language before you go. Some universities also have links with America, particularly for Engineering and Business courses, and of course American Studies. Many sandwich courses allow the option of a work placement abroad.

- **HND and Foundation Degree:** These courses are normally a year shorter than an honours degree, and the entrance requirements are lower. Students who do well can transfer easily onto a degree programme, and there are even some special one-year conversion programmes.

Choosing a Place:

It is important to start by deciding **what** you want to study, and with what kind of course structure. But you may find that the kind of course you want is available at a number of institutions, so you have to think about **where** to go. If you are going to spend three or four years of your life somewhere, it is important that you should enjoy being there.

- **Near or Far from Home?** For financial reasons you may need to live at home while you are studying, or you may want to be near enough to go home at weekends (although in practice university often takes over your social life, and you go home less and less often). You may want to break your ties with home completely, or just experience living in a different part of the country.

- **"Established" or Modern?** Some people like the idea of traditions and old buildings. But even at the oldest universities traditions may be dying out, and there are plenty of modern buildings. At a newer institution there may be more scope for starting new activities yourself.

- **Campus or Spread Out?** Most universities and colleges are on a self-contained campus, but a few (e.g. Bristol, Edinburgh) are spread over a wider area. Many have several separate campuses. Accommodation may be on the same campus as the teaching facilities, or it may be some distance away. You may appreciate the convenience of a self-contained campus, or you may find it claustrophobic.

- **City Centre or Semi-Rural?** If you are in the middle of a big city, then shops and entertainment are close by, but you have to put up with traffic and there may be security risks. Out-of-town campuses are peaceful and safe, and often students are more active at creating their own entertainment, but it is harder to escape and the architecture may get on your nerves.

- **A "Good" University:** A lot is said about the reputations of different institutions. League tables are published, sometimes based on rather doubtful criteria of excellence. Some employers express preferences, often favouring the university they went to themselves and others they have heard of. It is certainly true that standards vary from one place to another, and that some institutions develop a particular ethos (good or bad). But within the same institution there can be big differences between departments. It is important to visit the places which interest you most, and decide for yourself whether you like the department which is going to teach you. Ask about employment records, and talk to current students. Don't assume that higher A-level grade requirements mean a better course: they usually mean it is more popular, but that can be for a variety of reasons. Above all, remember that there is no such thing as a good course or a bad course, but only one which is good or bad for *you*.

Use a calendar of Open Days to plan visits to the places which interest you most. Refer to the Open Days information on the UCAS website (updated every week) and take advantage of the Taster Course opportunities, which allow you to spend several days living the life of an undergraduate.

Self-Select

Helping you choose the right course at the right institution to meet your personal needs

One of the key features of higher education in the UK is freedom of choice. You are free to decide what you want to study and where you would like to pursue your studies.

The system works very well for most people but it can sometimes be difficult to know where to start. The choice is simply so great that narrowing things down to one course in one place appears overwhelming.

Given that there is so much emphasis on individual choice and decision-making, we suggest the term 'Self-select' as a handy way of remembering ten key factors in the process of researching ideas and information to help you find your way through the fantastically rich maze of opportunities in our higher education system.

We'll run through the headings briefly at first before taking each in turn to explore in more detail exactly what we mean.

- Subject
- Employment prospects
- Location
- Finance

- Status
- Entry requirements
- Living arrangements
- Entertainment
- Community
- Time

Subject

We start with this because we feel that it really must be the starting point for most people. Once you have decided on this top priority, other things begin to fall into place behind it.

Of course, it's easy for us simply to say 'choose your subject' but the reality is much tougher for you. With some 37,000 different programmes of study on offer at 370+ institutions, you need to get down quickly to some hard thinking!

Here are some of the questions you should be asking yourself, together with our comments on the issues they raise:

Do I want to study a single subject or do I want to combine two or more subjects for my degree studies? If you are unsure, look for universities that offer a broad-based first year, allowing you to keep your options open while you find out what degree-level work is all about.

Do I want to continue with a subject I know from my school or college experience - English, Chemistry or French for example - or do I want to start something new at university - such as Film Studies, Medicine or European Law? An advantage of sticking with something you know is that you will already have a 'feel' for the subject and the confidence that comes from already having done well in it in recent exams. On the other hand, you may decide that you have gone far enough with that subject and are eager to seek stimulation in something entirely different.

Do I want to study a subject for its own sake - History, for example - because I like it or am I considering higher education purely as a route to obtaining a specific professional qualification? This is clearly related to the previous question and could be critical in helping you refine your choices. There is a world of difference between an academic degree in Biology and a vocational qualification in, say, Physiotherapy - even though the entry requirements may look broadly similar. The Physiotherapy course no doubt has a very focused employment record but this is only relevant if you are sure that you want to work as a physiotherapist!

Don't assume, by the way, that subjects with similar titles have the same content or are taught in the same way at different institutions. There are often considerable variations and it is up to you to find out what they are.

Employment prospects

You'll be investing a lot of time and money in your higher education and you need to be sure why you are considering it. If your top priority is to qualify for a graduate job, make certain that the course you choose has a good employment record. Some courses are 100 per cent vocational, which is perfect if you are similarly 100 per cent committed to the relevant career path - Dentistry if you want to practise as a dentist, Veterinary Science if you aspire to become a vet - but of limited value if you are not. Some courses appear to offer virtually nothing in terms of related graduate employment but could give you the opportunity to delve deeply into a subject - Philosophy perhaps or Anthropology - that seriously engages your intellect.

Always ask for details of the destinations of previous graduates for any course you are considering. At the same time, you can find out if any periods of work experience are included as part of the course.

There is particular emphasis in the UK now on teaching employability skills - communication, presentation, team work, problem solving and information technology - as part of any undergraduate course and you should, once again, enquire about how these skills are delivered on the courses you are considering.

Motivation is a key element here. By all means, if you really know what you want, go for the course that will get you a professional qualification in the shortest possible time. But don't make the mistake of forcing yourself to endure the drudgery of a subject you dislike simply because you hope it will be good for you at some later stage in your life!

Location

Many students are drawn to the obvious appeal of London but you should be warned that London and the south east of England can be exceptionally expensive and suitable accommodation may be difficult to find.

It is worth taking some time to explore the geography of the entire United Kingdom and to experience the joy of discovering that there really is life outside London (although many native Londoners do not appear to be aware of this!).

You can decide whether to base yourself in a big city centre, in a quiet country setting or beside the sea. You may have particular reasons for choosing an industrial, cultural, agricultural or commercial environment.

If you follow our advice of selecting a subject first, then location may be determined by the number of institutions offering relevant courses. English, for example, can be studied almost anywhere but a specialised course in, say, Meteorology, African Studies or Naval Architecture would immediately restrict your options in terms of location.

Finance

How much will your studies cost and how are you going to pay? You need to establish the total cost of tuition fees and your own living expenses. You might also want to find out if there are ways of meeting some of the costs through grants and bursaries or by working part-time while you are a student.

You then need to add the cost of accommodation, food, travel and whatever luxuries you permit yourself. It is hard to generalise about personal living costs because some people have more expensive tastes than others but it would be difficult to survive as a student anywhere in the UK for less than £10,000 a year...and you may need considerably more than that. You should add another £5-6,000 a year if you are heading for London. These figures are based on what you might need for roughly nine months rather than a full calendar year.

It is absolutely essential that you calculate - long before you even think of applying - the total financial implications of your higher education needs. It is equally essential to be clear about how you plan to meet the cost.

Status

All degree-awarding institutions in the UK must meet stringent quality criteria but it is evident that some universities are much more prestigious than others.

If you are an ambitious high achiever and set your sights on the best of everything, you will doubtless want to seek out the most highly rated places in the land. There are various league tables, both official and unofficial, ranking universities by such criteria as research, teaching quality and employment record, and they mostly feature similar groupings of institutions near the top.

Oxford, Cambridge, Imperial, London School of Economics, University College London, Durham, Edinburgh, Glasgow, St Andrews, Bath, Bristol, Nottingham, Warwick and York, for example, would be part of almost any top twenty UK universities.

It goes without saying, of course, that these are among the most difficult places to get into and you will need impressive qualifications to gain a place.

If, on the other hand, your achievements to date are more modest, you can still gain a very valuable university education but you would be well advised to avoid the most prestigious institutions and start your search rather lower in the league tables.

You may find, in any case, that Status is a less important factor than Subject and Location as described earlier in this article.

Entry requirements

You will often find the entry standard expressed in terms of UCAS tariff points based on grades achieved in GCE Advanced level (A level), Pre-U, Scottish Higher/Advanced Higher, International Baccalaureate, Irish Leaving Certificate or other equivalent examinations.

Each A grade at A level, for example, is worth 120 UCAS points (140 points for A*) and you will find that the standard Cambridge offer for 2015 entry, to quote one of the most prestigious examples, is A*AA or 380 points for Arts subjects and A*A*A or 400 points for Science subjects. By contrast, each E grade is worth only 40 points.

The UCAS tariff has recently been subject to considerable review and there will be changes to the existing system from September 2016 for the 2017 admissions cycle. See the UCAS website for full details.

The number of points needed beyond the elite institutions usually goes down roughly in line with the university's perceived status! This means that, as stated above under Status, you need to match your examination performance to date with the published entry standard of the institutions you are considering.

If you have pursued a pre-university course other than A level, Higher/Advanced Higher or equivalent, you can get detailed advice from the admissions office of your preferred university regarding the acceptability of your qualifications.

If your first language is not English, you may also have to take a test to demonstrate that you have sufficient language proficiency to complete a degree level course. Alternatively, you may take an English course before starting your degree.

Living arrangements

This is another issue that can vary according to your own personal circumstances.

The cheapest deal is almost always to stay with family or friends during your studies but this is rarely possible and may not be desirable because of the ways in which it could restrict your social life.

Finding the right place to live is almost as important as choosing the right course. If you get it wrong, it can have a seriously detrimental effect not only on your studies but also on your attitude to student life generally, making new friendships and even having the motivation to continue.

Evenings and weekends, for example, can be long and lonely if you're cut off from friends and fellow students.

Your chosen universities or colleges should each have an accommodation office to help with your living arrangements. Use their services to the full, asking especially about such things as:

- **Cost** - not just the weekly rent but whether you have to pay for 52 weeks a year or just the number of weeks per term

- **Number of rooms** - whether you have your own room or have to share with somebody else

- **Food** - does the rent include all meals (full board), some meals (half board) or no meals?

- **Facilities** - is there an en-suite bathroom, a fully-equipped kitchen, a television and so on? Is the cost of heating and electricity included in the rent?

- **Location** - is the accommodation within walking distance of your study centre or will you need to travel by bus or train? If so, how long does it take and how much does it cost?

- **Shops** - are there enough in the immediate area to meet your needs?

Entertainment

It is important to establish the right life-work balance to suit your lifestyle and perhaps your cultural or religious expectations.

Whatever your personal priorities might be, most people agree that too much work can be just as bad for you as a surfeit of late-night parties. You may be shocked or delighted to discover just how much of student life revolves around drinking alcohol in bars and generally 'having a good time'.

Even if you don't wish to join in with the overall socialising, you may still want to visit the theatre, go to concerts, join a sports club or take advantage of other facilities on offer.

You will find that almost all UK universities boast an impressive range of things to do when you're not actually studying. Entertainment ought not to be right at the top of your priority list but the provision of facilities for leisure and recreation might just tip the scales one way or another if you are still undecided after considering issues such as Subject, Location and Living arrangements.

Community

You'll be living and working in the midst of a large student community and you may find it important to check out information on some of the following questions:

- Does the university recruit many other students from my part of the world?

- How many students are in the same age-range as me?

- Is there a religious community of people of the same faith as me?

- Is there access and support for people with disabilities?

- Is single-sex accommodation available?

- Who can I talk to if I feel lonely or have difficulty settling in?

Time

How long are you prepared to spend on your higher education? Most full-time degrees last three years (four years in Scotland) but there are foundation degrees and higher diplomas that can be completed in two years.

There are *sandwich degrees* that incorporate some time spent in industry, commerce or a clinical environment and usually last four years, while subjects such as Medicine and Veterinary Science require at least five years.

You may prefer a part-time course or one based on distance learning. These could offer advantages in terms of saving on accommodation costs or avoiding debt by working to earn enough to cover your immediate needs but you may find that your learning is spread over a considerably longer period of time.

If you enjoy your studies so much that you choose to stay on for a postgraduate course, you may be looking at several further years before you are in a position to earn some serious income. There is currently no standard time allocation for the purpose of acquiring undergraduate and postgraduate qualifications but most European countries are now working towards a common programme, often referred to as 3-5-8.

This means that you could expect to take at least three years to obtain a first or Bachelor level degree; you could then take another two years to pursue a Master level qualification and a further three to obtain a Doctorate. There are many variations on this theme, and it may not apply in your particular circumstances, but the 3-5-8 pattern should give you a broad feel for the shape of higher education provision not only in the UK but also across Europe.

One attraction of having broadly comparable Bachelor-Master-Doctor qualifications that transcend national boundaries is that they can enable you to travel widely, selecting different locations for different levels.

Have you thought about how long you will be away from home? Have you considered how often you might want to return to visit family and friends? Do you know how much travel costs will add to your financial calculations?

Further Information

The essential starting point for almost all higher education provision in the United Kingdom is the Universities and Colleges Admissions Service (UCAS) website at: **www.ucas.com**

The equivalent for students in the Republic of Ireland is the Central Applications Office (CAO) website at: **www.cao.ie**

Suggested Reading

Heap 2015: University Degree Course Offers - The Essential Guide to Winning Your Place at University
- Brian Heap, Trotman Education, 2014

The UCAS Guide to Getting into University and College: second edition
- UCAS Publications, 2012

Cut the Cost of Uni: Tips and Advice to make Uni Affordable
- Gwenda Thomas, Trotman, 2012

How to Complete Your UCAS Application: 2015 Entry
- Beryl Dixon, Trotman Education, 2014

60 Successful Personal Statements for UCAS Application
- Guy Nobes and Gavin Nobes, COA, 2012

Admissions Tests

There has been a marked trend in recent years for the most sought-after universities, or those offering some of the most popular subjects, to use admissions tests to help identify the strongest candidates. So, take special note if you are considering applying to Oxford, Cambridge, certain courses at Ulster or University College London, or to read a subject such as law, medicine, dentistry, veterinary science or maths elsewhere in the UK.

The most widely applied test is the *UK Clinical Aptitude Test* (UKCAT) for Medicine and Dentistry, currently used by 24 universities, while a further eight use the *Biomedical Admissions Test* (BMAT) for courses including Medicine, Veterinary Science and Biomedical Science. Nine UK institutions use the *National Admissions Test for Law* (LNAT) and two require the *Sixth Term Examination Paper* (STEP) for Mathematics, with a further six encouraging applicants to take the papers.

On top of that, certain universities also set their own exams for a range of other subjects such as accounting, classics, engineering, English, history, languages, teacher training and nursing. Some 85% of applicants to Oxford, for example, will take some form of aptitude test this year.

The Oxford exams are seen as part of the sifting process of identifying candidates to be shortlisted for a formal interview, allowing admissions tutors to compare the relative strengths of applicants offering a diverse range of academic qualifications.

We list below details of the best-known admissions tests, although we do not claim that our list is completely comprehensive. You must check carefully to see whether any courses you are considering require you to pass an admissions test.

Most admissions tests happen at the start of the academic cycle, so if you do need to take one you'll need to register for it early – possibly before you complete your UCAS application. This is particularly relevant in relation to courses and universities covered by the 15 October application deadline.

You should be aware that universities use test data in different ways. For some, your overall score is a significant factor in their consideration of your application; for others, it may be used only in marginal situations. In certain cases, there is a threshold score that candidates must achieve in order to be considered further in the admission processes. This score is often determined each year, although universities may indicate on their website the threshold scores used in previous years.

Other universities set test results alongside such factors as academic achievement, your personal statement and interview performance. The test factor may be significant or may contribute just a small amount to the final outcome. It may happen that an admissions tutor uses the test score to rank candidates who appear in all other ways equal. A few universities use tests to provide opportunities for candidates who might not have progressed to interview using traditional selection methods. This can be of particular benefit to candidates from schools with a poor academic record.

History, Languages and Literature

Classics Admissions Test (CAT): **www.catoxford.org.uk**

English Literature Admissions Test (ELAT): **www.elat.org.uk**

History Aptitude Test (HAT): **www.hatoxford.org.uk**

Modern and Medieval Languages Test (MML): **www.study.cam.ac.uk/undergraduate/courses/mml**

Modern Languages Admissions Test (MLAT): **www.mlatoxford.org.uk**

Oriental Languages Aptitude Test (OLAT): **www.olatoxford.org.uk**

Law

National Admissions Test for Law (LNAT): **www.lnat.ac.uk**

Cambridge Law Test: **www.study.cam.ac.uk/undergraduate/apply/tests/law.html**

Mathematics and Physics

Maths Admissions Test (MAT): **www.matoxford.org.uk**

Sixth Term Exam Paper Mathematics (STEP): **www.stepmathematics.org.uk**

Physics Aptitude Test (PAT): **www.patoxford.org.uk**

Medical courses

UK Clinical Aptitude Test (UKCAT): **www.ukcat.ac.uk**

Biomedical Admissions Test (BMAT): **www.bmat.org.uk**

Graduate Medical School Admissions Test (GAMSAT): **www.gamsatuk.org**

Health Professions Admissions Test – Ulster (HPAT Ulster): **www.hpat-ulster.acer.edu.au**

Thinking Skills Assessment

TSA Cambridge: **www.tsacambridge.org.uk**

TSA Oxford: **www.tsaoxford.org.uk**

TSA UCL: **www.tsaucl.org.uk**

University of Cambridge: BMAT, MML, STEP, TSA Cambridge, Cambridge Law Test

University of Oxford: BMAT, CAT, ELAT, HAT, LNAT, MAT, MLAT, OLAT, PAT, TSA Oxford

Top tips for test preparation

1) Do your research
We give a web link for every test we know about. Spend as long as it takes to explore the sites, finding out what to expect in any test, how long it lasts, where it takes place and so on.

2) Think about what the test is trying to measure
The point of most admissions tests is to assess how you think rather than to see how many facts you can memorise. Thorough research as in 1 above and test experience as in 3 below should put you on the right track.

3) Take some tests from previous years
Test providers almost always invite you to try a selection of past papers. Try to sit them under the same conditions as the real thing: give yourself only the normally allotted time and stick to whatever rules apply about using a calculator or dictionary.

4) Talk to previous candidates
Talk to any students in your school or college who have taken a particular admissions test before. An internet search will usually locate a chatroom or student forum where other candidates talk about their admissions test experience.

5) Register on time
This links back to 1 above. Your research will show that you need to register for many tests early in the school year. Make sure you don't leave things too late!

Background information

If you want to explore the thinking behind university admissions tests, visit the *Supporting Professionalism in Admissions* website at:
www.spa.ac.uk/information/admissionstests

The UCAS Tariff

UCAS currently operates a points system known as the UCAS Tariff for entry to higher education. This allows you to use a range of different qualifications to help secure a place on an undergraduate course. The Tariff has, however, been under review and major changes are being introduced for applications made from September 2016, for courses starting in 2017 onwards. Aware that some readers of this book will be applying for 2016 entry to higher education and some for 2017 entry, we give some examples of both the current and new Tariff figures. They are very different, so please make sure that you don't confuse them!

Universities and colleges use the UCAS Tariff to make comparisons between applicants with different qualifications. Tariff points are often used in entry requirements, although other factors are often taken into account. You will usually find that details on the UCAS database provide a fuller picture of what admissions tutors are seeking.

The Tariff helps universities and colleges when deciding on course entry requirements and making conditional offers, although conditional offers that use Tariff points will often require a minimum level of achievement in a specified subject (for example, using the current Tariff, '300 points to include grade A at A level chemistry', or '260 points including SQA Higher grade B in mathematics').

Use of the Tariff may also vary from department to department within any one university or college, and may in some cases be dependent on the programme being offered.

It is important to emphasise that the methodology behind the new Tariff is entirely different from the current version. This means that points under the two systems are not comparable. For example:

Qualification and Grade	Current Tariff	New Tariff
A level grade A*	140	56
A level grade A	120	48
A level grade B	100	40
A level grade C	80	32
A level grade D	60	24
A level grade E	40	16

Qualification and Grade	Current Tariff	New Tariff
Scottish Higher grade A	80	33
Scottish Higher grade B	65	27
Scottish Higher grade C	50	21
Scottish Higher grade D	36	15

Whilst many universities and colleges use qualifications and grades, others use the Tariff in their admissions activities, principally to inform and describe entry requirements and offers. Where the Tariff is used, you can often expect offers to include a mixture of Tariff points and qualification, subject and/or grade conditions.

The table below shows the difference in total points between the current and new Tariff points for two typical offers.

Example of offers	Current Tariff points total	New Tariff points total
Three A levels at grades A, B, B	320	128
Five Scottish Highers at grades A, A, B, B, C	340	141

Universities and colleges are free to choose whether or not to use the Tariff and how to deploy it. The introduction of the new Tariff does not alter this. UCAS recommends that admissions decisions should not be made on Tariff points alone.

References to the Tariff on university and college websites for entry in 2015 and 2016 can be found on the UCAS website at: **www.ucas.com/how-it-all-works/explore-your-options/entry-requirements/ucas-tariff**

Which qualifications attract points?

The new Tariff contains only qualifications at Qualification Credit Framework (QCF) Level 3 and Scottish Credit and Qualification Framework (SCQF) Level 6 or equivalent. This means that, for example, it does not include Key Skills qualifications at Level 2 or 4. For EU qualifications this is the European Qualifications Framework (EQF) Level 4 or equivalent - therefore the Irish Leaving Certificate at Higher Level is included, whilst the Ordinary Level is not. For qualifications outside the EU, evidence is reviewed to make a judgement about their equivalence to this level.

For composite qualifications the new Tariff allocates separate points to each separate constituent qualification rather than the overall qualification. For example, for the International Baccalaureate (IB) Diploma, the new Tariff allocates separate points to the Higher Level, Standard Level, Extended Essay and Theory of Knowledge qualifications. There is no overall allocation to the whole IB Diploma.

Using the new Tariff tables

The Tariff tables contain the new Tariff points for all of the qualifications that are currently on the UCAS Tariff. They are arranged in three sections:

1. *UK benchmark qualifications*: the qualifications most frequently held by applicants from each of the UK countries. They are called 'benchmarks' because they are often used as a reference point by higher education providers when looking at less-familiar qualifications.

2. *Other UK qualifications*: these are the bulk of qualifications on the Tariff, presented in alphabetical order. This section also includes historic UK qualifications which are no longer taught to learners.

3. *International qualifications*: qualifications awarded and regulated outside the UK that have been allocated Tariff points.

You can consult all of the new Tariff tables at:
www.ucas.com/sites/default/files/new-tariff-tables.pdf

If you have any questions or feedback regarding the new Tariff, contact:
newtariff-feedback@ucas.ac.uk

Applying for Art and Design Courses

Original article by Tony Charlton - Professional Development Officer, UCAS

Have you ever imagined yourself working as a website designer, an animator or a packaging designer; or as a sport and fitness equipment designer, a magazine photographer, film set designer or a fashion illustrator? The key to success in these and literally thousands of other jobs is that career advancement is increasingly dependent on gaining a degree, foundation degree or higher national diploma (HND).

In choosing any career, it is vital to separate fact from fiction. With art and design, some students (and their parents) have misgivings about its suitability due to a lack of first-hand experience and an over-reliance on misleading media reporting. The true picture, however, is much rosier. The creative industries are a significant contributor to the economic wealth of the UK and employ more than 1 million people. The influence of artists and designers is so all-pervasive that it would be hard to imagine our world devoid of their creative inputs. If you doubt this, just take a moment and look around you, at items in your home, place of work, study or leisure environment. Consider, for example, furniture in your home, the 'white goods' in the kitchen (i.e. cooker, fridge etc.), soft furnishings such as carpets and curtains, the adverts on your TV, your weekend mountain bike or, on a personal note, the clothes and shoes that you are wearing today. In all likelihood, the vast majority will have been designed by art and design graduates.

The sort of person you need to be

An ability for sustained effort and a willingness to work, on occasion, in a non 9 to 5 environment are both important. It is vital to realise that the art and design job market is extremely competitive and that a high level of commitment is needed. Increasingly, work opportunities are offered on a short-term contract or self-employed basis and, to secure work, you must be prepared to market yourself. The importance of self-promotion, for even the most gifted students, is recognised by most colleges and universities and forms part of supporting studies.

How important is drawing ability?

The ability to express yourself through the medium of drawing is still viewed as essential for most art and design courses. Do not be beguiled into thinking, as some school pupils sometimes do, that drawing is somehow yesterday's skill and that a computer can 'do it all'. It can't, and your progress in art and design will be severely limited, if not totally jeopardised, unless your portfolio contains sound evidence of competent drawing skills.

Study options

Art and design has expanded to embrace an enormous range of study opportunities at degree level. Choices vary from 'Fashion Merchandising' to 'Digital Imaging', and from 'Calligraphy' to 'Museum and Exhibition Design'. In total, there are over 70 specialisations on the art and design subject menu. This means, in reality, that a significant number of schools are hampered in offering the full spectrum of art and design possibilities through lack of specialist resources.

Do I need to take an Art Foundation course?

In England, Wales and Northern Ireland, a significant number of students who take A levels choose, before applying for degree level studies, to take a one-year art foundation course. Usually this is done at a college or university near the student's home and, in reality, most students live at home whilst taking their art foundation course. For application purposes, apply direct to your chosen course and not through UCAS. In Scotland, the first year of a four-year degree has a similar purpose.

Choosing the right course

With more art and design courses in the UK than in any other country in Europe, a snap decision could prove costly. Instead, take time to research your options fully and, whenever possible, try to make a personal visit. Before doing so, you will find it useful to visit a UCAS *Design Your Future Fair*. Taking place annually in London and Manchester, and exclusively for UCAS art and design applicants, the Fairs are a golden opportunity to meet staff and students from all major art colleges and university art departments. Admission is free but attendance figures usually exceed 10,000, so it is essential to book a place online via the UCAS website. When making subsequent university and college visits, remember to check the studio and workshop facilities very carefully (this is of course where you will spend most of your time as an art and design student).

Making a UCAS art and design application

The Universities and Colleges Admissions Service (UCAS) annually handles applications from more than half a million people for places at UK colleges and universities. Of these, just under 40,000 students apply for one or more art and design courses.

Applications for studio-based art and design courses should reach UCAS between early September and either 15 January or 24 March. (The only exception is Fine Art at the Ruskin School of Art, University of Oxford, which requires applicants to apply by 15 October).

The deadline applicable to each course is clearly given in UCAS Course Search and is also embedded into the Apply software. Online notification of interviews, including the date, is available for applicants through Track.

May I apply for courses with both dates?

Yes, this is perfectly acceptable. You may make up to five choices overall, with any combination of dates permissible.

Do I have to express any preference in my choices?

No, art and design applications now follow standard UCAS procedures in being considered on a simultaneous basis. You therefore should not express a preference for a particular college or university in your personal statement (unless, of course, you are applying as a single choice applicant).

Suggested reading

Getting into Art and Design Courses
- James Burnett, Trotman Education, 2014

Further information

Artquest
www.artquest.org.uk

Universities and Colleges Admissions Service
www.ucas.com

Institute of Designers in Ireland
http://idi-design.ie

Visual Artists Ireland
http://visualartists.ie

Gap Year Considerations

Original article by Ken Reynolds, specialist writer on careers and higher education

Organisations in the business of setting up gap year activities are very skilled at promoting the idea that a year out between school or college and higher education and a job can offer you, as one website puts it: "an EXCITING, CHALLENGING and VALUABLE opportunity, be it in the UK or OVERSEAS. It can and probably will ENRICH YOUR LIFE FOREVER, aside from broadening your view of the world and those around you."

The gap year is portrayed as a light at the end of the tunnel; a vision of freedom after exams; a break from academic goals and pressures. Get set, trills the enticing publicity, for the adventure of a lifetime; the chance to 'find yourself' as you battle in the heat and dust against poverty, famine and injustice; the opportunity to live your dreams and make the world a better place.

All of this undoubtedly turns out to be true each year for some among the 200,000 or so young people from Britain who decide to bite the bullet, pack their rucksack and head for the hills. Yet a very different overall picture emerges from a three-year study of the habits and experiences of gap year participants published by Lucy Huxley, a sociologist at Manchester Metropolitan University.

Lucy's report - **Seeing the World: an Examination of Backpacking as Global Youth Culture** - claims that most gap year travellers rarely interact with local people, learn nothing about the countries they visit, hang out only with fellow backpacking Brits and stay in constant contact with home via mobile phones and the internet. Rather than exploring the tropical rainforest or learning an obscure language, they are more likely to be downloading the latest plot twists in Eastenders or checking the scores in the Premier League.

The findings led one newspaper columnist to write that adventure and education are no longer part of the gap year. "It's about pretence," she maintains, "the pretence of independence. The advent of the e-mail has made that pretence increasingly difficult to uphold, but we do it anyway."

Her rather harsh conclusion is that: "gap years have forfeited any claim to be an essential part of the maturing process. For middle-class British students, the best that can be said is that a gap year begins, very gently, to wean them away from the culture of the risk assessment exercise and the health and safety checklist that has cosseted them all their lives so far. Though insured to the last strand of designer-straightened hair, gap-year students must, I hope, take at least a smidgen more responsibility for themselves than they did in their school sixth form."

Perhaps surprisingly, Lucy Huxley herself is more positive about the benefits of a gap year, saying that the students she interviewed felt the experience had been worthwhile and had given them new confidence.

"They are getting a sense of confidence and maturity. It's a cliché about finding yourself," she says, "but that still seems to be apparent and they are certainly getting something from it. They enjoyed it and got something out of it."

Similar worries about so-called 'voluntourism' are expressed by ethical tourism campaigners Tourism Concern. Executive director Mark Watson says that, whilst the desire to help others is commendable, too many expensive commercial volunteering opportunities end up exploiting those offering help whilst harming the lives of those meant to be on the receiving end.

"Volunteers often have unfulfilling and disappointing experiences," he says. "Volunteer placements can prevent local workers from getting much-needed jobs; hard-pressed institutions waste time looking after them and money upgrading facilities; and abused or abandoned children form emotional attachments to the visitors, who increase their trauma by disappearing back home after a few weeks.

"We feel that there are many opportunities for people to undertake meaningful volunteering in their own community, where they will receive proper training, support and supervision – without the need to pay a tour operator for the privilege. In the majority of cases, people would do far better - and have a more rewarding experience – to volunteer at home and spend their money travelling afterwards."

Personal Development Guide

These are important issues for you to consider, and you must reach your own conclusion about what is best for you. If you feel that a gap year would be of benefit, spend some time exploring the COA *Personal Development Guide*. The sheer number of gap year agencies can be bewildering, so we have grouped them under headings to help you become aware of the range of opportunities available and decide what sort of gap year activity best meets your needs.

Internet links are provided for all the organisations listed. The websites will provide detailed information on the type of experience offered, the likely demands on your character and abilities, and the potential benefits for you and/or the community involved.

You can spend your time in the UK or overseas; you may be paid or you may have to pay a considerable sum in order to participate; you may choose a course of study or you may go on an expedition. The choice is yours.

Medicine Dissected

How medical degrees vary from one university to another

A medical degree is a university course lasting from four to six years that, on graduation, allows you to register and practise in the UK as a medical doctor. Medical degrees vary enormously between medical schools, and the same medical school may offer several different types of medical degree. There are three main types of medical degree: standard, foundation and graduate entry.

There are 34 medical schools in the UK: 26 in England, 5 in Scotland, 2 in Wales and 1 in Northern Ireland. Most offer standard courses, 13 offer foundation courses and 15 offer graduate entry courses. Some medical schools have all three types of course, while others may have only one type.

Standard courses may be five or six years in length, and most medical students study on this type of course.

Foundation courses are six years in length and are designed to widen access to medicine to those without science A-levels or to those from less privileged backgrounds. They are generally open to school leavers, mature students and sometimes graduates. The course usually involves a foundation year (hence the name) in which the basic sciences (especially chemistry and biology) are taught. Some medical schools also cover clinical teaching in the foundation year. On successfully completing the foundation year, students simply progress to the first year of their medical school's standard course.

Graduate entry courses are open only to applicants who already have a university degree. They all last four years and are generally very competitive, having a very high number of applicants for each place.

Standard courses in the UK can be said to fall into three different categories: traditional, integrated and problem-based. The main differences between them lie in the way they organise 'pre-clinical' and 'clinical' teaching, although we should stress that the 'clinical' element - based in hospitals or in primary care with teaching carried out by clinicians leading small groups - is ultimately similar for all three types of course. It is also true that the categories are not rigid and that there is some overlap between, for example, integrated and problem-based courses. What is vital is that you research the full range of courses on offer, talking to practitioners and advisers, reading prospectuses and checking out websites, before you draw up a shortlist for your application. In the process of doing this, you should find that the categories we mention here will help you identify courses that correspond to your preferred personal learning style. Different types of people suit different types of course and only you can decide which one might suit you best. Wherever you study medicine, you should end up with a broadly similar qualification - but it is wise to pick a university where you perceive that you will have the best chance to flourish both academically and socially.

- *Traditional, or subject-based*, courses are now something of a rarity in the new world of medical education, being limited to venerable establishments such as Oxford, Cambridge and St Andrews. There is a clear pre-clinical/clinical divide and the pre-clinical years are taught very rigidly in subjects. In some of these institutions, you may have to apply again for a clinical place and this could be somewhere very different from your original location. Some Oxbridge students, for example, finish their clinical years in London, while many St Andrews medics migrate to Manchester. This type of course tends to appeal to exceptionally academically able, scientifically minded applicants, although there is the potential risk of losing motivation due to the complete lack of patient contact in the pre-clinical years.

Also, students can sometimes feel a little unprepared and isolated when they take their first steps into hospital in the clinical years. This type of course offers considerable scope to complete research (such as a Masters or PhD) without overly disrupting your degree. In summary, traditional courses are well worth considering if you are highly confident about your long-term motivation and like the idea of taking a science degree before embarking on your clinical studies.

- *Integrated, or systems-based*, courses are run at the majority of UK medical schools, such as Birmingham and Leeds. Devised under the recommendation of the General Medical Council (GMC), these courses may be said to occupy a mid-way position between traditional styles and problem-based learning. A key feature is that they generally claim to have patient contact from day one, although this varies in amount from place to place and may be limited in the first year to local community visits. Patient contact increases as the years progress, with what could still be seen as a sort of division between pre-clinical and clinical years. Many students, it should be said, are happy with relatively limited contact with patients in year one as they feel that at this point they do not have sufficient clinical knowledge to approach patients on the wards. Teaching is based on body systems such as the digestive system, learning the anatomy, physiology, pharmacology and biochemistry of the relevant system, and supplementing clinical knowledge. There is also an emphasis on communication skills and understanding the local community. Teaching is a mixture of lectures, tutorials, self-directed learning and hospital work in later years. Integrated courses tend to appeal across the board to all types of aspiring doctors.

- *Problem-based learning (PBL)* is a new, dynamic style of course, pioneered by medical schools such as Liverpool and Manchester. Taught with a patient-orientated approach from day one, students are heavily involved in clinical scenarios even in the first year. This type of course, with its emphasis on self-directed learning, can require a great deal of self-motivation, especially for students expecting to be spoon-fed large doses of information. Teaching generally revolves around small, tutor-led groups, with computer work, practical sessions and a large amount of time for personal study. As to whether this type of course offers a better way of teaching medicine than the others mentioned above, the jury is still out. Indeed, some of the new schools are only now producing their first doctors. Medical schools offering this type of course include the new ones such as East Anglia, Hull and York, Keele and Peninsula, together with Barts and the London (Queen Mary), Glasgow, Liverpool, Manchester and Sheffield.

Four other factors to consider

As is clear from our brief analysis of different types of course, not all medical degrees are taught in the same way. The GMC also accepts that there is simply not enough time in the day to teach medical students everything they need to know. It has therefore identified a 'core' curriculum, which all medical schools must follow, supplemented by *student-selected components* (SSCs). Given that SSCs can form as much as 25-30% of the course at some universities, you should check carefully what might be available at any medical school you are considering. SSCs generally reflect the way in which medical teaching is currently developing, with a diverse range of projects, which not only give you the opportunity to study areas of interest in some depth but also equip you with the skills to source information for yourself.

Another feature to look out for is *Intercalating*, the opportunity to incorporate a degree (BSc or BA) into your medical course. It takes one year, which is often completed after your second or third year. At some medical schools it is compulsory (most of the 6 year courses), some offer it as an option to all students and at some places it is only offered to the most academically able students. The degrees can range from the more traditional science topics such as biochemistry, anatomy or physiology to more unusual subjects such as medical law, ethics, journalism and even history of medicine. There are many reasons why you might intercalate: to extend your knowledge of a particular subject or to gain more experience in carrying out research or laboratory work. The main downside is the extra time and money it takes, adding a year to an already long degree, and carrying implications for what might already be a precarious bank balance! If you have no interest in research, there might be little point in applying to a medical school where intercalating is compulsory; conversely, if you seriously want to intercalate, it may be risky to apply to a school that offers intercalation only to, say, the top 10% of the year group.

Thirdly, an *elective* could give you the opportunity to practise medicine anywhere you want in the world for two months during your clinical years. Electives range from running outreach clinics in developing countries to accompanying flying doctors in Australia. Most medical students see their elective as a wonderful opportunity to visit some exotic destination before they qualify, although you can opt to stay at home if you wish.

Finally, there was a time when all medical schools undertook full body *dissection*, although many now use videos and computers for their anatomy teaching. Some teach from prosections only (parts of the body dissected by a professional anatomy teacher), while some still do full body dissection. Because it is very practical, dissection is often a welcome break from lectures and most students get a lot out of it. It also helps to make clear the differences in the human body between different individuals. If you want to become a surgeon, dissection would be really useful and you should look for courses where this is a strong feature.

Exploring medicine courses

A group of medical students at Leeds University has created a very useful website to help future candidates. Visit it at: **www.wanttobeadoctor.co.uk**

Another option is to visit the website at: **www.medschoolsonline.co.uk** and explore the options available. You can even register to join in debates about various issues related to studying medicine.

You should also spend some time exploring the Medical Schools Council website at: **www.medschools.ac.uk**

For the most reliable, up-to-date, official information, visit the GMC website at: **www.gmc-uk.org** and click on Education and Training. You can download *Tomorrow's Doctors* in PDF format.

The GMC sets the knowledge, skills and behaviours that medical students learn at UK medical schools: these are the outcomes that new UK graduates must be able to demonstrate. The GMC also sets standards for teaching, learning and assessment. These outcomes and standards are laid down in *Tomorrow's Doctors* (2009), which you can consult online or download in PDF format.

The same applies to *Tomorrow's Doctors* supplementary advice, produced by the GMC in response to requests from medical schools.

The advice covers:
- Assessment in undergraduate medical education
- Clinical placements for medical students
- Developing teachers and trainers in undergraduate medical education
- Patient and public involvement in undergraduate medical education.

Study programmes taught in English across Europe

Original article by Ken Reynolds, with additional material supplied by Guy Flouch of Eunicas

Are you aware of the rapidly growing range of undergraduate study opportunities taught in English across the European Economic Area (EEA)?

There are now very many such programmes, characterised by excellent quality, realistic entry requirements and outstanding value for money. Where tuition fees exist at all, they are almost invariably lower than those that now apply in the UK. On top of this, the cost of living is generally no greater than in Britain.

You could, for example, study European Law at Maastricht in the Netherlands, Civil Engineering at Via University College in Denmark or Biology at Sundsvall mid-Sweden University.

Currently, the majority of the UK and Irish students crossing the Channel to take up these opportunities head for the Netherlands: the Dutch authorities report over 3,000 applications this year from UK students alone. However, increasing numbers of programmes are also available in countries such as Denmark, Sweden, Finland, Austria and Germany.

There are no fees for EEA nationals on first degree programmes in Denmark, Finland, Sweden and Norway. In Germany, Austria and Switzerland, fees at state-sector universities are between nil and about €1,500 a year. In the Netherlands, standard tuition fees for EU students are €1951, plus €3225 for some liberal arts courses, but you are automatically entitled to a student loan from the Dutch state to cover these.

A further attraction is that entry requirements tend to be low in comparison with the points needed to enter equivalent programmes in the UK or Ireland. It is important to understand that this is not a reflection on the quality of the programmes, rather a difference of admissions philosophy.

How can I find a good university?

Some of Europe's top universities are now offering programmes in English. Examples include: Leiden, Eindhoven, Utrecht, Maastricht and Groningen in the Netherlands, Aarhus and Southern Denmark, Gothenburg in Sweden, Aalto in Finland, Johannes Kepler Linz in Austria, Milan and Politecnico di Torino in Italy.

There are also Universities of Applied Sciences/University Colleges, which traditionally combine theoretical study with practical application in a range of subject areas. Work placements are usually included in their programmes, preparing you to enter specific careers.

Look out too for private universities and business schools across the continent. Some of these offer excellent programmes but they can be expensive.

What can I study?

Unsurprisingly, there is a wide choice of programmes including the word 'International' in the title. International Law, Business, Politics or Tourism are prominent here, but you can also consider the full range of degree provision, including Economics, Applied Sciences, Engineering, Media or Sports Management.

If you don't have a particular subject in mind, there are some impressive Liberal Arts and Sciences programmes, particularly in Dutch universities, where you can design your own course and specialisations.

Special cases

In cases where UK provision is exceptionally heavily oversubscribed, notably in Medicine, Dentistry and Veterinary Science, certain Central and Eastern European countries are more than happy to fill the training void. Fees for some of these courses are higher than those quoted earlier in this feature.

For example, you can study Veterinary Science at Szent István University in Budapest. The course is fully accredited by the European Association of Establishments for Veterinary Education (EAEVE), which means that a veterinary diploma awarded in Budapest is equivalent to that of any Western European veterinary school. You can find full details on the website at: **www.univet.hu/en**

Meanwhile, both Pleven Medical University, in northern Bulgaria, and Varna Medical University, on Bulgaria's Black Sea coast, offer a six-year medical programme in English. The MD conferred upon graduation is the equivalent of a UK MBBS/MBChB plus the first foundation year (F1) of the NHS foundation training scheme.

Among the Dentistry programmes available across Europe is the five-year DDS degree at the Poznan University of Medical Sciences in Poland.

Interestingly, several Italian universities are now offering Medicine in English, with fees significantly lower than those in Central and Eastern Europe.

Further information

A good starting point for exploring higher education opportunities across Europe is to visit some of the following websites:

Netherlands: **www.studyinholland.nl**

Denmark: **http://studyindenmark.dk**

Finland: **www.studyinfinland.fi**

Norway: **www.studyinnorway.no**

Sweden: **www.studyinsweden.se**

Germany: **www.study-in.de/en**

France: **www.campusfrance.org/en**

Ireland: **www.educationinireland.com/en**

Italy: **www.study-in-italy.it**

Malta : **www.um.edu.mt/int-eu**

Information on courses taught in English across Europe – including a database of available programmes, entry requirements and course content – can be found on the European Universities Central Application Support Service (EUNICAS) website at: **www.eunicas.com**

For a registration fee of €28, Eunicas will support and advise you on your application to up to eight programmes in Europe.

Undergraduate study in the United States

Lauren Welch, Director Advising and Marketing, US-UK Fulbright Commission, London

Study in the USA is an option increasingly favourable to UK students. There were 9,467 UK students at American universities in 2012-13, around 50% of whom were taking a first degree. These numbers mark a 3.1% increase from the previous year. If you think US study may be a good fit for you, read below for factors you should consider as you research American universities.

Getting started

The best starting point for information on study options in the US is the US-UK Fulbright Commission. The US-UK Fulbright Commission is a not-for-profit organisation, funded by both governments to promote educational exchange between the US and the UK. As part of the EducationUSA advising network, it is the only official source of US study information in the UK. Visit the website at: **www.fulbright.org.uk**

The Fulbright Commission in Ireland is also an EducationUSA advising centre. More information is available on their website at: **www.fulbright.ie**

Why study in the USA?

Why do so many students cross the Atlantic to pursue an undergraduate degree? In a recent survey, we found many students were most attracted to the ability to choose from the exceptionally wide range of universities on offer (over 4,500), as well as the opportunity to experience American university life. Students also cite the flexibility to explore their academic interests as another reason why US study is a good fit. Under the 'liberal arts' philosophy, students take classes from a variety of subjects during their first year before specialising in their major field of study.

Additional reasons include the funding opportunities made available by US universities and external funding bodies, travel and cultural experiences, and the chance to internationalise and strengthen their CV.

Degree structure

The 'liberal arts' philosophy of American degrees requires that students gain a well-rounded education by taking a wide variety of courses in the arts and sciences before concentrating on one academic area. A bachelor degree following this philosophy will typically include the following:

- **Course or Class** - another way of saying 'module'

- **Core Courses (also known as 'General Education' classes)** - the foundation of the degree programme, required of all students. They take a variety of courses in mathematics, English, humanities, physical sciences and social sciences

- **Major** - the subject in which a student chooses to concentrate. Your major courses represent one third to one half of the total number of courses required to complete a degree

- **Double Major** - most students major in one subject. However, the flexibility of the liberal arts curriculum provides students this option. Double majors allow students to complete the full major degree in both subjects, usually within four years

- **Minor** - a subject in which a student may choose to take the second greatest concentration of courses. The number of courses required for a minor tends to be one-third the number for a major in the same subject

- **Elective courses** - may be chosen from any department. They offer opportunities to explore other topics or subjects you may be interested in and help make up the total number of credits required to graduate.

A degree is designed to be completed in four years, although there is no fixed timescale. Instead, a degree is awarded after a student has completed a required amount of coursework, expressed in terms known as credits/units or semester hours. Usually a student will need to accumulate approximately 110 to 130 credits in order to graduate, with each course on average earning 3 or 4 credits.

Admissions process

Application Timeline: Ideally, you should begin researching universities and the application process 12 to 18 months before you wish to attend. (For example: start researching universities during spring/summer 2015; apply during autumn/winter 2015, with the aim of starting university in August/September 2016). This will leave plenty of time to find a university that is a good fit and allow you to prepare for any admissions exams you may have to sit. However, if you are just starting the admissions process in the early autumn the year before you would like to attend, you will still have time to compile your application materials - you will just need to work at a faster pace!

Choosing a University: First make sure that US study is a good match for your goals. You should then begin researching universities with a view to narrowing your search to the universities to which you will apply. You should consider a range of factors, including the majors on offer, campus size and setting, availability of funding and competitiveness of admission. Remember that, in the US, it is more important to find the right fit than to apply only to a handful of 'name-brand' institutions.

The following are admissions process points to keep in mind as you get started:

- *Application Deadlines* - There is no one set date for US university applications, but deadlines generally tend to fall between mid-October (for early decision/early action applications) and the end of January (for regular decision applications) in the academic year before enrolment

- *Admissions Exams* - You will probably need to sit an admissions exam, most likely the SAT Reasoning Test (formerly the Scholastic Aptitude Test or Scholastic Assessment Test) or ACT (originally the abbreviation of American College Testing). The most competitive universities may require two to three SAT Subject Tests in addition to the Reasoning Test or the ACT plus Writing. If you need to take an exam, remember to register early as testing centres in the UK fill up very quickly

- *Application Components* - You must submit a transcript from your school with your marks, as well as up to three letters of reference from contacts who know you well both inside and outside the classroom. Two to three essays outlining your academic interests and providing insight into who you are as a person are also usually required. These essays should highlight your future goals and say why you are interested in that particular university/programme or field. Each university will specify how many letters of reference it wants, and will most likely provide essay prompts for you to answer. Check on the admissions pages of each university website.

Funding

As you research universities and complete your applications, you should not forget to investigate funding options. There are four main types of funding for study in the US: savings, loans and scholarships from a US university or from an external funding body.

US universities award funding on the basis of financial need (often called grants) and/or merit (scholarships), as well as sports scholarships. External funding bodies may include a wide range of professional, charitable or government organisations that have a vested interest in educating members of society. Often, scholarships from external funding bodies can be thought of as niche scholarships, as they may be based on very specific personal qualities outlined by the funding body in addition to academic merit or financial need.

Sutton Trust US Programme

The Sutton Trust, in partnership with the US-UK Fulbright Commission, is running a US Programme to give bright state school students interested in attending a US university a preview of life on a US campus and support in making high quality undergraduate applications to the US.

The programme will assist students through the process of applying to a US university - from introductory information sessions, to a week in the US visiting campuses, to admissions tests and completing university applications. All costs, including travel and accommodation, are met by the Sutton Trust.

For full details, visit the website at:
www.suttontrust.com/programmes/us-programme

USA Study Advice and Resources

- **Advising Website at: www.fulbright.org.uk** for a step-by-step guide to applying to US universities

- **Seminars** (monthly from March to October): attend an Undergraduate Study in the US seminar

- **USA College Day** (autumn): attend USA College Day, the only American university fair in the UK

- **Additional help:** the contact page of the Fulbright website offers email and phone details.

US-UK Fulbright Commission: **www.fulbright.org.uk**

Study in the USA Information: **www.fulbright.org.uk/study-in-the-usa**

Fulbright Commission – Ireland: **www.fulbright.ie**

Open Doors: **www.iie.org/en/Research-and-Publications/Open-Doors**

EducationUSA: **www.educationusa.info**

US-UK Fulbright Commission – EducationUSA London

> Battersea Power Station
> 188 Kirtling Street
> London
> SW8 5BN

Fulbright Commission - Ireland

> Brooklawn House
> Crampton Avenue
> Dublin 4
> Ireland

Studying in Canada

Original article written by Cathy Norris with assistance from Allison Goodings, Trade Commissioner for the Education Section at the Canadian High Commission, London.

Canada's universities offer degrees that are globally recognised. There is a full range of course options, from three- to four-year bachelor degrees to master and doctoral (PhD) levels. Other options include professional qualifications in such areas as medicine, law, architecture and dentistry, as well as certificates, diplomas and short career-focused programmes.

Where?

Canada is a vast country consisting of ten different provinces and three territories.

These all have their own colleges and universities and each province and territory is unique, from the Rockies on the west coast to Quebec, the heart of French-Canadian culture.

Application process

There is no centralised system for applications. Each university has its own policy regarding admission requirements. The process usually begins in the summer months (May/ June/ July) and application deadlines vary from institution to institution. For providers which accept students in September, deadlines range from the fall (autumn) to winter. For institutions with intakes in January or May/June, the deadline could be several months ahead. You should check the website of each institution in which you are interested and make direct contact for specific admission requirements and application deadlines.

For schools in Ontario there is an online application service, which allows you to apply to three schools for the same rate. Some other provinces also have common application procedures.

- Ontario: **www.ouac.on.ca**
- British Columbia: **https://applybc.ca**
- Alberta: **www.applyalberta.ca**

Cost of Studying

Canada claims to offer the lowest tuition rates for overseas students compared with Australia, New Zealand and the United States. You can calculate the projected costs for a specific course by using the *Step 1-2-3* option on the website at: **www.educationau-incanada.ca/educationau-incanada/template-gabarit/step-etape.aspx?lang=eng**

This will give you an estimate not only of fees but also of living costs.

Funding

Government scholarships are available but many are for postgraduate or research programmes. Most universities and colleges offer a variety of scholarships (entrance and continuing) to international students, including some at undergraduate level. You could choose to work while you study, either on or off campus. During term, students may work for 20 hours a week, but during scheduled breaks you can work full time. You can also apply, after completion of your degree or diploma, for a work permit, which would allow you to add valuable international work experience of up to three years to your CV.

Accommodation

Many post-secondary institutions have accommodation located on or near campus. Dorms generally have a shared kitchen, bathroom and laundry facilities. Some offer optional meal plans where you can pay a set price up-front for two or three meal tickets per day.

If staying for just one semester, choosing a residence can be easier than finding your own private, off-campus housing.

For a longer period, you could choose residence for your first semester and then make alternative long-term arrangements as you become more acquainted with your area.

Staying in residence is the preferred option for a majority of Canadian students in their first and second years of study. Many international students also find it allows them to make friends and find study partners more easily, saves on transport to campus, and generally enables a smoother social transition.

Study Permit

In order to study in Canada as an international student you may need a study permit. Canadian study permits are only issued after you have been accepted at a Canadian college, university or other accredited educational institution designated to receive international students.

Entry to Canada is dependent on you having sufficient funds to pay for tuition fees, living expenses and a return ticket home. Character and health checks are also made and may involve a police check or a medical examination, or both. Your study permit is issued on arrival against a written notification of acceptance on a course.

You can find out whether you need a study permit and check your eligibility via the Citizenship and Immigration Canada website at:
www.cic.gc.ca/english/study/study-who.asp

Healthcare

Canada's universal healthcare system is well developed, with each province/territory managing healthcare for its region, covering all citizens for hospital and physician care. Virtually all Canadian post-secondary institutions have medical insurance plans available to international students. Contact the Canadian educational institution you plan to attend for information about health insurance cover for you.

Whether or not you purchase this cover from your Canadian institution, it is highly recommended that you take out appropriate travel health insurance.

Further information

Find out more about studying in Canada from the official website at:
www.educationau-incanada.ca

You should also spend some time exploring the website of each institution in which you are interested.

Study options in Australia and New Zealand

Sarah Nash, Director of Study Options, a free advice and application service for UK and Irish students interested in studying in Australia and New Zealand

Over the past few years the number of British students looking to study at universities overseas - whether in Australia, New Zealand, the United States, Canada, Ireland, mainland Europe or elsewhere - has been rising steadily.

Now, the issues swirling around the UK higher education system - ranging from complaints about contact teaching hours and a lack of focus on students to the fact that most English universities now charge £9,000 a year as their standard tuition fee - have caused the number of people investigating university options overseas to jump sharply.

So what is drawing so many UK students to Australian and New Zealand universities? Here are just a few of the reasons:

- **High standard of education** - the quality of HE education available at Australian and New Zealand universities is excellent. In the *QS World University Rankings 2014*, eight Australian institutions are ranked among the top 100 universities in the world. New Zealand has one university in the top 100 and a further two in the top 250. To put those numbers into context, Australia has around 40 universities, New Zealand has just eight and the UK around 140

- **Based on UK system** - education in Australia and New Zealand is based on the UK system, with universities awarding Bachelor of Arts or Science degrees that are recognised by both employers and academics as being the equal of qualifications gained from a UK university. This recognition between systems is important if you want to study a professional degree such as nursing, veterinary science, social work or engineering

- **Less competition for places** - many subjects in the UK are so popular that places to study them at degree level are always oversubscribed. There are places available on many of these degrees in Australia and New Zealand, including subjects such as physiotherapy, dentistry, veterinary science, psychology, history and marine science. The academic entry requirements are often just as tough as they are here in the UK, but there are more places available overall, so students should have more chance of securing a place

- **Straightforward application process** - applying to Australian and New Zealand universities is very uncomplicated. With the help of Study Options, you simply apply direct to each university and can usually expect a response within four to six weeks

- **Best place for certain subjects** - Australia and New Zealand are recognised as world leaders in subject areas such as sports science, physiotherapy, marine science, geology, social work, tourism and environmental science. Marine scientists in Australia are always happy to report that they can use the Great Barrier Reef as a laboratory!

- **Candidates can hold up to five offers** - you are allowed to hold up to five conditional offers from Australian and New Zealand universities, alongside the two permitted by the UCAS system in the UK. This means that, when your A level or equivalent results arrive, you could have seven potential courses and universities from which to choose

- **Attractive lifestyle** - both countries offer an enviable lifestyle for students, one that is relaxed and outdoorsy, with enough cultural similarities to the UK to be reassuring, but enough differences to make living there an opportunity for extensive travel and endless new discoveries.

Five easy steps to making an application

1 Do plenty of research. Study Options can send you a free *Guide to Studying in Australia and New Zealand* to help you get started. Alternatively, visit the website at: **www.studyoptions.com**

2 Make a list of the courses available in your chosen subject. Make sure you specify what you want to study, what qualifications you have at the moment, and whether you have any particular requests – for example, if you want to be in a specific city

3 Check the content and structure of each course on your list, together with details of tuition fees, entry requirements, application deadlines and other key information. If you want to do a professional degree overseas, check with the relevant professional body in the UK that they will recognise your overseas qualification, and allow you to register and work when you return home

4 Once you have decided which universities to apply to, let Study Options know and they will send you the application forms and a guide to applying. Take particular care with your personal statement. Unless you're applying for a performance-based course such as music performance or fine art, which require an audition or portfolio, or a very competitive course such as medicine, it's unlikely that you will be required to attend an interview. Your personal statement is therefore your only real opportunity to set your application apart from all the others

5 Send the completed applications to Study Options, who check to make sure everything is correct and certify documents on behalf of the universities. Applications are then forwarded electronically to your chosen universities.

Bear in mind that studying in Australia and New Zealand is an HE option that requires you to fund your own tuition fees and living costs. There are no grants or loans available and very few scholarships. Student visas in both Australia and New Zealand allow you to work for up to 20 hours a week during term time and as much as you like during the long university holidays.

Further information

For full details, visit the *Study Options* website at: **www.studyoptions.com**

You might also explore

Hobsons Course Finder – comprehensive and independent information on higher education pathways in Australia, including postgraduate courses and career options: **www.hobsonscoursefinder.com.au**

Studies in Australia – the international student guide, including an online course search facility: **www.studiesinaustralia.com**

Think New: **http://studyinnewzealand.com**

Degree Course Descriptions

The following pages contain the Degree Course Descriptions, carefully selected to give a flavour of each major course area.

The articles are written in most cases by professors and lecturers at leading UK universities. These people know the courses from the inside and understand the difficulties facing students who are about to make choices that could have a lasting influence on their future.

Each Degree Course Description contains:

· an introductory overview of the course area

· details of a typical course structure

· information on potential career opportunities

· suggestions for further reading

· website links to sources of more detailed information

Accountancy

Original article by Ken Pratt, University of Stirling

Introduction

Few organisations survive or prosper without financial information for planning, decision-making and control. Accountants are the skilled professionals who provide and verify this information. Accounting has been described as 'the language of business' and the ability of managers to communicate and co-ordinate their activities depends in part on their ability to understand and use that language. Accountants liaise with managers in all functions, which makes the work endlessly varied and provides a broad experience of the workings of the organisation. This breadth of experience makes them valuable to many different organisations and opens up a wide choice of careers.

Degree Courses

To pursue a successful career in accountancy you are likely to need both a university degree and a recognised professional accountancy qualification. Your university degree could be in almost any subject: it does not have to be in accountancy or a related discipline. A degree in a subject other than accountancy is commonly referred to in an accountancy context as a 'non-relevant degree' but this is perhaps an unfortunate and misleading term. Some employers are very keen to recruit applicants with non-relevant degrees, say for example in engineering, computer science, mathematics or languages, because these can bring additional skills which will be very useful in the work they will do. Most employers are pleased to recruit able students no matter what their degree subject, arguing that graduates in, for example, philosophy or anthropology or English literature bring variety and a wider education to their workforce.

There are also good reasons for choosing to take a university degree in accountancy: it is an indication that you are clear about your intended career and it allows you to study the subject in much greater breadth and depth than is possible in study for professional examinations, where study is often completed in short intensive blocks or in the limited time available outside the demands of busy and sometimes long working days. A university honours degree provides not only practical technical competence but also a thorough grounding in the theoretical and conceptual context of accountancy, not to mention powers of inquiry. Graduates with a recognised degree in accountancy who go on to pursue a professional qualification will be required to take fewer professional examinations than those with a non-relevant degree. A number of trends, such as the almost universal use of computers, wider concepts of financial accountability and greater regulation, have increased the level of knowledge required by accountants and make studying for an accountancy degree a desirable first step for would-be accountants.

As is the case with most subjects, there is considerable variation between the courses at different universities. At some, there is a greater emphasis on the use of computers; at some, certain aspects (taxation for example) are a compulsory part of the course, whilst at others the aspect is an option.

Expect degree courses to include a basic core of accounting, finance, taxation and business law. Another likely part of the core is operations research, which employs mathematical methods to assist in making decisions. You will often find that accountancy courses are combined with other subjects that have a clear connection with accountancy. Economics, marketing, computing and management science fall into this category. Many universities offer degrees in accountancy with a modern language. These combined degrees often enable students to work in areas other than accountancy when they obtain their degree. There are many alternatives in degrees involving accountancy and also finance. This makes it even more important than usual to study university prospectuses carefully and to find out which option suits you.

The major companies and professional firms normally expect applicants to graduate with a good Honours degree. An Honours degree in England is normally completed within three years. In Scotland, however, it is often necessary to stay on for a fourth year.

Career Opportunities

There are very many openings in the accountancy profession, in industry, government and commerce for well-qualified graduates. These include financial and management accounting, auditing, taxation, consultancy and financial services. Accountants may also choose to work in organisations or industries which particularly interest them or match their career goals including, for example, international oil companies, high-street retailers, health care, sports organisations, local and national government and charities.

Related Degrees

International Accounting; Accounting for Management; Business Accounting.

Suggested Reading

Working in Accountancy 2015
- Sherridan Hughes, Trotman Education, 2014

Accounts Demystified: the Astonishingly Simple Guide to Accounting
- Anthony Rice, Prentice-Hall, 2011

Accounting
- Michael Jones, John Wiley, 2013

Further Information

Association of Chartered Certified Accountants (ACCA)
www.accaglobal.com

Chartered Institute of Management Accountants (CIMA)
www.cimaglobal.com

Chartered Institute of Public Finance and Accountancy (CIPFA)
www.cipfa.org

Institute of Chartered Accountants in England and Wales
www.icaew.com

Chartered Accountants Ireland
www.charteredaccountants.ie

Institute of Chartered Accountants of Scotland
www.icas.org.uk

Institute of Certified Public Accountants in Ireland
www.cpaireland.ie

Acting

Original article by Malcolm Griffiths, Nottingham Trent University

Introduction

This article is primarily about courses at drama schools - usually but not always at degree level - designed to offer vocational training for aspiring actors. See the separate article on Drama for more academic degrees exploring the history and development of drama and analysis of texts. There are also performing and creative arts courses, which offer opportunities for more experimental approaches to performance in conjunction with, for example, dance, music and visual arts studies. These courses do not claim to provide the kind of training found at drama schools but to encourage students to create their own performance events and to learn through both practice and the wider debate on the arts.

Degree Courses

Drama schools are a comparatively recent phenomenon and have largely replaced the actor's traditional apprenticeship on the job with opportunities for developing skills, learning techniques, making mistakes and acquiring self-confidence before trying to survive in a highly competitive market. Although there will always be room for people with irrepressible natural talent, the importance of drama schools in nurturing ability and improving standards is now recognised. Schools are acutely aware that a professional actor needs to be adaptable to all kinds of theatre - compelling a pub audience in cabaret, projecting the nuances of a character's psyche in a large auditorium, devising a show with disabled children and so on. Each school will try to prepare students to meet the exceptional range of responses and skills required, but each will have evolved its particular philosophy and style. It is here that care needs to be taken in selecting a course. All drama schools provide tuition in voice, movement and acting but how these three fundamentals are taught will differ widely. Movement teaching, for example, can vary from exercises drawn from gymnastics or acrobatics to precise schooling in dance. One school may place great emphasis on a highly individualistic approach focusing on students' technical and expressive proficiency and on the production of play texts in order to give the student the experience to develop as a flexible and disciplined instrument of interpretation. Another will stress the essential collaborative aspect of theatre and develop work from a basis of group improvisation in order to increase students' creative responsiveness and social awareness. No drama school would claim to be able to turn you into a great actor but it can help you further your ambition by providing a thorough grounding, expertise and time.

Before deciding which course to apply to, you should consider what facilities the school has and how much work is done on radio, television and film as these will become a crucial source of your future livelihood. Also find out whether the school employs visiting professionals for projects or productions and whether it covers both past and contemporary theatre forms.

Career Opportunities

The image of the successful actor or actress projected by the media and magazines is one of often far-fetched glamour. Real success can mean being able to afford to choose between work in theatre, films or television or to remain with a company over a number of years developing a particular form of theatre. The majority of performers, however, face a harsher reality where stretches of unemployment are broken by the occasional television engagement, promotional video or short repertory season. A career in acting requires a special toughness and determination in addition to real talent. If you succeed, it will be very rewarding. Should you fail, nobody else will shed a tear.

Related Degrees
Drama, Performing Arts; Performance and Live Arts; Theatre (Acting).

Suggested Reading
So you want to Tread the Boards
- Jennifer Reischel, JR Books, 2007

Being an Actor
- Simon Callow, Vintage, 2004

Year of the King
- Antony Sher, Nick Hern Books, 2004

The Making of the Professional Actor
- Adrian Cairns, Peter Owen, 2001

Other People's Shoes: Thoughts on Acting
- Harriet Walter, Nick Hern Books, 2003

So You Want To Be An Actor?
- Timothy West and Prunella Scales, Nick Hern Books, 2005

Actor's Guide to Auditions and Interviews
- Margo Annett, Methuen Drama, 2004

About Acting - Peter Barkworth
- Methuen Drama, 2001

Voice and the Actor
- Cicely Berry and Peter Brook, Harrap, 2000

So You Want to Be a Film or TV Actor?
- Lisa Rondinelli Albert, Enslow Publishers, 2008

So You Want to Be a Film and TV Actor
- Anthony Brown, Infinity, 2009

How to be a Working Actor
- Mari Lyn Henry and Lynne Rogers, Backstage Books, 2008

An Actor's Guide to Getting Work
- Simon Dunmore, Methuen Drama, 2012

Further Information
Drama UK
www.dramauk.co.uk

British Actors' Equity Association
www.equity.org.uk

Creative and Cultural Skills
http://ccskills.org.uk/careers/advice/any/theatre

National Association for Youth Drama in Ireland
http://nayd.ie

Aeronautical/Aerospace Engineering

Original article by Professor Donald McLean, University of Southampton

Introduction

Aeronautical engineering is not easy to describe in just a few words because it is a very big subject embracing a large number of specialised technical disciplines. Each of those disciplines can become a lifetime study for some of us, yet to be any good at aeronautical engineering means that you must have some understanding of all of them. You must learn about the physical principles involved when anything flies, or when it moves through space where there is no real atmosphere. You have to learn the techniques needed to analyse and design aerospace vehicles for specific tasks.

It is that very variety and the corresponding great complexity of these vehicles that gives aeronautical engineering its special dimension: as an engineering subject it calls forth the greatest imagination and enthusiasm from everyone who works in it. The kind of vehicles you may deal with can range from those which operate in the earth's atmosphere to those which go beyond it. There are the single- and twin-engined general aviation aircraft, which don't fly very fast, very far or very high, but which are the most common aircraft type in the world; commercial jet transports fly millions of people daily in safety and comfort over millions of miles at affordable cost; and the different types of military aircraft must have a performance which is evidently a function of the intended mission. Although each of these aircraft types has its special problems, because each operates in a different speed regime, and although research is carried out continuously on them in industrial design offices, university laboratories and military research establishments, each type is linked by a common core of technical specialisations and disciplines which are used as the basic subjects of any British aeronautical degree.

Degree Courses

Traditionally, 'aeronautical' engineering has a mechanical focus, covering the various aspects of conventional flight in the atmosphere and the manufacture of aircraft, while 'aerospace' engineering encompasses aeronautical engineering together with other aspects, such as space, automated flight control systems and avionics. However, the distinctions between the two are now disappearing, with course content often overlapping. You might consider a three-year BEng Bachelor level degree or an MEng, which involves an integrated additional year of study leading to a Master level qualification. Many universities also offer work experience opportunities, either through a one-year 'industrial' placement between the second and third year of your course, or through project work or summer placement schemes. All courses cover applying maths, science and technology to the research, design, manufacture and maintenance of airborne products. Areas of study include aerodynamics, structures, fluid dynamics and avionics, and examining manufacturing processes. To study aerodynamics effectively means that you have to be able to have access to a wind tunnel in which a model aircraft or an airfoil can be tested.

When an aerospace vehicle is moving around, it has to be structurally sound: its frame and surface must be strong enough to withstand the stresses which result from the very great forces to which a vehicle is subject whenever it is manoeuvred, or whenever it meets atmospheric turbulence. Even spacecraft orbiting outside the earth's atmosphere can be subjected to torque disturbances caused by gravity gradients and solar pressure. Thus, the study of the behaviour of materials, the stresses and strains within that material, the study of vibration, and the deflection and twisting of the structural elements, are referred to as structural analysis. It is an important subject for every aeronautical engineer and it is taught in every aeronautical engineering course. Equally important is the study of how a vehicle is accelerated: propulsion.

Aircraft and spacecraft carry a considerable amount of systems equipment for auxiliary power, heat exchanging, life support, fire extinguishing, communication, navigation, and flight control, not to mention the wide variety of weapons systems fitted to military aircraft. Some of these systems are described by the term avionics, a compound word from aviation electronics. How such systems work, and how aerospace vehicles depend upon them, are usually covered in degree courses but there are also specialist courses in avionics systems or aerospace systems engineering. The core subjects of an aerospace systems course are likely to include mathematics, computation, communication theory, electromagnetism, system dynamics, signal analysis, power and actuator systems, as well as aerodynamics, propulsion and structural design.

Avionics systems courses involve the five principal areas of modern aeronautical engineering: aerodynamics and structures, propulsion, communication and guidance, flight control systems and information systems.

Career Opportunities

Current challenges for aeronautical/aerospace engineers range from developing more environmentally-friendly aeroplanes to imagining what might become safe and affordable space tourism vehicles. You might design and develop products such as airliners, helicopters, fighter jets, satellites and space vehicles, or you might work on components such as landing gear, engines and electrical/electronic systems.

Related Degrees

Avionic Systems; Space Technology; Aero Mechanical Engineering; Aerospace Technology; Aerospace Manufacturing Engineering.

Suggested Reading

Aircraft Structures for Engineering Students
- T H G Megson, Butterworth-Heinemann, 2012

Fundamentals of Aerodynamics
- John Anderson, McGraw-Hill, 2011

Aircraft Flight
- R H Barnard and D R Philpott, Prentice Hall, 2010

What Makes Airplanes Fly?
- P P Wegener, Springer, 2011

Further Information

Careers in Aerospace
www.careersinaerospace.com

Aerospace Defence Security Group
www.adsgroup.org.uk

Civil Aviation Authority
www.caa.co.uk

Royal Aeronautical Society
http://aerosociety.com

UK Space Agency
www.gov.uk/government/organisations/uk-space-agency

Engineers Ireland
www.engineersireland.ie

Agriculture and related courses

Original article by Professor W Holmes of the former Wye College

Introduction

The study of natural resources and their management to provide food, fibre, wood and other materials is of major importance throughout the world. The current emphasis on the environment makes it even more important that the physical, biological and economic principles underlying the production of crops, trees, and animals, and their interactions with the environment, are well understood.

Agriculture, horticulture, forestry and related subjects studied at degree level deal with these subjects in a very effective way. General courses give a broad training. There are also specialist courses in sciences (agricultural botany, agricultural biochemistry, agricultural zoology, animal science, horticultural science, wood science); courses emphasising economics (such as agricultural economics, agricultural business management, agricultural and food marketing); environmental courses (agriculture and environmental science, forestry and natural resources, terrestrial ecology) and in agricultural engineering.

Before you start, you must have a genuine interest in the subject. You might have grown up on a farm but this is certainly not essential. The subject may appeal because you like growing plants or working with animals. Alternatively, you may wish to apply your skills and interests in biology, chemistry, economics, geology, mathematics or physics to the real life situation. Or you may just like the countryside and country pursuits. Whatever your motivation, evidence of a keen interest and that you have read something about the subject, and preferably worked in it, will help to impress the selectors; a vague sentimental interest in nature and the open air is not likely to be enough.

For most courses, it is recommended that you spend at least one year after school gaining practical experience on a farm, a horticultural holding or an agricultural research station before you start. Even farmers' sons and daughters are encouraged to gain experience away from home. Many employers consider such experience to be essential. As an alternative, some courses provide for the student to take a sandwich year to gain his or her practical experience in the middle rather than before the course begins.

Degree Courses

Courses in the UK normally last three or four years, in addition to the practical year, with a progression from basic studies in the first year to more applied studies in the later years. For example, a course in *agriculture* will probably include the study of biology, biochemistry and economics together with introductory aspects of agriculture and statistics and computing in the first year. Soil science, crop production, animal production, farm mechanisation and farm management would be second-year courses. Advanced aspects of crop and animal production and of farm management, together with selections from more specialist topics (eg animal breeding, marketing, plant pathology or intensive horticultural cropping) might occupy the final years. In addition, most final year courses include a project, in which the student pursues a particular interest in some detail and submits a report or dissertation as part of the final examination.

Courses in *horticulture, plant science* and *agricultural botany* concentrate on plants. The horticultural courses include production and amenity horticulture, economics, management and marketing as well as the sciences of plant nutrition, plant physiology and plant pathology. Courses in plant science and agricultural botany are more science oriented: they omit management and use the additional time for experimental techniques and frequently for the conduct of small-scale investigations.

Similarly, courses in *animal science* and *agricultural zoology* provide for more detailed study of the anatomy, physiology, biochemistry and genetics of farm animals, and of the parasites and insects of agricultural importance, but omit some of the more practical aspects of animal husbandry and management. Since some of the work is conducted with smaller organisms, practical laboratory projects may be included.

Courses in *agricultural economics* are intended primarily for planners or consultants rather than for farm or estate managers, whose needs are usually met by courses in agriculture, agricultural business management or horticulture. These courses therefore start from a base of economics, mathematics and statistics and progress to advanced economics, agrarian development, agricultural policy, economic statistics, management and marketing with relatively brief reference to agricultural technology. Courses in *agricultural business management* and *land economy* depend more heavily on economics, management techniques and legal aspects, and they give less emphasis to scientific subjects.

Career Opportunities

A good degree gained opens a remarkable variety of career opportunities. Some graduates are soon running their own businesses in farming or horticulture; many are managing businesses for larger organisations, estates or conservation agencies. A further large proportion is involved in advisory work with national or international organisations or with commercial companies. Education, research and government posts at home or overseas also provide many opportunities.

Related Degrees

Agronomy; Organic Agriculture; Crop Science; Agricultural Science; Agriculture of the Environment; Agricultural Technology; Agricultural Biochemistry; Organic Agricultural Food and Marketing.

Suggested Reading

The Future of Farming, the Rise of the Rural Entrepreneur
- Edwin Van Raalte and Marjan Van Riel, AB Publishing, 2013

Adam's Farm: My Life on the Land
- Adam Henson, BBC Books, 2011

So shall we reap
- Colin Tudge, Penguin, 2004

Farmers Weekly
- magazine

Further Information

Farmers Weekly Interactive
www.fwi.co.uk

Department for Environment, Food and Rural Affairs
www.gov.uk/government/organisations/department-for-environment-food-rural-affairs

Grow Careers
www.growcareers.info

Lantra
www.lantra.co.uk

Irish Agriculture and Food Development Authority
www.teagasc.ie

American Studies

Original article by Mike Nicholson, University of Essex

Introduction

An important starting point here is to establish what exactly any particular university means by the term 'American'. You will find that most American Studies degrees in the United Kingdom restrict themselves to the United States (US), or possibly the US and Canada, while some have a wider vision in which you explore transatlantic issues as a whole, north and south of the Equator, looking at patterns of political frontiers and larger divisions based on language, religion or industrial development.

Degree Courses

Often offered as an interdisciplinary course, American Studies may be taken as a major subject (comprising 60% to 70% of the programme), as a minor subject (comprising 30% to 40% of the programme) or combined equally with another subject. It is typically linked with such subjects as Business, Computing, Education, English, Environmental Studies, European Studies, Film Studies, French, Geography, German, History, International Development, Media Studies, Portuguese and Spanish.

All of this means that American Studies courses vary considerably, not only from one institution to another but also from one student to another on the same programme. One university claims that you can "work in fields as diverse as the Hollywood cinema, the history of the ancient Aztecs and Incas, US social history, the history of slavery, the politics of contemporary Latin America, and contemporary Latin American and US culture". Another institution hints at certain themes by posing a series of questions: "How do we find meaning in the events of September 11th? Hollywood and the American Dream: the Americanisation of popular culture or cultural imperialism? The US economic blockade of Cuba: promoting or subverting democracy? What do the careers of Hillary Clinton and Barack Obama tell us about race, class and gender in the United States? What was the significance of the extradition proceedings against General Pinochet of Chile? What are the global implications of political and economic developments in Venezuela, Bolivia or Brazil? What does the new Mexican cinema tell us about contemporary Mexico?"

Many programmes provide an opportunity to study America at first-hand, allowing you to spend anything from a term or semester up to a full academic year abroad. While in America, you may be expected to complete a project that will count towards your final degree result. Before applying, you should note where in America a university has exchange partners and research what these institutions have to offer.

In terms of structure, the first year in most degree schemes encourages a broad study pattern covering several topics, to give you the opportunity to get a feel for the diversity and range of the programme. Specialisms usually start in the second year, often with an upper limit of three areas, e.g. American history, literature and film.

In the second year at one English university, for example, you are invited to choose from topics such as American Drama 1945-1970, America and Vietnam, American Bestsellers, the American 1960s, the American West or Native American Literature and Film.

The final year allows you to develop your particular interests to a more advanced level, and may include a dissertation on a topic agreed with your tutor.

Career Opportunities

While your American Studies programme may not be particularly vocational in nature, your wide-ranging studies should help you develop powers of critical and analytical thinking, the ability to apply these to primary and secondary texts, and skills in written and verbal forms of expression.

Research by the British Association for American Studies identifies career paths grouped into the broad categories listed below:

Business, Law and Accountancy (41.9%) Graduates pursue the full range of careers in these fields: in banking, large accountancy firms and other financial services, in management, marketing and retail for small and large firms.

Postgraduate Study (13.2%) While some graduates take MAs and PhDs in American (or Latin American) Studies, others go on to postgraduate courses in such varied areas as Cultural Studies, Social Work, Creative Writing, Development Studies, or even take an MBA (Master of Business Administration). American Studies graduates are more likely than their peers to undertake further study abroad - often, but not exclusively, in the United States.

Administration and Civil Service (10.9%) This includes charity organisers, immigration and other Civil Service officers, as well as local authority and health service administrators.

Teaching (9.9%) This category includes teaching at all levels from primary school to universities and colleges.

Arts, Media and Media Related (8.2%) This includes working for regional and national radio and television, film production, gallery work, acting and theatre management.

Publishing and Journalism (6.3%) This includes freelance writers and researchers as well as journalists for regional and national newspapers and magazines.

Public Relations and Advertising (2.2%) Graduates have secured PR and personnel jobs in many different firms, and have found work in both the creative and management aspects of advertising.

Teaching and Other Work Abroad (3.3%) Careers abroad range from teaching English as a foreign language to working for the EU in Brussels, internship programmes in the US Congress, and administrative posts in various multinational companies.

Other (4.4%) There are many career paths not covered by the categories above. These include nursing, the Armed Services, speech therapy, the police and leading expeditions as well as temporary employment.

Related Degrees

Comparative American Studies; English and United States Literature; United States and Latin American Studies; North American Studies; American and Canadian Studies; Hispanic Studies (Latin America).

Suggested Reading

The Cambridge Companion to Modern American Culture
- Christopher Bigsby, Cambridge University Press, 2006
Penguin History of the United States of America
- Hugh Brogan, Penguin, 2001
A New Introduction to American Studies
- Christopher Bigsby and Howard Temperley, Routledge, 2006
Get Set for American Studies
- Edward Ashbee, Edinburgh University Press, 2004

Further Information

Transatlantic Studies Association
www.transatlanticstudies.com
British Association for American Studies
www.baas.ac.uk
Irish Association for American Studies
http://iaas.ie

Anatomy

Original article by Professor Anthony Firth, St Mary's Hospital Medical School, London (now part of Imperial College School of Medicine)

Introduction

The anatomical approach is to explore the structure of living organisms as a way of getting at how they work. Anatomists tend to think in terms of shapes and relationships in space as the most striking and exciting aspects of living things - their imagination tends to be visual and spatial rather than abstract.

The earliest anatomists relied on dissection of dead organisms ('dissection' is another word meaning 'cutting apart') as their main method of study, and dissection of the dead bodies of people or of domestic animals still forms the core of many anatomy courses in medical, dental or veterinary science.

Whether or not students of biology, outside the health sciences, come across anatomy as a formal subject in their courses, they use the methods of structural study which typify the anatomical approach to biology. These now range from naked-eye observations during dissection to high-resolution microscopic examination of cells and their components. The first effective use of the electron microscope on biological materials in the 1950s both emphasised the power of the visual approach and also underlined its limitations. With these instruments it is possible to reveal the organisation not only of cell interiors but also of the large molecules such as DNA and proteins which characterise living tissue, but until quite recently this ability to see fine structural detail has been offset by the maddening difficulty of finding out anything precise about the chemical nature of the structures so revealed.

Over the last generation, and particularly in the last ten years, biologists have learned to characterise the molecular composition of microscopic structures by a range of methods which allow the presence of specific molecules to be revealed by light or electron microscopy. This hybrid science of histochemistry is an extraordinarily powerful tool, for it has allowed specific chemical information to be obtained with all the precision about structure and spatial relationships which characterises microscopic science. At first this could only be exploited for a fairly limited number of biologically interesting chemicals which were sufficiently distinctive for them to be stainable by chemical reactions which failed to stain other substances: starch and neutral fats are good examples. The most interesting molecules of living systems, the nucleic acids and proteins, could be identified as classes but it seemed impossible to label selectively a single species of protein or a single gene in a chromosome. Something could be done with those proteins which happened to be catalysts, the enzymes, as they could often be manipulated to yield a visible and insoluble reaction product which could be recognised by light or electron microscopy. Enzyme histochemistry has been with us for about thirty years and grows in subtlety and usefulness every year; it can show us not only where enzymes are within a cell, but also which reactions they can catalyse and even how fast they can do it.

Degree Courses

For students entering biology these are exciting times. Those training for medicine and allied professions meet both the traditional and the new anatomy. They study the human body by dissecting the dead, by examining pictures generated by an ever-growing range of non-invasive imaging methods such as x-radiographs, computerised tomography, ultrasound and magnetic resonance imaging. They explore living anatomy by examining their own bodies and those of other students. They study the mature and the developing body by microscopic means, which increasingly depend on the chemically specific and functionally informative methods of histochemistry. For all biologists, form and function are becoming unified by new methods in microscopy.

Whether we work on the unfolding of the genetic programme of development, the functional organisation of the brain, the subtly disordered biology of cancer cells, or the means by which an amoeba achieves the extraordinarily complex task of crawling across a piece of glass, our approach leans heavily on the central insight of anatomy: that form is the visible aspect of invisible functions and so can serve as a road to understanding them.

Career Opportunities

Anatomical science provides an ideal training for those students wishing to pursue a research or other career based on the biomedical sciences. Typical employers offering laboratory-based careers are the universities, government establishments, the National Health Service and the pharmaceutical and food industries.

Anatomy also provides an excellent basis for careers in education, biomedical information services and scientific management. Graduates can register for higher degrees (PhD, MSc), or take further training for a career in, say, physiotherapy or osteopathy; in exceptional cases they may gain admission to medical, dental or veterinary programmes.

Related Degrees

Anatomical Science.

Suggested Reading

Gray's Anatomy for Students
- Richard Drake et al, Churchill Livingstone, 2014

Molecular Biology of the Cell
- Bruce Alberts et al, Garland, 2008

Atlas of Human Anatomy
- Frank Netter, Saunders, 2014

Further Information

Anatomical Society of Great Britain and Ireland
www.anatsoc.org.uk

Gray's Anatomy Online
www.bartleby.com/107

Royal Society for Public Health
www.rsph.org.uk

National Health Service Careers
www.nhscareers.nhs.uk

Anthropology

Original article by Professor Adam Kuper, Brunel University

Introduction

Anthropologists have a romantic image. They are pictured camping in an Amazonian rain forest, or sailing on a frail barque between two little Pacific islands. But few people have much idea what anthropologists are really up to, and they are surprised to discover that we may also do field studies rather closer to home, in Greek islands, Irish villages or even Midlands factories.

Anthropology is about the evolution, unity and diversity of the human species. One branch of anthropology, physical anthropology, is concerned largely with the biological evolution of human beings. Archaeologists drive deep shafts back in time, reconstructing cultural processes in the distant past. Social or cultural anthropologists study contemporary human communities, charting their customs and practices and attempting to explain them.

The central experience of social anthropologists is always fieldwork. Devoting one or two years to any study in the field, the researcher participates as far as possible in the life of the people, speaking their language and forging bonds of friendship and trust. This sometimes trying, often inspiring, always important experience of immersion in a strange way of life is then translated into a formal analysis either of the community or, more usually today, of an aspect of its life. (But a number of anthropologists do slip the academic restrictions and produce lively impressionistic and personal accounts of their experience, such as Nigel Barley's humorous reminiscences of fieldwork in West Africa and Indonesia.)

Fieldwork - ethnography - is only one aspect of the anthropologist's work. The challenge to field-workers is not only to make sense of their observations, but to relate what they have seen to studies made of similar institutions elsewhere. The ultimate goal is to further our understanding of social and cultural processes at large. Social anthropology is therefore a comparative social science. It has particularly close ties with history and sociology, though there are also fecund links with other disciplines. It can often be studied in association with another subject, sometimes in the traditional company of physical anthropology and archaeology, but otherwise together with ancient history, linguistics, African or Asian languages, psychology or sociology, or in more and more new combinations.

Degree Courses

At a typical university, the first two years of study of anthropology would be devoted to outlining the variety of cultures and customs which are to be found in the societies around the world, and to introducing the students to the main philosophers of society, such as Durkheim, Weber and Marx. These are at a more advanced level in the second than the first year. During each year, teaching would cover five main areas: (i) the study of family and kinship systems in human societies, (ii) the study of economic life in human societies, (iii) the study of political life, (iv) the study of systems of religion and ideology, and (v) the study of language in society. A major question running through all these sections is whether the findings of economists, political scientists and others in western industrial society are going to be relevant to the study of tribal and peasant communities in the Third World.

Among topics covered at the Honours level would be 'nationalism and ethnicity', 'sex roles in human society', 'communication in human and animal society', 'representation and narrative' and 'linguistic anthropology'.

Career Opportunities

First year students are sometimes shocked by their sudden exposure to the variety of ways in which people think it proper and sensible to order their lives, but this is itself a profoundly educational experience and the discipline provides rich insights into other cultures. Students are also given a training in social science approaches and techniques, which often provides a basis for further independent academic development or opens the way to careers in the media, market research, social work, teaching or, in some cases, to the adventure of anthropological research.

Applied anthropology is a growing field. Government departments or development agencies are the usual employers, but in the USA more than half of professional anthropologists are employed by the private sector. Anthropologists advise on problems of development abroad and are often to be found on teams of planners associated with development projects. Others have come to specialise in community relations at home, particularly in multi-cultural environments and they may contribute to policy-making in fields as diverse as medical or educational services and town planning.

For some anthropologists, the ultimate justification of their studies is a moral one. Levi-Strauss has suggested that the study of anthropology offers two advantages: first it encourages us to take a level-headed and unbiased view of customs and ways of life remote from our own; second, it dissuades us from taking for granted the 'rightness' or 'naturalness' of our own customs.

Related Degrees

Social Anthropology; Forensic Anthropology.

Suggested Reading

Anthropology and Anthropologists: the Modern British School
- A Kuper, Routledge 1996

History and Theory in Anthropology
- Alan Barnard, Cambridge University Press, 2000

Small Places, Large Issues
- T Hylland Eriksen, Pluto Press, 2010

The Innocent Anthropologist: Notes from a Mud Hut
- Nigel Barley, Eland, 2011

Encyclopedia of Social and Cultural Anthropology
- Alan Barnard and Jonathan Spencer, Routledge, 2011

Anthropology Today
- International journal published by Wiley for the Royal Anthropological Institute:
http://eu.wiley.com/WileyCDA/WileyTitle/productCd

Further Information

Royal Anthropological Institute
www.therai.org.uk

Anthropological Association of Ireland
www.anthropologyireland.org

Aquaculture

Original article written with help from the University of Stirling

Introduction

In recent years there has been great progress in the cultivation of organisms and plants that live and grow in water-based environments. Whilst we tend to associate cultivation of organisms in water with fish farming, aquaculture or aquatic agriculture is concerned with the culture or artificial development of many aquatic organisms. These include not only fish but also molluscs such as mussels and oysters, crustaceans like prawns and shrimps, as well as crocodiles, turtles and algae.

Degree Courses

It is important to look very carefully at the different courses under an aquatic heading as their content is quite varied. A course in aquaculture will include courses in cell biology, physiology, ecology and evolution, molecular biology and genetics, followed by a varied programme including a core subject 'aquatic science' in which you will learn about aquatic environments and the management of living aquatic resources, as well as aquaculture and marine biology. The problems of disease and reproduction associated with this form of culture will also be studied as well as nutrition and biotechnology in aquaculture. You will then be able to choose optional courses such as freshwater science and ecotoxicology before carrying out a project over 12 to 14 weeks.

During the first year and a half (Semesters 1 to 3) at Stirling, for example, you take core modules in Oceanography, Introduction to Aquatic Environments, Cell Biology and Physiology, Ecology and Evolution, Genetics, Practical Skills in the Natural Sciences, People and Environment, Global Environmental Issues, and Earth Science. Honours students continue in Semesters 4 to 8 with core modules in Managing Aquatic Resources, Coastal Marine Biology, Biodiversity, Biosphere, Aquaculture, Pelagic and Benthic Processes, Aquaculture Field Course, Aquaculture Assignments and a final year Aquaculture Project. Optional modules can be selected from those available in: Fish Development, Fish Nutrition, Aquatic Diseases, River Ecology and Management, Animal Physiology, Ecology, and Environmental Sciences. Overseas projects are encouraged and past final-year projects have been located throughout Europe, North and South America, the Indian subcontinent, Asia, Oceania and Australasia.

The degree shares a common foundation with programmes in Marine Biology. Because of this, the option to take a degree in Marine Biology is retained until the middle of the third year.

Career Opportunities

Graduates in Aquaculture are well equipped to enter the expanding field of Aquaculture or to follow any other career in which there is a need for scientifically trained personnel. Graduates can expect to seek employment in government and private laboratories, including environmental protection agencies and consultancy organisations.

A second degree (PhD or MSc) may often be required for more senior research posts or for senior management in the industry. Many graduates do therefore go on to pursue further study. Alternatively, a wide range of more general biological posts is available, including those in ecotoxicology and environmental impact assessment. A degree in Aquaculture can also be used to gain entry to careers outside science, such as those in management and finance, computing, and the leisure and tourism industry.

Related Degrees
Aquatic Sciences; Aquaculture & Fisheries Management; Aquatic & Fisheries Management; Freshwater Science; Applied Marine Biology; Aquatic BioScience; Aquatic Zoology; Coastal and Aquatic Science; Fisheries and Aquaculture; Marine and Freshwater Biology.

Suggested Reading
Aquaculture: Farming Aquatic Animals and Plants
- John S Lucas and Paul C Southgate, Wiley-Blackwell, 2012

Aquaculture: Principles and Practices
- T Pillay and M Kutty, Wiley-Blackwell, 2005

A Student's Guide to the Seashore
- J and S Fish, Cambridge University Press, 2011

Marine Ecology: Processes, Systems, and Impacts
- Michel Kaiser et al, Oxford University Press, 2011

Aquaculture: the Ecological Issues
- John Davenport et al, Wiley, 2003

Ecology of Aquatic Management
- Michael Dobson and Chris Frid, Oxford University Press, 2013

Further Information
Institute of Aquaculture
www.aquaculture.stir.ac.uk

Centre for Environment, Fisheries and Aquaculture Science
www.cefas.defra.gov.uk

Irish Aquaculture Industry
www.marine.ie/home/Aquaculture.htm

Aquaculture and Fisheries Development Centre, University of Cork
www.ucc.ie/en/afdc

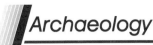

Archaeology

Original article by Dr S W Hillson, Institute of Archaeology

Introduction

Lost cities, great ancient works of art in gold and precious stones, the sumptuous tombs of forgotten kings. If you study archaeology, you can certainly learn about such exciting and exotic things, but most archaeologists spend most of their time dealing with much more mundane objects such as broken pottery and bones - the accumulated waste of ordinary households, farms and towns. What keeps us fascinated is the light that archaeology can shed on everyday life in ancient communities, rather than the lives and works of the great and powerful. This is one of the major differences between archaeology and history. Written history is mostly about rulers and the nobility, military and religious life. Archaeology is based on physical remains rather than records and the great bulk of the material which survives from the past represents ordinary people. Most ancient objects, even those which may seem to us to be ugly, poorly made or badly damaged, have a story locked up in them. There is a real thrill in taking a small, broken fragment out of the ground and bringing its story out with careful detective work. If you want to find out how people live, a good way is to look in their household refuse, and much of archaeology is tied up with the recovery and sophisticated analysis of ancient domestic rubbish.

Archaeology is an unusually broad subject, bridging the arts and the sciences. It ranges throughout the world, wherever people have lived, and extends from the earliest artefacts made by our extinct relatives some two and a half million years ago, through the period of historical records, including the industrial revolution and up to the present day. The basic approach is scientific, because objects must be excavated and studied in as methodical and objective a manner as possible, but there is also room for the artistic appreciation of beautiful artefacts and for interpretations, which involve history, philosophy and sociology. An expanding field is 'science-based archaeology'; applying techniques which originated in the more traditional sciences. Physics is used to date objects and to locate buried sites. Chemistry helps to discover ancient methods of manufacture and trade routes. Biology is applied in the study of health, hygiene and diet in ancient communities. With all these different strands to archaeology, it can be difficult to define the core of the subject.

Although not a course requirement, it is a good idea for those thinking of embarking upon a degree course in archaeology to join an archaeology society, take part in a dig or other fieldwork or do voluntary work in a museum.

Degree Courses

If you apply to study archaeology, you will find a bewildering range of degree courses and options. Some courses are highly specialised, such as classical archaeology, medieval archaeology, Egyptology, Near Eastern archaeology and archaeological conservation (the restoration and preservation of artefacts). These are really for people who already know the area of archaeology in which they would like to concentrate. The majority of people are less sure and apply for general archaeology courses, but the coverage of these also varies considerably. The subject is so wide that very few institutions have the staff to cover the full range, or even a substantial part of it. Look very carefully at what options are available before you apply. The majority of courses deal with the archaeology of Europe, Mediterranean and Middle Eastern countries. It is much harder to find course options on the archaeology of Africa, eastern Asia and Australasia, and the Americas. Some departments specialise in prehistory, whilst others concentrate on the classical or medieval periods. Relatively few institutions have specialist options in the various science-based archaeology subjects but some departments concentrate on them and several BSc degrees in archaeology are offered. Because of all these variations, it is a good idea to visit archaeology departments in good time before you apply. Most departments will be very pleased to arrange this.

Despite the rather exotic nature of the material, much of an archaeology course follows the traditional pattern of classes but one of the distinctive features of the subject is practical work. You are likely to do a lot of fieldwork because it is the basis of all archaeology. Fieldwork is one of the main attractions for most professional archaeologists and students, ranging from a regional field survey to full excavation of a particular site. Depending on the course, you may travel widely with your fieldwork. There may also be a lot of practical work in the drawing office and laboratory. You could be identifying and piecing together shards of pottery, learning to interpret aerial photographs, practising drawing site plans, learning to sort and identify animal bone fragments, or using a microscope to identify pollen grains. Archaeological conservation involves a specialised training with a great deal of laboratory work, learning various treatments and restoration techniques. Most students enjoy handling ancient objects very much. The fieldwork and practical content of courses varies, and it is well worth finding out what facilities are available in a particular department and how much hands-on experience of artefacts and other remains there is.

Career Opportunities

There are many archaeology graduates but fewer than 5,000 professional archaeologists employed in the UK. The main areas of work for archaeologists are in commercial archaeology units, museums, providing planning and development control advice through local authorities or specialist consultants. Many also work for the national heritage agencies (English Heritage, Historic Scotland, Northern Ireland Environment Agency and Cadw) or conservation charities, of which the National Trust is probably the biggest employer. A number of archaeologists continue with academic research after graduation and some of these go on to teach in colleges and university departments. Some archaeologists are self-employed and many of these work as specialist consultants in their particular field, such as pottery or bone analysis. Most archaeology graduates enter the general graduate market, taking up commercial, financial, managerial and teaching careers (eg history, ancient history or classical studies).

Related Degrees

Archaeological Science; Environmental Archaeology; Classical Archaeology; Archaeological Conservation.

Suggested Reading

Archaeology: An Introduction
- Kevin Greene and Tom Moore, Routledge, 2010

Archaeology: Theories, Methods and Practice
- Colin Renfrew and Paul Bahn, Thames and Hudson, 2012

British Archaeology
- bi-monthly journal published by the CBA: **www.britisharchaeology.org**

Sampling in Archaeology
- Clive Orton, Cambridge University Press, 2000

Further Information

Council for British Archaeology
http://new.archaeologyuk.org

Institute of Archaeologists of Ireland
www.iai.ie

Architecture

Adapted, with permission, from material supplied by the Royal Institute of British Architects (RIBA)

Introduction

At the forefront of designing the built environment that surrounds us in the 21st Century, architects are professional experts in the field of building design and construction, using their unique creative skills to advise on the design and construction of new buildings, the reuse of existing buildings and the nature of the spaces surrounding buildings in our towns and cities.

Society looks to architects to define new ways of living and working, to develop innovative ways of using existing buildings and creating new ones. We need architects' understanding of the complex process of design and construction to build socially and ecologically sustainable cities and communities. Architects can be extremely influential as well as being admired for their imagination and creative skills.

Architects design by drawing. This is their chief means of communication though they need to be able to speak and write well too. You will be taught how to do the necessary technical drawing; this is not a subject you need to study beforehand but you should enjoy drawing. At interview, most schools of architecture will want to see a portfolio of drawings and sketches but it is not essential to take Art as an examination subject.

Degree Courses

Training to become an architect takes a minimum of seven years, but only five of those are spent at a school of architecture. The **first three years** are normally spent working towards a degree at your chosen school, where the object will be to develop your sensitivity to people, places and technology in order to help you understand the ways in which buildings and their surroundings are affected by social, cultural and material factors. You will be taught the practice of design.

The **fourth year** is normally spent working in an architect's office under the general direction of your school of architecture. Some students also travel during this year or work in parts of the building industry. You then return to a school of architecture for **two further years** to obtain a diploma or higher degree; this does not have to be at the same school where you took your first degree.

After the **seventh year**, which is again spent working in an office, you take a professional practice examination. If you pass, you can become a full member of the Royal Institute of British Architects (while studying you can become a student member). The title 'architect' is protected in the UK by law and you must register with the Architects Registration Board before you can start to practise professionally.

Much of the time in architecture school is spent on projects rooted in building design. By the time you reach the final year, you will also have touched on many related subjects such as urban design, town planning, landscaping and interior design. One day a week is generally spent at lectures or seminars which cover the history and theory of architecture, all aspects of building construction and technology, computer systems, professional practice and many other topics.

All RIBA-validated courses are designed to ensure that students achieve the required standard in the core areas of study. Some courses also offer specialist areas of study or have developed strengths in particular areas, for example: technology, environmental design, history or theory. As a prospective student, you should research course options carefully in order to establish what best suits you.

There are also architectural studies courses designed for those who wish to study architecture as a non-vocational subject. Such courses do not give exemption from RIBA professional examinations but can be of interest if you wish to enter related areas such as conservation, planning or landscape architecture.

Career Opportunities

Like the construction industry generally, architecture has highs and lows reflecting the state of the national economy. Since the recession of 2008, the building sector has shrunk considerably and with it opportunities for architects. However, the UK construction industry has turned around in 2014 to become one of the fastest-growing sectors in the economy, offering new hope for architecture graduates in the years to come.

Training is very long with no guarantee of employment at the end. Most architects work in small private practices with usually fewer than ten staff. To start with, you might be on a short-term contract and then progress with experience to junior and then senior partnerships. Alternatively, you could start your own practice. The environmental field is a growing area of work, offering opportunities for professionals to become involved in the planning process for environmentally sensitive development schemes.

Related Degrees

Interior Architecture; Architectural Engineering; Naval Architecture.

Suggested Reading

Architecture: Form, Space and Order
- Francis Ching, John Wiley, 2014

Introduction to Architectural Science: the Basis of Sustainable Design
- Steven V Szokolay, Routledge, 2014

101 Things I Learned in Architecture School
- Matthew Frederick, MIT Press, 2007

Architecture Now! 8
- Philip Jodidio, Taschen, 2012

Mastering Architecture
- Leon von Schaik, Wiley, 2005

Further Information

Architects Registration Board
www.arb.org.uk

Royal Institute of British Architects
www.architecture.com

Royal Incorporation of Architects in Scotland
www.rias.org.uk

Royal Society of Ulster Architects
www.rsua.org.uk

Royal Institute of the Architects of Ireland
www.riai.ie

Art and Design

Original article by Norwich School of Art and Design

Introduction

Art and Design can appear a bewilderingly complex subject. A vast range of courses at various levels prepares the student for a lifetime of professional practice and by far the best way to ensure compatibility is to undertake a preparatory diagnostic course prior to application for higher-level study. In England, Wales and Northern Ireland, full-time courses of one or two years' duration usually fulfil this important function, though some are available part-time. They include: Foundation studies in Art and Design and Access to Art and Design. Some specialist National Diploma courses are also offered at Further Education level. In Scotland, the first year of a four-year degree has a similar purpose.

Degree Courses

At Higher Education (Bachelor of Arts, Foundation Degree and Higher National Diploma) level there is a vast menu of specialist courses and broad-based programmes from which to choose. Many Graphic, Textiles, Fashion and 3-Dimensional Design courses arrange work experience in the industry, as well as business and professional studies to prepare for the world of work.

Fine Art courses are primarily aimed at supporting the student in the development of individual creative practice within contemporary and historical contexts. They may have a structured initial phase where skills are taught and many contain specialisms like painting, sculpture, printmaking and time-based media.

Graphic Design and **Visual Communication** courses prepare graduates for a range of professional opportunities as advertising designers, publishing designers, illustrators, animators, photographers and many other commercial disciplines. Some courses have a common first year, when students are able to experience the disciplines before specialisation, others specialise from day one.

Animation, Illustration and **Photography** are also offered as degree courses in their own right.

Film and **Video** courses prepare students for careers in film, broadcasting and independent production. Some concentrate on producing students with specialist knowledge and experience of production team roles such as camera, editing, or production design, while others take a more broad-based approach.

Textiles and **Surface Pattern** courses may emphasise commercial design, individual creative development, or craft practice, though these aspects frequently overlap. There may be a further specialism into printed or woven textiles, or specific applications of textile design, like textiles for fashion. Like other degree programmes, there may be a broad introductory phase followed by an opportunity to specialise.

Fashion Design courses are sometimes allied to textile courses, though some are independent. They prepare the student for the highly competitive commercial world of fashion design and usually provide an intensive training in all aspects of the business.

Many offer options in Marketing and may include foreign languages. Students undertake work placements and must be prepared to work to deadlines. Like other degree programmes, there may be a broad introductory phase followed by an opportunity to specialise in areas like knitwear, swimwear or millinery.

Three-Dimensional Design courses include product, automotive, furniture, model-making, ceramics and jewellery design. These courses usually contain strong technical elements. A basic ability in mathematics may be required. 3-D design courses prepare graduates to take up positions in the design industry and all will have a strong industrial or craft profile.

Broad-Based courses are available with titles like Visual Studies, or Art and Design. These courses suit those who have made an informed decision to undertake a high level of broad-based or comparative study. Such courses can prepare graduates for specialised study at post-graduate level, careers allied to art and design like teaching, or suit those driven by each new concept they encounter.

Additional Specialist courses may combine disciplines to a specific end (as conservation courses do) or allow for the study of historical and contemporary practices (History of Art and/or Design) or may be highly specialised, such as wildlife illustration.

Career Opportunities

Getting established as an artist or designer can be difficult - but increasingly industry and commerce need artists to design their products and literature. Teaching can also provide a stable career. It helps to have talent and determination and to lay out your plans in advance of graduation.

Suggested Reading

To find out how to apply to art and design courses, see the introductory article **Applying for Art and Design Courses**

The Art of Looking Sideways
- Alan Fletcher, Phaidon Press, 2001

What is Graphic Design?
- Quentin Newark, Rotovision, 2007

Graphic Design: a Concise History
- Richard Hollis, Thames and Hudson, 2001

Modern Art: Impressionism to Post-Modernism
- David Britt, Thames and Hudson, 2007

Isms: Understanding Modern Art
- Sam Phillips, A and C Black Visual Arts, 2012

How to Be a Graphic Designer, Without Losing Your Soul
- Adrian Shaughnessy, Laurence King, 2010

Further Information

Artquest
www.artquest.org.uk

Arts Council England
www.artscouncil.org.uk

Artists Information Company
www.a-n.co.uk

Creative and Cultural Skills
www.ccskills.org.uk

National Society for Education in Art and Design
www.nsead.org

Creative Scotland
www.creativescotland.com

Visual Artists Ireland
http://visualartists.ie

Astronomy/Astrophysics

Original article by Dr George Lafferty, Department of Physics and Astronomy, University of Manchester and Professor Chris Kinchen, University of Hertfordshire

Introduction

Astronomy and Astrophysics mainly involve the application of known physical laws to distant regions of the Universe, which cannot be accessed directly by man-made apparatus and in which the physical conditions can only be inferred from the electromagnetic radiation emitted. This radiation may be visible light, detectable by optical telescopes; or radio waves detected by giant radio-telescopes; or it may take the form of more energetic radiation, such as gamma rays. Courses in Astronomy and Astrophysics include study of the sun and the solar system, the stars and the galaxy, distant galaxies and quasars and the beginning of the universe in the Big Bang. Training in mathematics, physics, information technology and computing would be involved. Universities that offer the subject either have their own or have close connections with other observatories, and an important part of courses involves work in these observatories. Obviously, time spent in observatories will usually be when it is dark and relatively cloudless, and courses have to be flexible so that laboratory work takes the place of observatory work when it is cloudy.

Degree Courses

Astronomy is a branch of physics and most astronomers of today took their first degree in physics, mathematics or a combination of physics and astrophysics.You can, if you are keenly interested, choose a course with a strong astronomy content, but a pure physics course will give you a firm basis for the postgraduate studies which are a pre-requisite for entry to a research career in astronomy. Only a minority of those graduating in astronomy, or physics with astronomy options, will spend their whole lives working in astronomy, but the training in scientific, mathematical and computing techniques, in either field, forms a sound foundation for many different careers. It is vital for aspiring astronomers to study prospectuses to be able to make an informed choice from the varying courses with an astronomical content offered by different universities.

The course structure is very flexible at many universities, with physics and astronomy degree programmes frequently sharing a common first year. The range of modules available in the first year is designed to stimulate your interest in physics, whilst giving you a sound foundation upon which to build in later years. Modules might include Atoms, Nuclei and Matter, Cosmos, and Astrophysical Concepts. It is often the end of the first year before you have to decide whether to continue with your original degree choice or choose another within the range of physics and astronomy degrees.

In the second and third years, you would take a selection of advanced modules that would allow you to practise and consolidate new skills by applying them to a wide range of astrophysical problems. In the final year, you could concentrate specifically on, say, astrophysics, spending half your time completing taught modules and half working on a major astrophysics project.

Career Opportunities
Very few careers are available in the astronomy or astrophysics fields - but the training you receive can open up careers in satellite technology, physics research, industry and in many branches of technology, as well as in finance, banking, industry, management and so on.

If you want to become a professional research astronomer, you must aim for a really good honours degree - a first or upper second class in an MSci or MPhys course - so that you can gain a postgraduate place on a doctoral degree course. It is almost unknown for anyone with 'only' a first degree to obtain a professional post.

Related Degrees
Planetary Science; Geophysics/Planetary Physics; Space/Astrophysics.

Suggested Reading
Cambridge Illustrated Dictionary of Astronomy
- Jacqueline Mitton, Cambridge University Press, 2007

The Elegant Universe: Superstrings, Hidden Dimensions and the Quest for the Ultimate Theory
- Brian Greene, Vintage, 2005

The Fabric of the Cosmos: Space, Time and the Texture of Reality
- Brian Greene, Penguin Books, 2005

So you want to become an astronomer
- Leaflet written by Cardiff Astronomical Society, downloadable from the website at:
www.rmg.co.uk/upload/pdf/So_you_want_to_become_an_astronmer.pdf

Further Information
Royal Astronomical Society
www.ras.org.uk

British Astronomical Association
www.britastro.org

Royal Observatory Greenwich
www.rmg.co.uk/royal-observatory

Royal Observatory Edinburgh
www.roe.ac.uk

Institute of Physics
www.iop.org

Students for the Exploration and Development of Space
http://seds.org

International Space University, Strasbourg, France
www.isunet.edu

Astronomy Ireland
www.astronomy.ie

Audiology

Original article by Ken Reynolds, specialist writer on careers and higher education

Introduction

Audiology is the field of clinical science and technology that is concerned with hearing and balance. As a healthcare profession, it also involves the assessment, management and therapeutic rehabilitation of people with hearing and balance problems and associated disorders. This includes patients of all ages, from newborn babies and children through to working adults and the elderly.

Your role as an audiologist would be to recommend and provide appropriate assessment, rehabilitation and management for people referred to you, applying a scientific approach in a caring and patient-focused way.

Degree Courses

Guidance on courses and professional training in Audiology has been complicated in recent years because of the gradual implementation of the Department of Health Modernising Scientific Careers (MSC) programme. The previous four-year BSc (Hons) Audiology has been replaced by a three-year degree (practitioner training programme) in Healthcare Science (Neurosensory Sciences, specialising in Audiology). The degree combines both academic and work-based learning. Within the first year, the work-based learning provides a broad experience, with short 'tasters' in the specialisms (Audiology, Neurophysiology and Ophthalmic and Vision Science), which should give a holistic view of the areas which together contribute to high quality care. There is a greater focus in the second year on specific areas of audiology, including the more complex aspects of hearing and balance assessments, adult aural rehabilitation, and digital technology, including hearing aids and cochlear implants. The final year allows you to develop your specialist knowledge and understanding in audiological science and to apply this to clinical practice. In addition to an optional study module, you would undertake a 25-week clinical placement. At the end of the programme, you will be able to carry out the role of a Healthcare Science Practitioner in Audiology.

There is also a postgraduate route, allowing graduates with a science-based first degree (2:1 or above) to apply to the Scientist Training Programme. You would be employed by an audiology department, which would arrange your clinical training, including a three-year, part-time Master in Neurosensory Sciences programme.

When you have completed your degree or postgraduate programme, you will be eligible for voluntary registration with the Council for Clinical Physiologists. Whichever training route you follow, you will need Disclosure and Barring Service clearance, as you could be working with children and other vulnerable groups. As a clinical scientist in audiology, you would have to register with the Health and Care Professions Council.

In a related but separate field, several universities offer a foundation degree in hearing aid audiology.

Career Opportunities

Once qualified, most audiologists work in a hospital, assessing and treating patients, and may reach consultant level. Some audiologists work in a university, where their job is primarily concerned with teaching and research. There are also opportunities available in the private sector.

NHS audiologists work closely with ENT consultants, health visitors and speech and language therapists to provide the appropriate assessment and intervention for children and adults of all ages. They may also work with a range of other professionals to address the needs of groups with special requirements such as children and adults with learning difficulties.

Audiology is a rapidly developing field, and the need for audiological services is well documented. A national study of hearing shows that approximately 16% of the population have a significant hearing loss, indicating that working in this field is an important area of the NHS. With experience, many audiologists develop a special interest and expertise in one area of audiology, such as paediatrics or balance.

The profession of audiology is currently undergoing a period of considerable change and it is very difficult to determine how career prospects will develop over the coming years. You should regularly check the British Academy of Audiology and NHS Careers websites to keep abreast of the very latest analysis of the implementation of the MSC programme.

Related Degrees
Human Communication (Speech and Language Therapy).

Suggested Reading
Introduction to Audiology
- Frederick N Martin and John Greer Clark, Pearson, 2014

Audiology: the Fundamentals
- Fred Bess and Larry Humes, Lippincott Williams and Wilkins, 2008

Handbook of Clinical Audiology
- Jack Katz, Lippincott Williams and Wilkins, 2014

Fundamentals of Hearing: an Introduction
- William Yost, Academic Press, 2006

Further Information
British Academy of Audiology
www.baaudiology.org

NHS Careers
www.nhscareers.nhs.uk

Registration Council for Clinical Physiologists
www.rccp.co.uk

Health and Care Professions Council
www.hcpc-uk.org

Disclosure and Barring Service
www.gov.uk/government/organisations/disclosure-and-barring-service

Irish Society of Hearing Aid Audiologists
www.ishaa.ie

Irish Academy of Audiology
www.iaoa.ie

Biochemistry

Original article by Dr Louise Banton, Lancaster University, with additional material supplied by the Biochemical Society

Introduction

Biochemists study the most basic of life processes. For example, identifying the ways in which DNA is transferred between cells and can be manipulated. This has led to the development of new technologies such as Molecular Biology and Genetic Engineering. The resulting recombinant DNA technology has formed the basis of modern biotechnology (e.g. production of human insulin), medical developments (e.g. prenatal diagnosis and genetic counselling) and forensic science (e.g. DNA fingerprinting).

DNA directs the production of proteins. These have diverse functions, such as catalysing biological reactions (enzymes), carrying oxygen round the body (haemoglobin), protecting us from infection (antibodies) and holding us together (collagen). Using both simple and high-technology methods, biochemists work out how these proteins function. Biochemists also develop methods for making use of proteins, such as enzymes in biotechnology and antibodies in hormone analysis.

With knowledge of the basic molecular mechanisms, biochemists study how life processes are integrated to allow individual cells to function and interact to form complex organisms. They work with all sorts of organisms, from viruses and bacteria to plants and man.

Degree Courses

At a typical university, the biochemistry degree will be made up of modules, which enable you to construct the most suitable course of study for your degree.

The emphasis of the subject will be medical and will include courses in immunology, blood biochemistry and genetic diseases. Later in the course, you will undertake projects, in which you may collaborate with a local industry or school; you will also be able to specialise in areas that interest you, such as biomedicine, immunology, genetics and microbiology.

The modules in all courses are likely to include genetics, the molecular design of life, introduction to the cell, nervous systems, biomedical physiology, protein structure, enzymes metabolism, bio-energetics, physiology, blood biochemistry, glycobiology, immunology, enzymes, biotechnology and cell signalling. There will be modules in organic, physical and inorganic chemistry, together with an introduction to spectroscopic theory and techniques.

University courses vary and it is very important that you look at a range of prospectuses and visit as many universities as possible. Many universities offer sandwich courses, which give the opportunity to spend a year working in industry. Because biochemistry is a research-based discipline, many graduates continue into postgraduate training.

Career Opportunities

There are many areas of everyday life in which biochemists are employed.

Industry - Pharmaceutical, food, brewing, biotechnology and agrochemical companies.

Medicine - Hospitals, public health laboratories, medical research institutes, and the pharmaceutical industry.

Education - All levels of education offer prospects for biochemists.

Away from Science - Biochemists can be employed in sales and marketing, finance, journalism and patent work.

Related Degrees

Molecular Biosciences; Applied Biochemistry; Medical Biochemistry; Molecular Medicine; Biochemistry with Industrial Placement; Nutritional Biochemistry; Biochemical Engineering; Biomedicine; Agricultural Biochemistry; Biochemistry with Biotechnology.

Suggested Reading

Schaum's Easy Outline of Biochemistry
- Philip W Kuchel, Schaum, 2011

Biochemistry: International Edition
- Lubert Stryer et al, W H Freeman, 2011

Molecular Biology of the Cell
- Bruce Alberts et al, Garland, 2008

Biochemistry
- Donald and Judith Voet, John Wiley, 2011

Further Information

Association for Clinical Biochemistry and Laboratory Medicine
www.acb.org.uk

Society of Biology
www.societyofbiology.org

Royal Society of Chemistry
www.rsc.org

Bioindustry Association
www.bioindustry.org

Biochemical Society
www.biochemistry.org

Biotechnology and Biological Sciences Research Council
www.bbsrc.ac.uk

Institute of Biology of Ireland
www.ibioli.net

Irish BioIndustry Association
www.ibec.ie/ibia

Biology

Original article by Professor N Maclean, Southampton University

Introduction

Biology, the study of life and living things, occupies a unique position in the spectrum of human interest and knowledge. Although undoubtedly a science, it has much in common with the arts, partly because nature appeals to our aesthetic as well as our rational senses, and also because we ourselves are part of nature. For this reason many people who would not otherwise choose to study science finally settle on biology. On the other hand, with the rapid growth of molecular biology over the last decade, some who would previously have chosen to study physical sciences are now considering biology as a possible and challenging alternative. Many departments now offer a choice of degree options in eg biology, botany, zoology, cell biology and applied biology, the choice of degree title depending on courses chosen for study.

Thus, if you find yourself subscribing to any of the following categories then it may mean that biology should be your prime choice of subject:

(1) Your interests straddle the two cultures of science and arts

(2) You are very keen on natural history, birds, plants, insects or whatever

(3) Your greatest passion is conservation of the planet and its natural resources

(4) You are not at all keen about natural history or conservation, but you are intrigued by problems of living systems and how they work

(5) You are interested in medicine but don't want to become a doctor.

Degree Courses

Biology is often taken to represent 'soft' science rather than 'hard' science, that is a science where the number of variables in any one situation may be so great that the construction of an equation or formula is impossible. Although with the recent growth of molecular biology and biotechnology this is much less true than it once was, it is still sufficiently true to mean that biology may appeal to those with limited expertise in the physical sciences. But do not be beguiled into thinking that the softer science indicates a softer option. The ability to analyse and understand complex situations such as arise, for example, in evolutionary genetics, requires a sharp mind as well as considerable breadth of knowledge.

The central core in most departments would consist of cell biology, genetics, ecology, and the form and function of living organisms; students will often be encouraged or compelled to study computation and statistics on the one hand and biochemistry and physiology on the other. From this basic groundwork will stem a range of optional specialisations in, for example, parasitology, taxonomy, evolution, cell and molecular biology, developmental biology, immunology, applied ecology, animal behaviour and advanced courses in genetics or comparative physiology. Of course many departments have their own special areas of research expertise, but these are reflected more in higher degree course structures than in undergraduate ones. When you visit a department as a prospective student, you should enquire about the areas in which the research strengths of the department lie. They may not coincide at all with the topic in which you would want to specialise.

Many of the key questions facing mankind now and in the future are essentially biological. How can we control our own population, avoid war, cure disease, conserve nature? To my mind one of the most exciting things about being a student of biology is that one learns so much more about oneself. You learn to understand your own anatomy, physiology, behaviour and evolution, and you also come to see yourself in the context of nature, as one amongst many other species, as a member of an evolved and evolving population of organisms, interacting at all times and all levels with the other diverse organisms with which we share the planet. Whether you are managing staff in Marks and Spencer or running field trials of agricultural crops, there is much to be gained from the bracing sense of perspective, both evolutionary and ecological, shared by those who have learned to think deeply about biology.

Career Opportunities

Some biology graduates enter research or continue with further academic or professional training, but the majority find employment in finance, administration and operational management, marketing/buying, medical and technical sales, computer programming, environmental health, laboratory work, technical journalism etc. Biology graduates are attractive to employers because they are normally well trained in communication skills, numeracy, scientific method and how to best deal with complex problems in management.

Related Degrees

Human Biology; Biotechnology; Tropical Disease Biology; Forensic Biology; Applied Biology; Medical Biology; Animal Biology; Computational Biology; Behavioural Biology; Biology with Overseas Study; Food Biology; Palaeobiology; Cancer Biology; Biophysics; Cell Biology; Developmental Biology.

Suggested Reading

Life: The Science of Biology, International Edition
- David Sadava et al, Sinauer Associates, 2013

The Selfish Gene
- R Dawkins, Oxford University Press (revised edition), 2006

Wonderful Life: Burgess Shale and the Nature of History
- Stephen Jay Gould, Vintage, 2000

The Language of the Genes
- Steve Jones, Flamingo, 2000

Biology: a Global Approach
- Neil Campbell, Jane Reece et al, Pearson Education, 2014

Practical Skills in Biology
- Allan Jones, Rob Reed and Jonathan Weyers, Pearson, 2012

Further Information

Society of Biology
www.societyofbiology.org

Biotechnology and Biological Sciences Research Council
www.bbsrc.ac.uk

Institute of Biology of Ireland
www.ibioli.net

Biomedical Science

Original article by Dr Christopher Smith, GKT School of Biomedical Sciences, King's College, London

Introduction

Different universities tend to use the term biomedical science in very different ways: some centre on the teaching of topics such as haematology and transfusion science, medical microbiology, pathology and clinical biochemistry. The Institute of Biomedical Sciences has approved these programmes with the aim of graduate entry into hospital and other diagnostic organisations as laboratory scientists. Other universities, mainly those with associated medical schools, have a different objective. They offer combinations of the science subjects that form the basis of biomedical research, such as physiology, pharmacology, molecular biology, anatomy, genetics, developmental science and neuroscience. The first biomedical science degree of this kind was a response to the increasing trend of joint-subject degrees such as physiology and pharmacology, recognising that - especially at research level - there is an important and essential integration between the traditional disciplines. A study of pain would nowadays be hard to fund with neuroscientists alone; a combined molecular pharmacological and developmental approach would be more likely to succeed.

Degree Courses

It is of course impossible to study at an advanced level all the subjects mentioned above. Most universities offer an integrated first year, usually with the emphasis on the base subjects of physiology, pharmacology, cell biology and molecular biology. In the second and third years, increasingly you will be asked to specialise. At some universities this may be by formal transfer to a specialist programme such as neuroscience. In other cases you will be required to make your own choice of individual units so that you can either develop a detailed knowledge of your chosen area, such as cardiovascular science, or follow a traditional specialist degree. Finally you might choose a wide range of topics including some outside biomedical science such as languages, management, environmental science or philosophy. This last pattern would be appropriate for jobs such as the management of science, science journalism or teaching. One factor to note is that the larger the size of the biomedical department, the larger the range of course units that can be offered. Larger schools, however, also have larger class sizes (rising up to 500 in first year courses): you must choose the style and options that suit your personal needs.

Career Opportunities

Biomedical science could well become established as a prime route to the rapidly growing field of graduate-entry medicine. Medical schools feel happier with graduates who have proved their ability for advanced study and also had time to develop their interest in medicine through extended work in the healthcare system. Please note that 'transfer' to medicine is not offered: you would apply to several medical schools at the beginning of your third year via UCAS. Most medical schools do not specify the exact degree programmes required but biomedical science at a university with a medical school clearly is a very good start. Biomedical science also offers you entry, depending on your chosen specialisations, to the bioscience careers detailed elsewhere in these Degree Course Descriptions, including biochemistry, physiology and molecular biology. Finally you should not forget that close to 50% of graduates move into the general job market, including management, the Civil Service, the Armed Forces and finance. It is for you to consider this range of careers and what type of biomedical science programme will best help your aims.

Guidance on training as a healthcare scientist in the NHS has been complicated in recent years by the gradual implementation of the Department of Health *Modernising Scientific Careers* (MSC) programme. The main MSC entry points are either the *Practitioner Training Programme*, which combines academic study on an accredited three-year full-time BSc Healthcare Science degree with practical experience in the NHS, or - if you have a first or upper second degree in a relevant subject - the *Scientist Training Programme*: a three-year programme which includes practical experience and academic study leading to a specialist diploma or Master of Science qualification. There will also be Higher Specialist Scientific Training at consultant level, although this is still under development.

Related Degrees

Clinical Sciences; Clinical Physiology; Biomedical Materials Science; Life Sciences; Medicine; Pharmacology; Genetics; Pharmacy; Molecular Biology; Neuroscience; Haematology; Medical Microbiology; Chemical Biochemistry.

Suggested Reading

Biomedical Sciences Explained - Series of books designed specifically to meet the needs of undergraduates studying biomedical sciences. Each volume covers a key topic, such as Clinical Biochemistry, Haematology, Cellular Pathology, Transfusion Science.
- C J Pallister, Series Editor, Scion Publishing, 2010

Essentials of Human Anatomy and Physiology
- Elaine N Marieb, Pearson, 2013

Biology of Disease
- Nessar Ahmed et al, Taylor and Francis, 2006

Further Information

Institute of Biomedical Science
www.ibms.org

National Health Service Careers
www.nhscareers.nhs.uk

Health and Care Professions Council
www.hcpc-uk.org

Wellcome Trust
www.wellcome.ac.uk

British Pharmacological Society
www.bps.ac.uk

Physiological Society
www.physoc.org

Royal Society
http://royalsociety.org

Academy of Medical Laboratory Science, Ireland
www.amls.ie

Biotechnology

Original article by Dr J H Parish, Leeds University

Introduction

Biotechnology is concerned with the application of the biological sciences to manufacturing. Some of the processes themselves (especially those concerned with the food and drink industries) are thousands of years old but scientific analysis of these processes is relatively recent. This involves the application of scientific method and the use of scientific enquiry to expand the variety of biological products.

Degree Courses

There are four major academic foundations of biotechnology:

Biochemistry emphasises a certain unity among living organisms. Organisms have energy-yielding metabolisms whereby substrates are converted to products and energy is trapped by the synthesis of Adenosine Triphosphate (ATP). This invariably involves oxidation/reduction (in our species reduced substrates such as cream cakes and fish and chips are oxidised to carbon dioxide and water) but the variety in different forms of life is considerable. All organisms use enzyme catalysts to convert substrates to the chemicals required for growth by processes that involve expenditure of ATP.

Genetic engineering Classical genetics is limited by the 'breeding barrier' (you can cross barley and rye, horses and donkeys, but not diverse species - such as carrots and elephants). There are techniques for introducing genes (i.e. a piece of DNA) from one organism into cells of a totally unrelated host. The hosts are commonly microbes but can be animal or plant cells.

Cell culture Bacteria, yeasts and moulds have been the organisms used in industrial fermentations. To these can now be added cells of animals and plants; specialised examples of these are used to produce vaccines, antibodies and natural products. Photosynthetic microbes suggest an alternative for the large scale fixation of CO_2.

Fermentation engineering and reactor design are specialised engineering subjects and biotechnology presents engineers with problems concerned with sterilisation, stirring, heat exchange and downstream processing of large volumes of aqueous materials.

The following examples are necessarily incomplete. Genetic engineering allows the construction of micro-organisms and animal and plant cells in culture that contain cloned genes from a variety of sources. Further manipulation allows the expression of these genes. We can construct a bacterial or fungal strain that will produce proteins of animal origin and which is of established value. Examples are chymosin (an enzyme used in cheese manufacture obtained otherwise from calves) and several human proteins of medical importance. The benefits of using fermentation technology vary between the economic, humanitarian and medically desirable. The implications of the ability to introduce and express foreign genes into cells are rather different. If these cells are used to generate whole plants or if their genetic information is introduced into embryonic animals we obtain 'transgenic' higher organisms. A transgenic plant might have properties of resistance to pests, diseases or herbicides. Transgenic animals might be used to generate recombinant proteins in their milk. The ability to manipulate DNA in the laboratory provides a method for altering or improving the performance of a protein for specific purposes. Such activities are referred to as 'protein engineering'. One example of protein engineering is the modification of the enzyme present in biological washing powders to allow it to perform better in washing machines. More important for the human race is the modification of proteins for medical use.

The science of molecular biology has generated a technological revolution. Just as organic chemistry generated novel chemicals, such as dyestuffs and plastics, molecular biology has entered a synthetic or creative phase that is leading to a domination of parts of the fermentation, pharmaceutical and agricultural industries.

Career Opportunities

A biotechnology degree can lead to careers in the NHS, the Medical Research Council and the food and pharmacology industries, where the techniques involved are at the forefront of many new technical developments, eg in using enzyme systems in yeasts or bacteria to produce useful substances such as penicillin, antibodies (needed to fight specific diseases), foodstuffs, proteins, enzymes, carbohydrates or alcoholic drinks.

Biotechnologists are employed by breweries, for example, to optimise the performance of their companies by applying such subjects as fermentation technology and the molecular genetics of yeast to the brewing process.

Related Degrees

Environmental Biotechnology; Medical Biotechnology; Biotechnology with a year in Europe.

Suggested Reading

Basic Biotechnology
- Colin Ratledge and Bjorn Kristiansen, CUP, 2006

Environmental Biotechnology
- Alan Scragg, OUP, 2005

Biotechnology for Beginners
- Reinhard Renneberg, Academic Press, 2007

Brock Biology of Microorganisms
- Michael Madigan et al, Pearson Education, 2011

Further Information

BioIndustry Association
www.bioindustry.org

Biotechnology and Biological Sciences Research Council
www.bbsrc.ac.uk

Irish BioIndustry Association
www.ibec.ie/ibia

Botany

Original article by Dr Julie Hawkins, University of Reading

Introduction

Botany encompasses all aspects of plant biology, from molecular biology to ecosystems, from the smallest green unicellular organisms to the tallest forest trees. In a world which is likely to become increasingly dependent on threatened plant resources for food security and even for maintaining the composition of the air we breathe, the subject is bound to assume ever greater importance in future years.

As you read this article, botanists are busy collecting and describing the plants of the rainforest, designing conservation strategies for urban nature reserves, examining peat cores to determine the effects of past climate change, cross-pollinating crop plants to breed new drought resistant varieties, managing museum collections, using electron microscopes and automated DNA sequencing for cutting-edge research into fundamental processes, extracting and investigating the useful chemicals that plants produce, advising customs officers trying to stop the illegal export of rare plants, reconstructing fossil plants, determining the extent of gene flow between GM crop plants and their wild relatives, optimising greenhouse conditions for ornamental plants, identifying plant fragments as part of forensic investigations to determine the scene of a crime, participating in ethnobotanic surveys to record how tribal peoples use local plants, and studying the genetics of plant metabolism. Botanists are certainly never short of challenges!

Degree Courses

As a botany undergraduate, you should find that your degree programme includes most or all of the elements listed below. Each of these elements impinges on and assists in understanding and interpreting the others. **Plant Ecology** is the study of the interactions of plants with each other, with other organisms and with their physical environment. The theory of evolution is the foundation of modern biological science; studies in **Plant Evolution** would include plant adaptation, the origins of land plants and of flowering plants as well as **Palaeobotany** - the study of fossil plants. **Plant Systematics** is the biodiversity science of naming and description, classification and documentation of plants. **Economic Botany** describes the study of past and present use of plants and plant products, from hunter gatherer societies, through Neolithic farming to contemporary initiatives to conserve plant genetic resources. **Plant Genetics** includes a range of pure and applied topics such as biotechnology and plant breeding, population genetics, genomics and cytology. **Plant Biochemistry**, the study of metabolic pathways and the use of techniques such as nuclear magnetic resonance and X-ray crystallography to study protein structures, also includes **Phytochemistry**, the study of the defence and attractant chemicals. **Plant Geography** - often using Geographical Information Systems (GIS) - is the study of the distribution of plants, and explains the current distribution of plants in terms of evolutionary history, geological and climatic history and plant dispersal mechanisms. **Plant Morphology and Anatomy** is the study of the diverse and constant features of plant structures, such as fruits, flowers, shoots and roots. **Plant Development and Physiology** includes the study of transitions such as breaking of seed dormancy or flowering. The determination of the genetic basis of these transitions has become an important area of research. **Plant Conservation Biology** is the applied science which incorporates genetics (population genetics), vegetation survey and Environmental Impact Assessment, and applied ecology.

Universities with schools of soil science, zoology, meteorology, agriculture or geography would usually offer modules in these subjects to botany undergraduates.

Career Opportunities

Botanists are employed by botanic gardens and museums in Britain and overseas, by showcase educational attractions, such as the Eden Project, by conservation organisations such as Natural England, in public sector research (e.g. by universities and research centres such as the John Innes Centre in Norwich) and in the private sector. Industries and organisations related to horticulture, including the Royal Horticultural Society, are important employers. Botanists are also employed by international projects to reduce hunger and poverty, improve human nutrition and health, and protect the environment, such as those of the Consultative Group on International Agricultural Research (CGIAR). Many graduate botanists continue with further academic study before taking up a job with one of these employers. Other botany graduates use their degrees to enter other professions such as teaching, finance, administration, environmental health or science publishing.

Related Degrees

Plant Science; Environmental Biology; Conservation Biology; Soil Science.

Suggested Reading

Botany: an introduction to Plant Biology
- James Mauseth, Jones and Bartlett, 2012

Raven Biology of Plants
- Ray Evert and Susan Eichhorn, W H Freeman, 2012

Plant Physiology: international edition
- Lincoln Taiz and Eduardo Zeiger, Sinauer Associates, 2010

Further Information

Royal Horticultural Society
www.rhs.org.uk

Natural England
www.naturalengland.org.uk

John Innes Centre
www.jic.ac.uk

Internet Directory for Botany
www.botany.net/IDB

Royal Botanic Garden Edinburgh
www.rbge.org.uk

United Nations Environment Programme World Conservation Monitoring Centre
www.unep-wcmc.org

Consultative Group on International Agricultural Research
www.cgiar.org

Royal Botanic Gardens Kew
www.kew.org

Natural History Museum Botanical Collections
www.nhm.ac.uk/research-curation/scientific-resources/collections/botanical-collections/index.html

Eden Project
www.edenproject.com

Royal Horticultural Society of Ireland
www.rhsi.ie

Building, Surveying and Construction

Original article by K Hutchinson, Department of Construction Management &
Engineering, University of Reading; Martin Simons, School of the Built Environment,
Coventry University; John Pearson, Department of Quantity Surveying, Northumbria
University

Introduction

Imagine a building such as a new sports stadium: it must be planned, designed,
engineered, constructed and maintained. A host of skills are involved ranging from
the selection of the most appropriate material through to ensuring that the structure is
totally safe when there are extremes of temperature.

Degree Courses

Universities offer a wide variety of modular and linear degree courses in the areas of
Building, Surveying and Construction but certain aspects are common to all.

Building Construction and Management is likely to appeal to students who see
their future in planning, executing and managing the construction of building and civil
engineering projects. Courses give a deeper understanding of the entire construction
process, from the brief given to an architect through all the design and planning
stages to the completion of the project on site. In addition, students follow courses in
management, economics and law related to construction. Final year students usually
undertake a major project that integrates all aspects of the course.

Building Environmental Engineering Design and Management covers all the
environmental services (air conditioning, ventilation, heating, lighting, sound) and
utility services (electrical power, communications, fire protection, water, lifts) which
usually make a building function. Courses include: mathematics, thermal engineering,
electrical engineering and building technology management. Some are continued
with the addition of environmental engineering, lighting and acoustic utility and space
engineering, computer-aided design and human factors.

Building Surveying deals with the technological and managerial aspects of
construction in relation to existing buildings. It is a base for careers in built facilities
management including maintenance, refurbishment and rehabilitation of buildings.
Building surveyors require creative design ability and technical and managerial
competence.

A modular course in **Building Surveying**, at a typical university, has a common theme
in Construction and Design. Level 1 deals with the domestic construction, developing
at Level 3 into highly specialised systems and modular building components. Level
1 aims to lay the foundations with modules such as building mechanics, building
materials, environmental studies, economics, information technology, building law and
town and country planning. Level 2 builds upon these foundations with construction
and design taken into the commercial and industrial property areas. Aspects of the
specialist nature of building surveying are developed in property studies, planning and
property development, and management principles. Practical skills, such as building
and land surveying, are practised in the field course. At Level 2, a project brings these
together to explain the integrated nature of the construction industry and the people
and services which have an input into it. After a voluntary year of professional training,
the major themes of Level 3 construction and design are aspects of innovative
construction.

Quantity Surveying provides a sound foundation in the basic principles of quantity
surveying practice and gives an intellectual challenge which equips students with the
main problem-solving techniques needed in modern construction management.
The course at one typical university has a total of 36 units spread over three years.
Sandwich students spend a period of 12 months in industry in which students work

in private practice, for a local authority, in a commercial setting or in a construction company. Examples of units include measurement and appraisal, building technology, economics of the built environment, computing for the built environment, introduction to law for the built environment, town and country planning, civil engineering technology and measurement, applied economics and cost studies.

Construction Management Engineering and Surveying courses are for students who aspire to senior management positions in the general area of building, construction and management. Courses have been designed to open up a comprehensive range of options for practice in the construction industry as project managers, cost managers or property managers.

Career Opportunities

The majority of graduates in these disciplines enter the construction industry. Few enter research, design, development and financial fields. The demand for building, surveying and construction graduates depends to a great extent on the state of the construction industry and the picture in 2014 is starting to look encouraging, as the sector recovers from the severe downturn that started in 2008. Indeed, the UK construction industry has turned around in 2014 to become one of the fastest-growing sectors in the economy, offering new hope for graduates in the years to come.

Related Degrees

Building Services Engineering; Construction Management; Construction Engineering; Building Surveying Management; Quantity Surveying Management; Architectural Technology; Building Conservation; Building/Environmental Service Engineering; Estate Surveying and Evaluation; Fire Safety.

Suggested Reading

Collaborative Working in Construction
- Dino Bouchlaghem (Ed), Routledge, 2011
BIM Handbook: a Guide to Building Information Modelling
- Chuck Eastman et al, John Wiley, 2011
Barry's Introduction to Construction of Buildings
- Stephen Emmitt and Christopher Gorse, Wiley-Blackwell, 2014
Building: Penguin Dictionary of
- John Scott and James Maclean, Penguin, 1993
Building Construction Handbook
- Roy Chudley and Roger Greeno, Routledge, 2014
The Housebuilder's Bible
- Mark Brinkley, Ovolo, 2013

Further Information

Chartered Institute of Building
www.ciob.org
Royal Institution of Chartered Surveyors
www.rics.org
Construction Industry Training Board
www.citb.co.uk
Chartered Association of Building Engineers
www.cbuilde.com/home
Society of Chartered Surveyors, Ireland
www.scsi.ie
Construction Industry Federation, Ireland
www.cif.ie

Business Management

Osama Khan, Tutor in Accounting and Finance and Director of Undergraduate Studies, University of Surrey

Introduction

Business Management is a multidisciplinary subject that aims to provide you with a broad, analytical study of the theory and practice of running an enterprise. It may appeal to you if you wish to gain a general management degree with the option of specialising in certain key areas. An enterprise could be an organisation in pursuit of profit-making business or one involved in non-profit-making activities, such as a government institution. Every organisation has certain fundamental aspects crucial for its survival: the core organisational culture, human resources, business processes, systems and operations, accounting mechanisms and finance, marketing activities, and strategies. An organisation also has multiple stakeholders, including its suppliers, its customers and the environment in which it operates.

Business Management covers all the fundamental aspects of an organisation and how it manages relationships with stakeholders. A typical Business Management programme will build on essential skills in management and quantitative methods and progress to subject areas like organisational behaviour, human resource management, management information systems, operations management, marketing, accounting, finance and strategy. These programmes will also offer modules in entrepreneurship, law, ethics and international business. Most of the generic business management programmes will have substantial internationalisation in different subject areas. Given that many enterprises are multinational, graduates of business management programmes need to be aware of different cultures, traditions and business environments. Other modules might include advertising, managing change, innovation and business planning, all key features of the race to be competitive in the global business market.

Degree Courses

Almost all British universities have a School of Management or School of Business offering business studies or business management. Certain management schools, including Warwick, Bath and Aston, have a long tradition of excellent provision in business management. Others offer programmes increasingly comparable in quality to the top business schools, including Surrey, Bristol, Nottingham, Leeds and Manchester. Many universities offer business management jointly with pure sciences like physics and mathematics; there is also a popular marriage between business management and languages. In fact, you can combine the subject with almost anything you can think of in joint or mixed degrees, so you do not have to give up subjects that fascinate you just to pursue a degree with better job prospects.

Some courses offer sandwich arrangements, where you spend time (watch out for exactly how long and what you would be doing) in an organisational placement to develop practical experience of management. Surveys suggest that prospective employers really value this experience element, although it can be gained in other ways too, such as vacation work, project work based on real cases, or a gap year.

Many courses now provide opportunities to spend some time (from a few weeks to a full year) studying management in overseas partner universities. This does not always mean studying in a foreign language - as some foreign universities teach management in English - but you should expect to be treated in the same way as an indigenous student. Studying overseas is also valued by many employers, not least because it takes maturity, self-management and confidence to get the most from such opportunities, while the experience also develops sensitivity to cultural differences, boosts language skills and generally broadens your horizons.

Business and Management are complex mixes of many other subjects. Some see Economics as perhaps the most important component, reflected also in such topics as competition in markets, business efficiency, and the effect of the general economic climate on business. Mathematics and statistics are important too, for example in helping to forecast market changes, understanding the vast amounts of data available to managers, and in choosing between alternative investment decisions and strategies. Psychology, sociology and management of people are central to the study of management because of the necessary focus on organisational behaviour, leadership and group work. Finance and accounting cover the ways in which organisations, markets, sectors and economies are regulated and monitored, as well as how alternative investment opportunities are evaluated. Legal issues are important to management too, especially with respect to the increasing influence of EU and international law.

Career Opportunities

A degree in business management could almost be described as a career deferment programme, in the sense that it allows you to explore a whole range of professions before making a final choice. You might become a management consultant, an accountant, a banker, a marketing or sales executive, a human resources manager, a generic administrator, or you might start your own business.

Related Degrees

Business Analysis; e-Business; Business Administration; International Business Management; International Business; Business Management and Languages; Business Management and Physics; Business Management and Mathematics; Management Science.

Suggested Reading

The International Business Environment: Challenges and Changes
- Ian Brooks, Jamie Weatherston and Graham Wilkinson, Financial Times/Prentice Hall, 2010

Corporate Finance and Investment: Decisions and Strategies
- Richard Pike, Bill Neale and Philip Linsley, Pearson, 2012

Organisational Behaviour and Work: a Critical Introduction
- Fiona Wilson, Oxford University Press, 2013

Foundations of Economics
- Andrew Gillespie, Oxford University Press, 2014

Service Operations Management
- Robert Johnston, Graham Clark and Michael Shulver, Pearson, 2012

Frank Wood's Business Accounting Volume 1
- Frank Wood and Alan Sangster, Financial Times/Prentice Hall, 2011

Marketing: an Introduction
- Gary Armstrong, Philip Kotler, Michael Harker and Ross Brennan, Pearson, 2012

Further Information

Business Management Association
www.businessmanagement.org.uk
Association of Business Executives
www.abeuk.com
Association of Business Schools
www.associationofbusinessschools.org
Irish Management Institute
www.imi.ie

Chemical/Process Engineering

Professor R B Thorpe, University of Surrey

Introduction

Chemical engineers are involved with processes that can alter the chemical, biochemical or physical state of a substance, changing raw materials into useful products. They might create anything from food to pharmaceuticals, face creams to fuels.

Industrial manufacture imposes a commercial discipline on both the chemistry (or biochemistry) and the engineering that can be employed in these processes, challenging chemical engineers on a daily basis to design and operate systems that are both commercially viable and environmentally sustainable. Engineers may find themselves in the research laboratory, at the computer writing mathematical models or on the shop floor managing production, process improvement or plant maintenance. Because of the economies of scale, most chemical manufacturing plant is much larger than the glassware of the chemistry laboratory and operates at higher temperatures and pressures. This can require some serious engineering. Nonetheless, chemical engineers must also understand what is happening at the molecular level in chemical reactions and in the intra-molecular bonding that can make the separation of products in distillation columns complex, or at the cellular level if a biochemical route to manufactures is being taken.

Degree Courses

Relevant degree courses are available at some 40 universities in the UK and Ireland. Most courses lead either to the BEng degree (or similar bachelor level degree taking 3 years[1]) or the MEng degree (or similar master level degree, 4 years[1]). The MEng degree, if accredited, satisfies the educational requirements set by the Institution of Chemical Engineers (IChemE) to become a corporate member of the IChemE and a chartered engineer. Chartered engineers can progress to become Euro Engineers (Eur Ing), a professional accreditation that allows holders to practise throughout the EU. Some degree courses offer variants in which you might spend a year working in a relevant job in the middle of the course. These are sometimes called sandwich courses and usually take an extra year to complete.

Chemical Engineering courses have a significant content of chemistry, which means that advanced[2] level Chemistry or equivalent is usually an entrance requirement. The engineering content of the courses also requires a facility with certain aspects of Physics, although Physics at advanced level is not always required. Some engineering requires Mathematics well beyond advanced level, so an advanced qualification in Mathematics is almost always required at entry. Chemical Engineering degree courses also contain elements of Biology, Economics and Design and Technology, so advanced qualifications in these subjects could also support an application. It is also very useful for engineers to speak and write well and in some circumstances speak a foreign language, so strength in these skills is also positive in the eyes of admissions tutors.

The first year of most chemical engineering courses extends learning in chemistry and mathematics beyond A level. There will also be some fundamental engineering such as thermodynamics (the science of energy and heat) and fluid mechanics (how to move large quantities of material through a process). Some fundamental chemical

---

[1] Arrangements in Scotland and the Republic of Ireland may vary. Consult university prospectuses for confirmation.

[2] In England, Wales and Northern Ireland, advanced means A level or equivalent (e.g. the International Baccalaureate). In Scotland it means Higher level and in the Republic of Ireland Irish Leaving Certificate level.

engineering such as mass balances (what goes in must come out, somewhere) will also be taught. In the second year, courses on the design of chemical reactors and distillation columns, for purifying products, are commonly found. The design of whole chemical manufacturing processes is taught and examined through design projects. This activity usually occurs in the third year. The MEng year will usually contain more project work and advanced material. For further details, see the individual course prospectuses which are usually available online. Throughout the programme will be found courses on and examples of commercially driven decision making tempered by considerations of process safety and environmental and social impact.

All of the above is a preparation for the commercial world of the manufacture of chemicals in the broadest sense. Products made by processes designed, operated and maintained by chemical engineers include oxygen, pharmaceuticals, plastics, steel, silicon, petrol, diesel, natural gas, detergents, shampoo, cosmetics, perfumes, food oils, lubricating oils as well as the classical heavy and light chemicals such as sulphuric acid and dyes.

Career Opportunities
Chemical engineering graduates are highly prized and work in a wide range of industries including the chemical manufacturing sector mentioned above but also in air separation, water treatment and a range of commercial, management and banking companies, where the application of mathematics to the real world is key. A few years after graduation, chemical engineers can be in charge of plant and machinery worth tens or hundreds of millions of pounds.

Related Degrees
Any degree with the words 'Chemical' and 'Engineering' in the title is likely to be related. This includes Biochemical Engineering. Process Engineering is another variant. If any degree is accredited by the IChemE, it must have a very significant chemical engineering content. A full list of such degrees can be found at:
www.whynotchemeng.com/universities

Suggested Reading
Introduction to Chemical Engineering
- Kenneth Solen and John Harb, John Wiley, 2010

Chemical Engineering: an Introduction
- Morton Denn, Cambridge University Press, 2011

The Chemical Engineer
- online version at: **www.tcetoday.com**

Further Information
Whynotchemeng
www.whynotchemeng.com

Institution of Chemical Engineers
www.icheme.org

European Federation of Chemical Engineering
www.efce.info

Engineers Ireland
www.engineersireland.ie

Chemistry

Original article by Professor Paul H Walton, Department of Chemistry, University of York. With contributions by the School of Chemistry, University of Hull

Introduction

There were major changes a few years ago in the structure of Chemistry degree courses, the most fundamental of which was the introduction of four-year courses, most - but not all - entitled MChem or MSci, alongside the traditional BSc or occasionally BA courses. Don't be confused by the M in MChem: these are first degree courses, not postgraduate courses, with the same honours classifications (first, upper second, etc) as traditional BSc courses.

Degree Courses

The choice between BSc and MChem is an important one, but at most universities the two degree programmes are similar or even identical for the first two years, so that you may well be able to switch from one to the other as late as the end of year 2. Don't think simply in terms of 'MChem for the best and BSc for the rest': ask yourself whether what universities are offering you in the extra MChem year will (a) be interesting and challenging and (b) help you in your likely career after graduation. As a broad rule, you should consider studying for an MChem degree if you are planning a career as a professional chemist either at university or in industry.

Look carefully at what the additional year can offer. Usually it will provide you with another year of study at the same university, and most of the year will probably be devoted to a long research project, but you should also be given the chance to specialise in advanced aspects of chemistry which suit your own interests.

There is also, however, the prospect of spending part or all of the extra year studying chemistry at a university in another country so that you may develop language skills (and a vocabulary which includes scientific terms) likely to be extremely useful in career terms. Whatever the timing of your period of study abroad, it is important that the chemistry taught should fit in with what you do in the UK, and that you should not miss out on important features of the entirely home-based courses (for example project work). Another option offered by several universities is the chance to spend part or all of the extra year in paid industrial training (see below).

Most universities now claim to offer modular chemistry degree courses, although the freedom you have to select your own modules and the range from which you can choose varies enormously.

Many chemistry departments, through their industrial contacts, can help you in finding work, which not only brings in money but also gives you useful experience. With the advent of the four-year MChem courses, your chances of obtaining a paid placement, which counts towards your degree, are much greater. The chemical industry also encourages students to choose chemistry as their degree subject by offering sponsorship.

Two final pieces of advice: Firstly, 'If in doubt, ask!' There really is no excuse for failing to get the information you need. Secondly 'See for yourself'. All chemistry departments will arrange for you to visit them after they have received your application through UCAS: many will also be happy to see you individually or on Open Days. Make sure that you are happy with the surroundings in which you will be living and working and with the facilities which will be available to you!

Career Opportunities

The chemical industry was severely affected by the economic downturn that started in 2008 but has returned to sustained growth in 2014 and is committed to delivering by 2030 a 50% increase in the gross value it contributes to the UK economy. Positive prospects may be found in fields considered vital for the future, such as addressing climate change, providing energy, securing food and water or developing new technologies in healthcare, communication and security. Should you decide that you want to continue with postgraduate study, it is sometimes possible to get your research funded by your company once you start. Depending on the type of career you choose to pursue, you could find yourself working in a chemical production plant, a laboratory or an office.

Chemistry graduates also work in professions such as financial services, where their proven skills - not only data analysis and numeracy but an understanding of the physical world and providing robust intellectual challenge - are highly valued and well rewarded.

Related Degrees

Applied Chemistry; Chemistry with Management; Chemistry with Study Abroad; Biological Chemistry; Colour Chemistry; Analytical Chemistry; Forensic Science Chemistry; Chemistry with Industrial Experience; Chemistry in North America; Geochemistry; Computational Chemistry; Environmental Chemistry; Medicinal Chemistry; Industrial/Technical Chemistry; Pharmaceutical Chemistry; Chemistry with Materials; Chemical Physics; Biomolecular Chemistry; Polymer Science; Materials Chemistry.

Suggested Reading

Chemistry: Penguin Dictionary of
- D W A Sharp (Ed), Penguin, 2003

Chemistry: Molecules, Matter and Change
- Peter Atkins and Loretta Jones (Eds), W H Freeman, 2000

Accredited Degree Programmes in Chemistry
- see the Royal Society of Chemistry website below

Further Information

Royal Society of Chemistry
www.rsc.org

Chemical Industries Association
www.cia.org.uk

Institute of Chemistry of Ireland
www.chemistryireland.org

Chinese Studies

Original article by Ken Reynolds, specialist writer on careers and higher education

Introduction

China's rapid development as a global economic force presents many new study opportunities at both undergraduate and postgraduate level. Several universities now offer programmes enabling you to combine study of contemporary Chinese society, popular culture and media, economics, politics, geography and modern history with Mandarin Chinese from beginner to advanced levels. No prior experience of Mandarin is normally required, although students with existing language expertise can also be accommodated.

This article gives examples of courses available at three UK universities.

Degree Courses

We start with Nottingham, which offers three-year Bachelor and four-year Master undergraduate programmes. The first year at either level includes core modules on aspects of contemporary China together with Mandarin language from scratch, while the entire second year is spent at Nottingham's Ningbo Campus (UNNC) in China. This is a compulsory part of the course and all work in this year counts towards the final degree result. The third and final year of the Bachelor programme includes a 10,000 to 12,000 word dissertation on a China-related topic, with option modules available in further Mandarin and advanced translation.

The third year of the Master programme features a selection of option modules, including Further Mandarin, Mao's China, Globalisation and Innovation in China and China through Film and Literature, while the final year includes a dissertation and an optional internship. You may be required to study until September in the final year of this course.

There are also more specialised bachelor and master programmes focusing on the Business and Economy of Contemporary China, and a wide range of combined courses.

Sheffield has its own Confucius Institute, which provides both degree-related resources and extra-curricular activities, together with close links with Nanjing University and Beijing Language and Culture University.

Its single and dual honours degrees in Chinese Studies are all four years in length and include core modules in Mandarin Chinese. The second year is spent at the University of Nanjing in China and is a core requirement of the programme. Competitive scholarships are available to cover a large proportion of the costs of this year.

Language study continues to form an important part of the third year, using topic-focused materials drawn from newspapers, literature, films or radio broadcasts, combined with a selection of other modules.

In the fourth and final year, the language programme branches out into areas such as interpreting while continuing with reading, writing and speaking Chinese. There are also modules on topics such as modern-day Taiwan, late-imperial China and Chinese literature.

An important component of the final year of the single honours Chinese degree is a 15,000-word dissertation on a topic relating to any aspect of the Chinese world. Students taking a dual honours degree may choose a shorter dissertation (approximately 7,000 words in length), although this is not obligatory.

At Leeds, the deliberately modern bias of the four-year Chinese programme aims to produce graduates with an all-round proficiency in modern Chinese supported by a range of transferable skills and insights. Students begin the language from scratch (although there is provision for those with A level Chinese) and follow an intensive language programme in their first year. For the entire second year, students can choose to study in Taiwan (at National Chengchi University, Taipei) or at universities in mainland China located in Beijing, Tianjin or Shanghai. While abroad, they achieve a good level of day-to-day language ability and learn from the experience of living in another society.

Returning to Leeds in their third year, students continue with upper level language and non-language modules. By the final year of the programme, they are expected to be able to interpret relevant material in a wider sense, fitting it into the broader social, political, economic and cultural context of present-day China and the Asia-Pacific region.

Chinese can also be combined with a very wide range of other subjects.

Career Opportunities

Having acquired a detailed knowledge of contemporary China through disciplines including history, geography and economics, together with degree level language skills and the experience of practising Mandarin in its native context, graduates can consider a wide range of careers. Opportunities include teaching, translating, journalism, law, the City, and international marketing and sales.

In China itself, competition for graduate vacancies is intense. The main opportunities for foreign graduates in the Chinese labour market are in teaching, particularly English.

Related Degrees

Accounting and Finance for Contemporary China; Global Issues and Contemporary Chinese Studies; Chinese Studies with Economics, Film and Television Studies, Geography, History, International Development, Management, Music, Politics, South East Asian Studies, Arabic, French, German, Italian, Japanese, Russian, Spanish.

Suggested Reading

China: a New Cultural History
- Cho-yun Hsu, Columbia University Press, 2012

Multinationals, Globalisation and Indigenous Firms in China
- Chunhang Liu, Routledge, 2012

The Rise of Modern China
- Immanuel C Y Hsü, OUP USA, 2000

Penguin History of Modern China
- Jonathan Fenby, Penguin Books, 2013

Further Information

British Association for Chinese Studies
www.bacsuk.org.uk

Association for Chinese Studies in Ireland
www.chinesestudies.ie

Irish Institute for Chinese Studies
www.ucd.ie/china

Civil Engineering

Original article by John Oliphant, Heriot-Watt University, Edinburgh

Introduction

As a civil engineer, you could be involved in seeing projects through from design stage to construction and completion. Your projects might include the development and construction of bridges, tunnels, roads, railways, dams, pipelines and major buildings. At times, you might be in your office, working on designs at a computer or ensuring that your clients are kept up to date; at other times, you could be on site, leading teams, solving problems and literally being 'hands-on'.

Your first step is to study civil engineering at university to honours degree level (MEng or BEng) on a course recognised or accredited by the Institution of Civil Engineers (ICE). Having passed your course, your next important step is a professional qualification, which you can earn once you start working. This will define you as a true professional, capable of practising in most countries of the world.

There are three main types of professional qualification awarded by ICE. You can recognise who has these qualifications by letters (designations) after a name (e.g CEng MICE):

- An engineering technician (Eng Tech TMICE) applies proven techniques and procedures to solve engineering problems. They act as supervisors with technical responsibility

- An incorporated engineer (IEng MICE) is a professional engineer who promotes today's technology and applies and manages its use within the broad field of civil engineering

- A chartered engineer (CEng MICE) is an innovator who can lead teams of engineers and technicians developing solutions to civil engineering problems.

Degree Courses

The differences between courses at different universities can only be appreciated by reading prospectuses, and then visiting selected civil engineering departments. You must note clearly the strengths of each institution and its courses.

Some facts to find out are:

- What options are open to you later in the course?

- Does the course enable you to study for a time at a university abroad? This is of considerable importance to potential civil engineers, where firms are increasingly international.

- If you have the chance to study abroad, what arrangements are made for you to become competent in the appropriate foreign language?

- What does each university claim to be its strengths?

- Does the course involve any industrial experience, and if so how much?

- Is the course modular or is it linear?

Career Opportunities

Civil engineers can take advantage of work opportunities in both the private and public sectors, often changing jobs to gain more professional experience. They tend to specialise in areas such as roads and bridges, oil and gas rigs and pipelines, power stations, docks and harbours or public health and sewerage. There are courses run by the Institution of Civil Engineers for on-going professional development. UK civil engineering qualifications are internationally recognised and there are many opportunities to work on projects abroad. You could eventually become a director or partner in a civil engineering firm. Alternatively, you could become a university lecturer or set up as a consultant.

Civil engineering projects have been severely affected by the economic downturn that started in 2008. However, the industry is now recovering - boosted by the promise in the government Spending Review of 2013 of £50 billion of capital investment in 2015 to include roads to railways, bridges to broadband - and is once again investing in long-term planning, skills development and retention. The shift to a low carbon economy offers opportunities for innovative projects.

Related Degrees
Structural Engineering; Construction Engineering; Architectural Engineering; Civil and Coastal Engineering; Civil Engineering Surveying; Civil and Environmental Engineering; Civil and Structural Engineering; Offshore Engineering; Civil Engineering with Industrial Experience; Civil Engineering with Overseas Study.

Suggested Reading
Civil Engineering: a very short Introduction
- David Muir Wood, Oxford University Press, 2012

New Dictionary of Civil Engineering
- David Blockley, Penguin, 2005

The new science of strong materials: or why you don't fall through the floor
- J E Gordon, Princeton University Press, 2008

Structures: or Why Things Don't Fall Down
- J E Gordon, Penguin Science, 2009

Introduction to Architectural Technology
- Pete Silver and Will McLean, Laurence King, 2013

Further Information
Engineering Council UK
www.engc.org.uk

Institution of Civil Engineers
www.ice.org.uk

Institution of Structural Engineers
www.istructe.org

New Civil Engineer Magazine
www.nce.co.uk

Engineers Ireland
www.engineersireland.ie

Institution of Structural Engineers Republic of Ireland Branch
www.istructe.ie

Classics and Classical Studies

Original article by Dr Oswyn Murray, Balliol College, Oxford

Introduction

Classics is the study of the cultures of Greece and Rome. It was the original course in 'humanities' and is still a central arts discipline at most major UK universities. Its long tradition raises two questions: firstly, what is the justification of the classics in the modern world, and secondly, what are its strengths and weaknesses, both now and for the future?

The justification of classics lies in the nature of the Western cultural tradition. The essential characteristic of our culture, what the sociologist Max Weber called its 'formal rationality', is a creation of the Greeks. It was transmitted to the whole of Europe through the Roman Empire, and diffused through the rest of the world by the colonial expansion of Europe after the Renaissance, to become the basis of the first world civilisation. The Greeks were the first to separate clearly the three great functions of social civilisation - politics, religion and culture. In all essential aspects they set out the major branches of human investigation: biology, physics, medicine and mathematics in science; metaphysics, ethics, politics and logic in philosophy; sociology, psychology and anthropology in the social sciences; sculpture, pottery, architecture and the concept of representation in the arts; tragedy, comedy, epic, personal lyric, pastoral, history, biography and the divide between truth and fiction in literature. The Romans took over many of these artistic and intellectual pursuits from the Greeks but adapted them to the needs of their own younger and very different society. They made many original contributions, which remain central to our own culture, for instance legal science and public administration. In addition, many of the languages spoken on the continent of Europe are direct descendants of Latin. Of course many of these activities have transcended their beginnings, but the study of their classical origins reveals the interconnection between such different subjects and so the fundamental nature of the Western mind.

Degree Courses

For obvious reasons, therefore, the Western world has always looked back to the Greco-Roman past as an ideal and often sought to restore it in the present. One recurrent phenomenon in our culture is the creative importance of the renaissance or rebirth. The renewal of classical influences has marked every major new departure in culture from the fourth century AD to at least the nineteenth century. We cannot of course know the future. We may wonder if the chain has been broken, but even so its existence in the past is a fact, so that in the arts no major area of Western thought or literature can be understood without some knowledge of the classics. This explains the existence of classics courses in the majority of universities, for some access to the classics is presupposed for any serious arts studies; hence, too, the great popularity of foundation courses and of options covering classical history and literature in translation. Most classics departments now offer a variety of combined studies degrees in combination either with modern languages, or with philosophy, or with English.

Language requirements vary between courses and universities. For literary studies prior knowledge of Latin or Greek is an advantage, but all universities make provision for beginners in one or both languages. You need a keenness to learn. All universities teach in varying degrees in translation, often exclusively in translation for history and philosophy, while in literature a combination of survey in translation with in-depth study in the original is typical. Many universities also offer courses in classical studies, in which the thought, literature, art, history and archaeology of the classical world play a dominant role. The best preparation for classics at university lies in Latin and, where possible, Greek; the various ancient history and classical civilisation A level, Higher

Grade or equivalent courses are also useful. But all universities accept students from a wide variety of backgrounds, as long as they can show a genuine interest in the classical world. If there is no provision for language work at your school, get in touch early with the Joint Association of Classical Teachers for information on the many residential and non-residential courses for beginners in both languages.

Career Opportunities

Some 50% of classics graduates are in full-time employment or combining work with further study within six months of graduating. Of these, 14% choose professional roles within the business and financial sectors. With their ability to analyse and understand complex information and to research, document and present findings, Classics graduates are well-suited to professional services roles.

Communications-based roles are another clear option, drawing on an understanding of language and its power. Administrative roles can be an entry-level route for graduates who ultimately would like to work in creative, cultural and heritage-related positions.

Nearly a third of classics graduates undertake full-time further study. Often this is to enhance their understanding of a particular aspect of their degree course at Masters or PhD level, and might include classical archaeology, ancient history or Greek and Latin languages and literature. Becoming a specialist in an academic discipline, particularly at PhD level, can be the first step towards pursuing an academic career as a lecturer/researcher.

Other graduates opt for more vocational yet still subject-relevant courses, generally at Masters level, such as museum studies or records and archive management. Further study is also needed for a move into a profession such as law, teaching, librarianship or journalism.

Related Degrees

Classical Studies; Classical Civilisation; Greek Studies; Classics with Study in Continental Europe; Latin Studies.

Suggested Reading

The Oxford History of Greece and the Hellenistic World
- John Boardman et al, Oxford Paperbacks, 2001

The Oxford History of the Roman World
- John Boardman et al, Oxford Paperbacks, 2001

Early Greece
- Oswyn Murray, Fontana Press, 2010

Classical Art: from Greece to Rome
- Mary Beard and John Henderson, Oxford University Press, 2001

Renaissance and Renascences in Western Art
- Erwin Panofsky, Westview Press, 1991

Further Information

Institute of Classical Studies University of London
www.icls.sas.ac.uk

Classical Association
www.classicalassociation.org

Joint Association of Classical Teachers
www.jact.org

Classical Association of Ireland
www.classicalassociation.ie

Communications and Media Studies

Original article by Philip M Taylor, Institute of Communications Studies, University of Leeds

Introduction

Communications and media studies courses at British universities have expanded at a phenomenal rate in recent years. Frequently the object of unfair, not to mention ironic, derision in the media - largely on the grounds that they do not train graduates for the real world of the media, journalism or the communications industries in the broadest sense - these courses do in fact cover a variety of purposes. As a subject, communications is, by definition, multidisciplinary. Essentially, it involves the study of 'who says what to whom, when, with what purpose and with what effect'. Today's most effective communicators need to understand that although communication takes place in a technologically-driven environment, it requires creative applications that draw upon a number of traditional academic disciplines such as history, politics, sociology, law, psychology and even art, together with newer areas like cultural studies, graphic design and internet skills.

Degree Courses

Many university departments are interested in the media for their own sake, as part of an attempt to understand this significant aspect of our modern information society. These tend to concentrate on the theoretical aspects and should be of interest to students who want to be critics or analysts of the media, rather than practitioners. In the same way that students taking courses, say, in fine art, history or English literature, would not necessarily expect to make a career in those areas, these courses provide critical and analytical training of the mind and, as such, provide transferable skills that can be of use to many areas of society. Other departments concentrate largely on the practical or training aspects of the communications professions - from journalism to corporate or public relations. The most successful of these programmes do, in fact, have high rates of graduate employment in the media industries. Look for courses that enjoy accreditation with professional bodies - such as Creative Skillset or the Broadcast Journalism Training Council - or which have close relations (including attachments) with the media industries. Bear in mind that communications is one of the fastest changing employment environments of our time and that therefore academic departments that are well resourced with the latest digital and multi-media equipment are most likely to provide you with industry-ready skills.

More importantly, remember that communications is about communicating *something*. It is not just about the medium. The message is vitally important, and communicators who understand the skills needed to communicate also need the intellectual ability to understand what it is they are trying to say. Because communicators have enormous influence in our modern society, they carry considerable responsibilities. Programmes therefore that combine both theory and practice - although the balance is often difficult to maintain - tend to be the most successful of all.

But they are also the ones that attract the most applicants, and therefore they tend to require high examination grades for admission. On the other hand, because of their competitive nature, if you get in you will find yourself surrounded by many of the brightest and best students of your generation. Whether you are merely interested in understanding the media as a force which shapes so much of our perception about the world we live in, or whether you feel driven to become a driving force within our information society, make sure you choose the course that is right for you. Students who already know what they want to do in life can choose from a variety of specific courses on offer. Or if you don't know yet which aspect of this lively and expanding area you want to join, go for the more generalised courses that will help you make up your mind further down the road.

Career Opportunities

One thing is certain: communications and information are to the 21st century what oil and coal were to the 20th. Understanding this significance, as well as mastering its skills and matching up to the responsibilities involved, is as important now as it has ever been in a world in which 'information overload' is already one of its greatest challenges.

Related Degrees

Publishing; Public Relations; Communication Studies; Information Studies; Creative/Interactive/Design Media; International Business Communications; Media Studies.

Suggested Reading

Studying the Media: an Introduction
- Tim O'Sullivan et al, Bloomsbury Academic, 2003

The Media: an Introduction
- Daniele Albertazzi and Paul Cobley, Longman, 2009

The Media at War: communication and conflict in the 20th century
- Susan Carruthers, Palgrave Macmillan, 2011

Skills and Key Concepts for Media Studies
- Vivienne Clark et al, Hodder, 2002

Media Studies: Texts, Production and Context
- Paul Long and Tim Wall, Pearson, 2012

The Media Student's Book
- Gill Branston and Roy Stafford, Routledge, 2010

Further Information

Media and Communication Studies Site, Aberystwyth University
http://visual-memory.co.uk/daniel/media

Communication Advertising and Marketing Education Foundation
www.camfoundation.com

Creative Skillset
www.creativeskillset.org

Broadcast Journalism Training Council
www.bjtc.org.uk

National Council for the Training of Journalists
www.nctj.com

National Union of Journalists (UK and Ireland)
www.nuj.org.uk

Irish Film and Television Network
www.iftn.ie

Computing and Information Technology

Original article by Chris Kimble and Jeremy Jacob, Department of Computer Science, University of York and Professor David Arnold, School of Information Systems, UEA, Norwich

Introduction

The study of computation and computers is a broad and rapidly changing discipline. The subject has grown from one that was only of concern to a few mathematicians and electronic engineers to one where almost everybody's life is affected by computers in some way.

In taking a degree in computing, you should gain an education in a broad range of theory, tools and applications. You will also find that it has now become humanly impossible to know everything about computing, so you are likely to have to make choices about the areas you go into in most depth. As well as deciding between computing courses by choosing a university on a wider basis (e.g. the location, the reputation, the social life, the cost and availability of accommodation), there are a number of other ways by which you might differentiate between computing degrees. These include:

(i) Professional Accreditation by the Chartered Institute for IT (BCS) and the Institution of Engineering and Technology (IET)

(ii) Departmental Specialisations - usually demonstrated by the research interests of faculty

(iii) Balance between theory and practice; hardware and software; systems and applications

(iv) Lab provision - look at how much access undergraduates get

(v) Degrees with a year abroad (North America or Europe). This may affect the length and cost of the programme but also offers a wider educational experience

(vi) How much choice is there to take options in computing or options outside the faculty?

Traditionally, Computer Science has been the study of how to build machines that do computations efficiently. However, the term Information Technology (IT) is now used to describe the study of technologies used to store, communicate or manipulate information. Although related to computer science, the focus in IT is shifted away from technology used to process information and towards information and the uses that are made of it.

As a prospective student, you should make sure that you understand the different approaches to courses and course content before you apply.

Degree Courses

Growth and diversification in the Computer Science/IT area has led to the provision of a wide variety of courses and course names at universities. What is called 'Information Technology' at one university may be called 'Computer Science' at another. A course at one university called 'Software Engineering' may study more hardware in more detail than another university's 'Computer Science' course. Courses may be weighted towards the theory or more towards a vocational training in current techniques. How can you get behind the course title and find out what a degree is really about?

Is it a single subject, joint honours or an integrated degree?

Many Computer Science/IT degrees are single subject degrees, which tend to look at a particular subject area in greater depth than a joint honours or an integrated degree and often allow students to specialise in one particular area. For example, a single subject course may emphasise a particular sub-field such as artificial intelligence or computer graphics.

Joint honours degrees link Computer Science/IT with another subject. The usual partners are Mathematics, Electronics or Business Studies but other subjects can be linked to make some interesting combinations.

'Integrated' degree schemes attempt to overcome the problems that can be associated with joint degrees by teaching one or more topics as a single subject in a single department. 'Integrated' degrees may sound like a joint degree from their title but are more like single subject degrees. For example, Business Information Systems may be taught at some institutions as a joint degree, but be more integrated elsewhere.

Is it a sandwich course? Does it provide industrial experience?

Computer Science and IT are practical subjects; many universities will offer industrial experience as part of their course (a 'sandwich' course). In some sandwich courses the industrial experience will be a complete year (usually between the second and third years of study); in others a number of shorter periods are spent in industry. Engineering Council members, such as the BCS or the IET, set their own standards for training, and you are better off on a sandwich course whose training meets these standards.

Career Opportunities

The latest Technology Insights research report from e-skills UK reveals that IT employment through to 2020 is forecast to grow at almost twice the UK average. A record 129,000 new recruits a year are needed to fill IT and Telecoms jobs in the UK, both brand new jobs and replacements for those leaving the sector. The highest levels of employment growth are in high skill areas like software professionals, ICT managers, and IT strategy and planning professionals.

The technical skills most often requested by employers are: SQL, C, C#, .NET, SQL SVR, ASP, Java, HTML, JavaScript and Oracle.

Related Degrees

Software Engineering; Information Systems; Business Information Technology; Network Computing; Business Computing; Internet Computing; Computer Security; Computer Games; Artificial Intelligence; Medical Informatics; Computer Modelling; Business Systems Modelling; Computer Aided Engineering; Computer Science Informatics; Software Development.

Suggested Reading

Algorithmics: the Spirit of Computing
- David Harel and Yishai Feldman, Springer, 2012

Computer Science: an Overview
- Glenn Brookshear, Pearson, 2014

Get Set for Computer Science
- Alistair Edwards, Edinburgh University Press, 2006

The Passionate Programmer: Creating a Remarkable Career in Software Development
- Chad Fowler, Pragmatic Bookshelf, 2009

Further Information

e-skills UK
www.e-skills.com
BCS, the Chartered Institute for IT
www.bcs.org
Institution of Engineering and Technology
www.theiet.org
Irish Computer Society
www.ics.ie

Cybernetics

Original article by the University of Bradford

Introduction

Cybernetics is a broad subject, transcending traditional academic disciplines, and as such there are various ways of defining or commenting on it. The term was coined by a group of academics looking for a new name for the subject of the use of control and communication in different systems. They settled on cybernetics, derived from the Greek Kubernetes or steersman. As further justification for the name, the equivalent Latin word gives us the word governor, meaning a person in control. An early automatic control system was a speed governor for a steam engine.

It is sometimes called the 'science of interacting systems' - as cybernetics is not restricted to any one area, it can be applied to different systems - and typically these systems, or components within them, interact with each other. In a boat, for example, the steersman or controller interacts with the device being controlled (ie the boat), but the boat also interacts with the steersman. Ensuring that a boat reaches the correct destination is about much more than simply pointing it in the right direction and hoping for the best: the steersman must constantly check his position and make adjustments for the effects of winds and tides in order to maintain the right course.

One English university takes a broader, boat-free view, defining cybernetics as 'the acquisition, communication, processing and application of information'.

Degree Courses

Undergraduate courses incorporate many aspects of traditional disciplines such as computer science, information technology and engineering. Courses in cybernetics can include the study of control, computing, electronics, measurement, mechatronics, robotics, artificial intelligence, virtual reality and new technologies associated with the internet. The applications are varied: from automated transport systems, aeronautics and space systems to healthcare and entertainment. You could study cybernetics alone or combine it with control engineering, emphasising the technological aspects of cybernetics and incorporating practical and project work. In combination with biomedical engineering, it is possible to study more human aspects of the systems and combine this with biological, ecological and human systems. Medical cybernetics could appeal to you if you have an interest in medicine and computing and can equip you to incorporate IT into healthcare.

Cybernetics and virtual worlds allow you to explore worlds of the future and to interpret simulated worlds as a reality. Further possibilities include genome cybernetics, computer science and cybernetics, and electronic engineering and cybernetics.

You might expect your course to give you knowledge and understanding of:

- Appropriate mathematical techniques to help model and analyse systems, and use mathematics as a tool for communicating results and concepts
- Science underlying cybernetic systems
- Design of systems, including relevant design methods, and the use of appropriate technology
- Relevant management and business practices
- Engineering practice.

Check to see whether degrees you are considering are professionally recognised by bodies such as the Institution of Engineering and Technology (IET), the Institute of Measurement and Control (InstMC) or the Chartered Institute for IT (BCS). You could also explore the possibility of industrial sponsorship.

Career Opportunities

Career prospects for Cybernetics graduates tend to be good because the subject is very relevant to today's high technology society and opportunities are not dependent upon any one industry. Most graduates are employed in a technological capacity, either in a large company or a smaller company or consultancy; whereas others choose to further their research interests by undertaking postgraduate study.

If your course is suitably accredited, and you acquire the appropriate level of professional experience, you may apply for Chartered Engineer status.

Related Degrees

Artificial Intelligence and Cybernetics; Computer Control Engineering; Electronic Systems Control; Robotics and Automated Systems.

Suggested Reading

General System Theory: Foundations, Development, Applications
- Ludwig Von Bertalanffy, George Braziller Inc, 2003

Thinking in Systems: a Primer
- Diana Wright and Donella Meadows, Routledge, 2009

Artificial Intelligence: the Basics
- Kevin Warwick, Routledge, 2011

Mind, Man and Machine: a Dialogue
- Paul T Sagal, Hackett Publishing, 1995

Natural-born Cyborgs: Minds, Technologies and the Future of Human Intelligence
- Andy Clark, OUP, 2003

How We Became Posthuman: Virtual Bodies in Cybernetics, Literature and Informatics
- Katherine Hayles, Chicago University Press, 1999

Further Information

Cybernetics Society
www.cybsoc.org

Chartered Institute for IT
www.bcs.org

Institute of Measurement and Control
www.instmc.org.uk

Medical Cybernetics
www.medical-cybernetics.de

Institution of Engineering and Technology
www.theiet.org

Irish Computer Society
www.ics.ie

Dance

Original article by Dr Richard Ralph, formerly of Westminster College, Oxford (now part of Oxford Brookes University)

Introduction

I like to ask students coming to audition: 'Is there anything else you could possibly be happy doing as a career?' If the answer is 'yes' I tell the student to do that, as without any doubt it would be easier than a training and subsequent career in dance. For dancing, like a religious vocation with which it has many parallels, chooses you rather than you choosing it. Young people suddenly discover that they need to move their bodies, to reach deep into their reserves of stamina, strength and courage - and to dance. It can come upon you at the advanced age of sixteen or seventeen or it might be something you wanted to do since infancy.

Degree Courses

The basis of most professional dance courses is the learning of dance technique (this is usually either ballet or contemporary dance technique: other forms include jazz). This takes at least three hours of every day always following the same pattern and gives you a basic movement alphabet - the building bricks with which a choreographer will be able to express his or her art through you, or with which you will be able to communicate with others through movement.

Technique is a bit like doing scales if you are a musician. It is a daily routine, which keeps the body fit, supple and responsive to the instructions your brain gives it. Of itself it is not necessarily artistic, but it makes art possible: for the choreographer will paint and compose with the dancers' bodies. It is important to emphasise the place of technique in a dance school because it consumes many of the dance student's waking hours. As the body is trained to master the full range of dance technique, it changes shape as the muscle is developed. The way that the movement is timed and phrased gracefully and beautifully in relation to music will also be learned and the inner ideas or 'feeling tones' and muscular habits connected with certain sequences become second nature. But learning to dance is a mental and physical activity requiring ferocious concentration and considerable endurance. It tests commitment severely and many fall by the wayside. In any professional dance course the main credit will be given on the basis of progress made in technique classes.

Physical aptitude is important; your body has to be strong, but people with less-than-ideal or 'difficult' bodies can work wonders, especially if they undertake an appropriately supervised course of corrective strengthening exercises. But there are certain weaknesses which carry the risk of injury and which rule out rigorous training. So a proportion of students are not accepted at audition for physical reasons. In ballet the stereotyped look is more necessary than in contemporary dance, which tends to be more individual with less emphasis on the corps de ballet.

The most important qualification and the secret of eventual success in dance is an appetite for movement. Even in an untrained body this can show itself in the height of the leap, the length or depth of an extension, the follow through of a movement or exercise, or in a general sense of joy or even ecstasy. However, facial and physical beauty are of themselves not enough. The body as a whole must need to speak out in movement.

What I have described is a study in itself: a full-time job. But a course of theoretical studies as provided by most dance schools can speed your development as a dancer. Such subjects as music, anatomy and costume are relevant, dealing with the essential elements of the professional dancer's craft, but increasingly the dancer is being required to operate part-time as a community worker and teacher and so some preparation for teaching is necessary at dance school. A powerful sense of identity and self-confidence are necessary to contemporary dance in particular. The dancer is saying, 'Here I am; this is what I am doing; look at me.' And the 'I' is vital. There has to be somebody interesting to look at. All too often the hothouse intensity of the dance school produces a cold obsessiveness and a narrowing of horizons, which ends up by actually threatening artistic values. Keep your mind active and your interest in the world around you alive.

All the best dance schools have good libraries, record and video collections. It is vital that young dance students know something of the history of dance and about other art forms. Students need to go to museums, theatres, concerts and films, preferably with some guidance from the school. All of these art forms provide vital resources for any dancer.

Schools will give prominence to the creative and interpretative aspects of dance. Choreography is taught from an early stage. It is mainly a matter of individual ability, but there is a basic craft which will help dancers to understand the choreographers who will work with them in their professional careers. Even modest compositions can help dance students to develop as interpretative performers and to move creatively. It is an excellent preparation for professional life for students to work with other dancers on group pieces and to find ways of working through the inevitable artistic and personal tensions that arise.

Repertory - Once students have mastered the steps of a dance they learn how to perform it in front of other students and sometimes a public paying audience. It is important that students should always remember that they are studying a theatrical art form, which is designed to be performed, but too much performance early in the course is usually seen as inappropriate. The technical groundwork must be laid before it can be absorbed into interpretation.

Career Opportunities

The dancer's training is very tough and requires much dedication. Should you not achieve your ambition of dancing professionally, there is now a range of interesting dance-related careers open to the well-trained dancer. Careful course selection when you are applying for your dance course can keep a range of career options open.

Professional careers call for those with outstanding ability and depend on a great deal of luck and determination to succeed. Some enter teaching - others enter the general graduate market. The skills of self-expression and self-confidence can be a considerable asset in many unrelated careers.

Related Degrees

Performing Arts (Dance); Physical Theatre and Dance; Art & Teaching of Ballet; Dance and Culture; Dance Studies.

Suggested Reading

Conditioning for Dance: Training for Peak Performance in All Dance Forms
- Eric Franklin, Human Kinetics, 2003
Conditioning for Dancers
- Tom Welsh, University Press of Florida, 2009
Article 19
- Online contemporary dance magazine, accessible at **www.article19.co.uk**

Further Information

Dance UK
www.danceuk.org
Council for Dance Education and Training
www.cdet.org.uk
Dance Ireland
www.danceireland.ie

Dentistry

Original article written from material supplied by Dr S M Hooper, University of Bristol Dental School, and the British Dental Association

Introduction

There are 17 undergraduate and postgraduate dental schools in the UK and two in Ireland, each located in a major city. Dental courses last five years (four years postgraduate) and lead to a bachelor's degree (BDS). The courses include a sound academic education combined with theoretical and practical training in all aspects of dental practice. Subjects studied include anatomy, physiology, biochemistry, pathology, behavioural sciences and dental materials science, as well as clinical skills in all dental disciplines. Some dental schools offer a 'pre-dental' year for suitable candidates lacking the relevant science subjects. Entry requirements to typical courses are likely to include AS/A Level or H Grade or equivalent Chemistry and Biology. A broad range of other science and arts subjects is encouraged.

Degree Courses

Until relatively recently, the five-year course would start with two predominantly pre-clinical years, followed by three years of mainly clinical practice. Now, however, General Dental Council recommendations prefer early clinical exposure, together with integrated teaching of all subjects and a dimension of choice of special subjects by the student. The integrated nature of the programme means that basic science teaching relates to clinical practice and clinical teaching is underpinned by scientific understanding. This means that you should have contact with patients from the first few weeks of the first year and will be encouraged at an early stage to assume an appropriate level of responsibility for patient care.

A typical programme has three main components: the first consists of subjects common to medicine and dentistry, progressing from biomedical sciences through behavioural sciences, epidemiology, pathology and microbiology to human disease; the second includes oral and dental aspects of the biological sciences, leading to an understanding of the diagnosis, prevention and treatment of oral and dental diseases and disorders and the effects of systemic disease on the oral and dental tissues; the third consists of the clinical and technical aspects of dentistry, with the provision of comprehensive oral and dental healthcare for patients of all ages. These components are mainly integrated, although there is usually a larger proportion of basic sciences at first and a larger clinical component at the end.

In addition to learning the practical skills necessary to become a dentist, you would acquire communication, personal management and information technology skills, together with an appreciation and analysis of ethical and legal issues in dentistry.

At the end of year three, you may have the opportunity to take an 'intercalated' BSc degree, allowing you to pursue the subjects of your choice in greater depth.

You should note that, in addition to the normal academic entry requirements, most dental schools require you to take the UK Clinical Aptitude Test (UKCAT) as part of the admissions process. Visit the UKCAT website for full details.

Your personal statement is a significant factor in the overall assessment of your application. Schools will be looking particularly for evidence of appropriate commitment to, and realistic appreciation of, the academic, physical and emotional demands of a dental career. They would normally expect you to have undertaken some work experience in a caring environment and/or observation in a dental clinical setting. Communication skills and the ability to work successfully in a team are of great importance, while your interests, achievements and contribution to your community may be taken into account in addition to your academic ability.

It is rare for offers to be made without an interview, and you must be available for interview in order to be considered for admission. The interview is usually conducted by at least two senior members of the clinical and biomedical sciences staff, with the aim of assessing your personal qualities to find out whether you have the potential to become a successful member of the dental profession. In this context, strong interpersonal and communication skills are most important, particularly when you consider the relationships which dentists need to build with their patients.

Career Opportunities
After qualification there are a variety of areas in which you can choose to practise.

General dental practice - Most dentists choose to work as general dental practitioners (GDPs).

Hospital dentistry - This covers oral surgery, restorative dentistry, children's dentistry and orthodontics.

Community dental service - Provides dental care for patients with special needs.

Armed forces - Permanent commissions are available.

Dentists in industry - Some large companies (eg oil companies) offer a dental service to their employees.

University teaching/research - Research may be combined with teaching at the dental school.

Related Degrees
Dental Technology; Oral Health Science; Dental Materials.

Suggested Reading
Getting into Dental School
- Adam Cross, Trotman Education, 2013

C U @ Dental Skl
- Jenny Gallagher and Nairn Wilson, Stephen Hancocks Ltd, 2012

Clinical Problem Solving in Dentistry
- Edward W Odell, Churchill Livingstone, 2010

Oxford Handbook of Clinical Dentistry
- David and Laura Mitchell, OUP Oxford, 2009

Further Information
British Dental Association
www.bda.org

General Dental Council
www.gdc-uk.org

UKCAT
www.ukcat.ac.uk

Irish Dental Association
www.dentist.ie

Design and Technology

Original article by George Preston, Faculty of Applied Sciences, Bath Spa University

Introduction

If you are interested in studying an aspect of Design and Technology (D&T) in a higher education setting, do not restrict your research simply to courses that have D&T in their title. Many similar courses have titles as varied as electronic product design, fashion design technology, food technology and product design.

'Design' should be at the heart of all D&T courses, but what do we mean by 'design'? The term is unfortunately open to multiple interpretations. If we take as an example the design of an electric kettle, one interpretation of the design process can be considered to embrace everything to do with the development, production and marketing of the kettle. This will include technical aspects of the switch and heating element, the aesthetics and ergonomics of the body, the way the body will be manufactured, the way the product compares with other similar products, management of the development process, sourcing of materials/components and the environmental impact of the product.

If your interests are towards the technical aspects, you will be more interested in courses which focus on what is often referred to as engineering design. If, however, your interests lie in the aesthetic, functional and ergonomic aspects, you are more likely to be drawn to courses which emphasise industrial design. These are not the only aspects of design. Of increasing importance is the question of values in design that address the real impact, costs and consequences of a product. All products, for example, have an impact on the environment during every stage of their production, use and disposal. Considerable emphasis is now being placed on design which takes into account issues such as pollution and the use of finite energy resources. For example, if a component can be made from one material rather than two, there is a greater possibility that the component can be more easily recycled because expensive separation of the materials will be avoided.

There are few cases where one individual is responsible for the design, production and marketing of a product. Usually a number of people are involved in the development of a product and attention is given to the way people work together. *'Concurrent or simultaneous engineering'* sounds very technical and rather formidable but is primarily concerned with the way in which everyone with an interest can be involved in the design process at the same time. Traditionally, different aspects of the design process have tended to be dealt with in sequence. The concurrent approach makes the design process more effective and hence products can be brought to the market quicker with a greater degree of confidence that they will satisfy the needs of the user.

Degree Courses

In a typical course, first year students might take two very broadly based modules that give them experience of designing in a wide range of contexts such as food product development, resistant materials and textiles. Another important aspect of the modules is to ensure that students are familiar with a range of information technology tools that are increasingly important in all aspects of designing.

In the subsequent years, there is a range of modules that covers things such as design practice, working with resistant materials, materials and materials processing, design for manufacturing, control systems, designing with electronic multimedia, appropriate technology, product development in the food industry, marketing and satellite remote sensing.

Career Opportunities

Graduates enter specialist design studios, advertising agencies, teaching, newspapers, magazine and book publishing, product design in industry, printing, textile/fashion design, interior design and so on.

Related Degrees

Industrial Package Design and Technology; Textile Technology; Marine Sports Technology; Music Technology; Architectural Technology; Sustainable Technology; Paper Science; Environmental Technology; Industrial Product Design; Product Design; Theatre Design; Media Technology; Furniture Design/Production; Small Craft Design; Audio Technology; Sports Equipment Technology; Craft Design; Glass/Architectural Design; Model Design; Dental Technology; Prosthetics/Orthotics; Clothing Studies; Design for Digital Technologies.

Suggested Reading

Getting into Art and Design Courses
- James Burnett, Trotman, 2014

Design Uncovered
- Karen Holmes, Trotman, 2009

Making It: Manufacturing Techniques for Product Design
- Chris Lefteri, Laurence King, 2012

Becoming a Product Designer: A Guide to Careers in Design
- Bruce Hannah, Wiley, 2004

The Fundamentals of Product Design
- Richard Morris, AVA Publishing,2009

Product Design 01: Idea Searching
- David Bramston, AVA Publishing, 2008

Design Secrets: Products 2
- Lynn Haller and Cheryl Dangel Cullen, Rockport, 2006

The Career Guide for Creative and Unconventional People
- Carol Eikleberry, Ten Speed Press, 2007

Further Information

Institution of Engineering Designers
www.ied.org.uk

Design Council
www.designcouncil.org.uk

Creative Skillset
http://creativeskillset.org

Chartered Society of Designers
www.csd.org.uk

Institute of Designers in Ireland
www.idi-design.ie

Dietetics and Nutrition

Original article adapted, with permission, from material supplied by the British Dietetic Association

Introduction

Dietetics is the application of the science of nutrition to the management and prevention of diet-related illnesses. This article is about professional courses which, when successfully completed, will provide you with eligibility for state registration as a Dietitian with the Health and Care Professions Council (HCPC). These courses last three or four years. If you already hold a degree in a life science subject you may be eligible for a two-year postgraduate course in dietetics. The title dietitian is protected by law in the UK, which means that anyone using the title must be registered with the HCPC.

To start a degree course you will normally be expected to have obtained A Level, H Grade or equivalent passes in two or three subjects, preferably Chemistry or Biology plus another Science subject or Mathematics.

Remember that colleges and universities will consider each application individually.

Degree Courses

The dietetic degree programmes involves academic study and practical experience. Academic study involves:

- Biochemistry
- Human Nutrition
- Human Physiology
- Diet Therapy
- Food Processing, Preservation and Food Hygiene
- Nutritional Medicine
- Healthcare: Systems and Management Structures
- Epidemiology and Public Health
- Genetics
- Research Methods
- Data Analysis
- Behavioural Studies
- Pharmacology
- Professional Practice

You will be required to undertake practical placements, usually within the NHS and other health and care organisations, which are organised by the university. Placements allow you, under supervision, to develop practical skills and apply knowledge in a work environment.

Teaching is usually delivered over three to five days with 12 to 25 contact hours a week. Placements are full-time and approximately 37 hours per week.

The British Dietetic Association (BDA) holds responsibility for the curriculum, which describes what is expected of a newly-qualified dietitian and provides the framework for universities to deliver programmes that are responsive to the demands of dietetic employment.

In some institutions, where possible, the course is taught within the university's medical school. This means that you can learn to be a dietitian alongside your future colleagues: doctors, nurses, pharmacists and others.

Career Opportunities

Dietitians work with many different conditions and population groups. You may work with children, adults with diabetes, and people with food allergies. You could work with individuals or groups of people to help with their condition or plan healthy eating campaigns for a whole community.

As a newly-qualified dietitian, you would usually start your career in the NHS working in a general post within hospital and/or community. First posts often involve a varied caseload of general medical and surgical patients in wards, outpatient clinics and the community. You may also be involved in health improvement and other projects. After gaining experience, you would typically develop your career in a speciality such as oncology (cancer), diabetes, public health and health improvement, obesity, renal (kidney disease), cardiovascular, food allergy or an intensive care setting.

There are also opportunities to progress to management roles such as being responsible for controlling a budget and planning and marketing a dietetic service. Some dietitians choose to build on their NHS experience by moving to work in industry, education, the media or research.

Related Degrees

Public Health Nutrition.

Suggested Reading

Want a Career as a Dietitian?
- downloadable from the BDA website below

Manual of Dietetic Practice
- Joan Gandy, Wiley-Blackwell, 2014

Pocket Guide to Nutrition and Dietetics
- Sarah E Byrom, Churchill Livingstone, 2002

Oxford Handbook of Nutrition and Dietetics
- Joan Webster-Gandy et al, OUP Oxford, 2011

Further Information

British Dietetic Association
www.bda.uk.com

Nutrition Society
www.nutritionsociety.org

Health and Care Professions Council
www.hcpc-uk.org

Skills for Health
www.skillsforhealth.org.uk

Irish Nutrition and Dietetic Institute
www.indi.ie

Drama

Original article by John Marshall, Bristol University

Introduction

Of all the arts, drama is perhaps the most public and popular. In the various forms of live theatre, film and television, more drama is seen now than ever before. Although this popularity may, in part, be attributed to the greater accessibility afforded by television, it cannot disguise the very real significance of performed drama to society. Why should this be so? What made London audiences flock to the public playhouses in Elizabethan England? Why do millions of people watch *Eastenders*? How did Shakespeare ensure that the audience not only watched and listened to his plays but also returned to see his next one? How do soap operas work in terms of character, story line, dialogue, subject matter, setting, camera angles, editing and so forth? The serious asking of these questions and the rigorous thinking, exploring and analysis required to answer them is, in very simple terms, what constitutes the study of drama. To be able to comprehend fully the role of drama in society and to engage critically with text performance, it is necessary to gain knowledge and experience in a number of theoretical and practice areas which contribute to the informed study of drama. In the pursuit of textual analysis and practical criticism students may find themselves drawing on aspects of such diverse disciplines as art, architecture, history, religion, politics, physics, philosophy, psychology, sociology etc. This wide range of contributing knowledge is one of the exciting qualities of drama study at undergraduate level, which places it deservedly within the area of liberal arts education and distinguishes it from the more specialised and specific actor training with which it is sometimes confused.

Degree Courses

For the most part, drama degrees are not vocational; they are not designed to train students for particular professional posts in the theatre or television and should not be regarded as a fail-safe alternative to drama school. The candidate at interview who professes a yearning to act but wants a degree to 'fall back on' is unlikely to impress. It is rewardingly true that many drama graduates do proceed professionally but in most cases this follows an additional period of appropriate training. The number of degree courses available in the subject has grown considerably since the first, more than 40 years ago; and although many may have 'drama' in the title, the courses may be very different in context and approach. It is, therefore, extremely important that candidates read course outlines very carefully in order to select the type of course which best suits their interest. For example, many departments acknowledge the significant contribution of television and film to the drama of the twentieth century and may incorporate not only the theoretical study necessary for the critical analysis of text and screening but also a complementary element of practical film or video making. Other courses may concentrate entirely on the process and products of the theatre. Similarly, the variety of courses reflects the variety of approaches available to the study of drama and, while most will combine a number of these, the emphasis on the historical, critical, sociological and generic approach may be different in each case.

Drama study, in common with its professional relations, theatre, television and film, is apparently glamorous but in reality extremely hard work, not only intellectually, but physically and emotionally as well. It is demanding in terms of time as well as effort, but it is also sociable and pleasurable, and to the outsider, enjoyment can sometimes be confused with easiness. Don't be confused; be prepared to work long hours at reading as well as rehearsing and to give a great deal of yourself, not merely for your own benefit, but for the collective advantage and development of others.

Career Opportunities

The employment record for Drama graduates is relatively good. Approximately 17% enter further courses of study and training. Of those entering direct employment on graduation, 50% enter the creative and entertainment fields, whilst others might take a PGCE to become a teacher, or train for journalism, editing, languages or administrative work. The skills of persuasion and self-confidence, gained through acting, can be of considerable value in a wide range of unrelated career fields.

Related Degrees

Drama in the Community; Speech and Drama Studies; Acting; Theatre Arts; Film and Drama; Visual Performance.

Suggested Reading

So you want to be a Theatre Producer
- James Seabright, Nick Hern Books, 2010

So you want to be a Theatre Director
- Stephen Unwin, Nick Hern Books, 2004

Drama/Theatre/Performance
- Simon Shepherd and Mick Wallis, Routledge, 2004

The Career Guide for Creative and Unconventional People
- Carol Eikleberry, Ten Speed Press, 2007

The Field of Drama: How the Signs of Drama Create Meaning on Stage and Screen
- Martin Esslin, Methuen Drama, 1988

Modern Drama in Theory and Practice 1: Realism and Naturalism
- J L Styan, Cambridge University Press, 1983

The Empty Space
- Peter Brook, Penguin Classics, 2008

Further Information

National Drama
www.nationaldrama.org.uk

Creative and Cultural Skills: Theatre
http://ccskills.org.uk/careers/advice/any/theatre

Equity
www.equity.org.uk

TheatreNet.com - the Performing Arts Centre
www.theatrenet.com

Arts Council England
www.artscouncil.org.uk

Drama UK
www.dramauk.co.uk

National Association for Youth Drama in Ireland
http://nayd.ie

Irish Theatre Institute
www.irishtheatreinstitute.com

Ecology

Original article by Dr Louise Banton, Lancaster University

Introduction

Ecology is a complex area of biology concerned with how living organisms interact with each other and with the environment, including our own relations with other species and with the biosphere. It is an interdisciplinary subject drawing mainly from biology and environmental sciences but also from subjects like landscape history, economics, development studies and so on. It has its own rationale, methods and theory, particularly concerned with populations and communities. It is central to dealing with many problem areas such as pollution, climate change and resource conservation.

You may have the opportunity to specialise in different organisms (e.g. mammals, plants or insects) and in different environments (e.g. tropical or marine). You can study ecology to gain understanding of natural animal and plant communities and processes, and as the scientific basis for the sustainable management of the world's natural resources.

Degree Courses

At one UK university, the core first year units are based on workshops for numerical analysis, seminars and field trips, which play an important role in the programme. In the second year, you could take aquatic, marine, population and community ecology together with more ecology, evolutionary biology or environmental science units. Most third year units deal with applied aspects of ecology, such as fisheries, bioremediation and conservation. You would carry out a major independent research project during your third year.

At another university, 15 modules must be taken in the first year, including at least five in biology and five in environmental sciences. The remaining five modules can be chosen from biology, environmental sciences or other departments. There is a test at the end of each module. A similar pattern continues through the second and third years but the nature of the modules allows for increasing specialisation.

Some courses offer the chance of a year in another European state, in North America or in Australasia. There are also four-year industrial sandwich courses, in which you would spend the year between your second and final years working in a research laboratory or similar institution.

You may find it useful to look for a degree course that has received accredited degree or accredited degree pathway status from the Chartered Institute of Ecology and Environmental Management (CIEEM). These courses represent the first programmes to meet the standards of course content and delivery approved by the CIEEM Governing Board.

Degree accreditation was one of the recommendations of CIEEM's report into ecological skills gaps and shortages, published in 2011. *Ecological Skills: shaping the profession for the 21st century* identified degree accreditation as a means of supporting universities to teach students the knowledge and skills that employers are looking for. The degree accreditation scheme was accordingly developed in consultation with employers and recent graduates.

Career Opportunities

Many ecology graduates undertake postgraduate study, either as PhD students leading to a research career in some aspect of ecological research, or as Masters students in areas such as Biodiversity and Conservation. Some students proceed directly into applied wildlife or habitat management careers with conservation organisations or other public or voluntary sector organisations. Other careers are more generally related to biological sciences training, such as science communication and publishing (including media and journalism), science administration or public education (in zoos or museums).

Your career options need not be limited to the biological or environmental sciences. Increasingly, employers look to performance in undergraduate studies as evidence of an ability to work hard and master complex information, rather than seeking degrees directly relevant to the job. Consequently, ecology and environmental biology graduates may pursue careers in sales and management in science-based companies and in non-science-based areas such as finance, administration and management consultancy.

Related Degrees

Animal Behaviour; Countryside Conservation; Conservation Biology; Environmental Science; Natural History; Wildlife Biology; Zoology.

Suggested Reading

Rooting for a career in Ecology
- downloadable from the British Ecological Society website below

First Ecology: Ecological Principles and Environmental Issues
- Alan Beeby and Anne Maria Brennan, OUP, 2007

Ecology: From Individuals to Ecosystems
- Michael Begon et al, John Wiley, 2006

The Diversity of Life
- Edward O Wilson, Penguin, 2001

The Future of Life
- Edward O Wilson, Abacus, 2003

Ecology: Principles and Applications
- J L Chapman and M J Reiss, Cambridge, 1998

Conservation Biology
- Andrew S Pullin, Cambridge University Press, 2002

Further Information

British Ecological Society
www.britishecologicalsociety.org

Chartered Institute of Ecology and Environmental Management
www.cieem.net

Ecology Ireland
www.ecologyireland.ie

Economics

Dr Jo Blanden, Economics Programme Director, University of Surrey

Introduction

Economics is often described as the study of scarcity and choice. Given that the world's resources are limited, how should they be used to generate goods and services? Once these goods and services are produced, how should they be allocated among citizens? How are the economic systems of different nations interrelated?

Many important and topical questions can be considered from this viewpoint:

- How should the world respond to the threat of climate change?

- What is the best way to finance and organise schools and the NHS?

- What are the reasons for the recent financial crisis?

As students develop their study of economics, they are introduced to a very particular view of the world, with its own assumptions and structures. In particular, both firms and individuals are assumed to act to maximise their own wellbeing, either through profit or by enjoying their consumption. This means that problems can frequently be presented in mathematical form, which can lead to powerful conclusions. In addition, Econometrics, the statistical branch of Economics, provides a set of tools for discovering the relationships between real world data and finding out more about how the economy works. Economics is traditionally divided into two broad areas: *Microeconomics*, concerned with individual decision-makers, and *Macroeconomics*, which concerns the workings of national economies and the relationships between them.

The tools available to economists are powerful and in recent years they have been used to address many questions traditionally thought to be outside the usual economic sphere. Great examples of this trend can be found in Levitt and Dubner's Freakonomics which poses such questions as: 'Why do drug dealers live with their Moms?' or 'What do school teachers and sumo-wrestlers have in common?'

Degree Courses

The current UCAS website listing shows some 1300 different Economics degrees and foundation degrees spread over 110 different institutions. Careful research is therefore required to decide on the type of course which would suit you best. It is possible to combine Economics with one or two other subjects, such as Philosophy or Maths, for example, or alongside a language. It is also possible to specialise in a particular branch such as Economics and Finance, or to take a straight Economics course which will provide a solid foundation across the discipline. A common structure for a single-honours Economics course would be to start with an introductory first year, cover the core of Microeconomics, Macroeconomics and Econometrics in Level 2 and then use these skills to develop a specialism by choosing optional modules in the Final Year.

Economics degrees at some institutions also offer students the opportunity to engage in a work placement between their second and final years. This can be extremely valuable as it gives students the opportunity to relate their subject to the real world, to gain precious experience and skills and to return to their final year at university with new knowledge and motivation.

Career Opportunities

Undergraduate economists develop skills in three distinct areas, all of which are strongly valued by employers. The first is in logical thinking, giving them the ability to use mathematical techniques and apply theories to unfamiliar problems. The second is in data processing; they must work well with figures but also be able to seek out and interpret information from a wide variety of sources, often by making effective use of information technology. Finally, students must learn how to communicate ideas and arguments in plain English, both in written and verbal form.

Data on the earnings of graduates shows that those who studied Economics and Business have some of the highest earnings in the labour market (comparable with those for Medicine and Law). This seems likely to be connected to the strong numeracy skills of economists, which are highly valued by employers.

To give a few examples, recent graduates in Economics from the University of Surrey have found employment as analysts in financial companies and economists in the City, Government and Bank of England while others opt to pursue postgraduate studies either in Economics or in related areas such as Computer Science, Law and Investment Analysis.

Related Degrees

Business Economics; Economics and Economic History; Economics and Economic Psychology; Finance and Economics; Financial Mathematics; International Economics; Management Economics; Mathematical Economics and Statistics; Philosophy, Politics and Economics.

Suggested Reading

The Undercover Economist
- Tim Harford, Abacus, 2013

The Undercover Economist Strikes Back: how to Run or Ruin an Economy
- Tim Harford, Abacus, 2014

Freakonomics: a Rogue Economist Explores the Hidden Side of Everything
- Steven Levitt and Stephen Dubner, Penguin, 2007

The Economic Naturalist: Why Economics Explains Almost Everything
- Robert Frank, Virgin, 2008

Freefall: Free Markets and the Sinking of the Global Economy
- Joseph Stiglitz, Penguin, 2010

Too Big to Fail: Inside the Battle to Save Wall Street
- Andrew Sorkin, Penguin, 2010

Further Information

Why study economics?
www.whystudyeconomics.ac.uk

Biz/ed
www.bized.co.uk

Greg Mankiw's Blog - Random Observations for Students of Economics
http://gregmankiw.blogspot.com

Animation on the story of Economics
http://vimeo.com/23251216

The Economist Blog
http://www.economist.com/blogs/freeexchange

Economic and Social Research Unit, Ireland
www.esri.ie

Education (England, Wales, N. Ireland)

Original article by Professor Chris Husbands, University of Warwick

Introduction

This article is mainly concerned with programmes of teacher education in universities in England, Wales and Northern Ireland, since most education degrees fall into this category. Those aiming to work as teachers in the state system are required to have an appropriate degree and to have been awarded Qualified Teacher Status (QTS). There are two main ways of acquiring these qualifications: the postgraduate or the undergraduate route. (There are also employment-based and assessment-only routes but they are outside the scope of this article). For the postgraduate route, students can study for a degree in an appropriate subject, usually taking three or four years according to the discipline involved, and they can follow this by taking a one-year Postgraduate Certificate in Education (PGCE) which provides them with experience in schools, a grounding in professional practice and policy frameworks and knowledge of the public education system. At the end of the PGCE programme, students are considered for the award of QTS.

The undergraduate route is to take a three- or four-year concurrent degree: either a BA/BSc(QTS) or a BEd. A concurrent degree means that students combine academic studies in their specialist subject(s) with professional studies and experience in schools throughout the period of the degree. In practice, the three-year degrees are often based on a longer academic year than the four-year degrees, so that the time involved in study is roughly the same. It is vital to check on the details of course length and course requirements before deciding on whether to apply for a three- or four-year concurrent degree.

In Scotland and the Republic of Ireland a somewhat different system of qualification exists, see *Degree Course Descriptions*: **Education (Scotland)** and **Education (Ireland)**.

Degree Courses

All teacher training programmes are designed to equip you with the skills and knowledge you will need to teach successfully. Initial Teacher Training programmes focus on a number of themes, linked to the QTS standards. Whatever programme you choose, your initial teacher training (ITT) will involve:

- A knowledge and understanding of the relevant national curriculum programmes of study for your subject(s)
- Planning and preparing lessons and setting learning objectives
- Managing classes, promoting good behaviour and minimising disruption
- Using information and communication technology effectively
- Awareness of the professional values expected of teachers, in their attitudes and behaviour towards pupils and colleagues

Most trainee teachers (except for those on employment-based or assessment only routes) divide their time between a university or other higher education institution and a school, where they undertake supervised teaching practice.

All providers of teacher education work in close partnership with schools at all stages of the process: from curriculum design through to programme delivery and final assessment. Partner schools provide mentors from their staff to guide and develop students' work in schools.

All applicants for teacher education programmes must be interviewed to establish their academic, professional and personal suitability for teaching. As well as academic qualifications, applicants will be assessed at interview on their motivation and commitment to teaching as a career. Applicants are advised to gain some experience in an educational setting, possibly a local school, which will not only help them in making decisions about a possible career in teaching but will also provide valuable experience to discuss at interview.

You should note that a number of universities offer studies in education as a theoretical subject, which do not lead in themselves to qualified teacher status. For example, many institutions offer degrees in educational studies, business education, education and psychology, education and sociology.

Career Opportunities

There will always be a need for good teachers and there are sometimes shortages, although the situation varies from subject to subject and from area to area. At present, for example, those who want to teach secondary physics, maths, chemistry, computing, modern foreign languages, history, English, geography, biology, design and technology or music are in great demand in England and may be eligible for a scholarship or training bursary.

Teachers can be promoted to posts of responsibility in academic, administrative and pastoral roles - as heads of department or year group, personal tutors, heads and deputy heads. Allowances can also be offered for additional teaching and learning responsibilities.

Related Degrees

Primary Education; Early Childhood Studies; Upper Primary; Lower Primary; Nursery/ Infants; Physical Education; Secondary Education; Outdoor Education; Community Education; Educational Studies; Science for Education; English Language Teaching.

Suggested Reading

How to Survive your First Year in Teaching
- Sue Cowley, Bloomsbury, 2013

Teaching Uncovered
- Karen Holmes, Trotman, 2010

The Newly Qualified Teacher's Handbook
- Elizabeth Holmes, Routledge, 2008

Get Ready to Teach
- Verity Lush, Longman, 2009

Further Information

Get into Teaching (England)
www.education.gov.uk/get-into-teaching
Professional Skills Tests
www.education.gov.uk/sta/professional
National Curriculum
www.gov.uk/national-curriculum/overview
General Teaching Council for Wales
www.gtcw.org.uk
NASUWT
www.nasuwt.org.uk
Association of Teachers and Lecturers
www.atl.org.uk
National Union of Teachers
www.teachers.org.uk
Department of Education for Northern Ireland
www.deni.gov.uk
General Teaching Council for Northern Ireland
www.gtcni.org.uk

Education (Ireland)

Original article by Joyce Lane, educational consultant

Introduction

For almost all teaching posts in Ireland you need an eligible first degree and a recognised teaching qualification. This article gives some details of these qualifications and entry and training required. There is a lot of competition for teaching jobs so it is important to demonstrate interest and commitment. Relevant Work Experience such as time spent working voluntarily with children in schools or with youth people in clubs is recommended before application for teacher training.

Primary Teacher Training

Five Colleges of Education offer teacher training courses which last for four years and lead to a BEd degree. Up to 10% of places may be reserved for applicants from the Gaeltacht. Intake into the colleges is regulated by the Department of Education and Skills. It is also possible to qualify by completing a two-year Graduate Diploma after graduating with another degree. Four centres offer a full-time postgraduate course in Primary Teaching: St Patrick's College, Froebel Department, Coláiste Mhuire Marino Institute of Education and Mary Immaculate College, Limerick. In addition, an online Higher Diploma in Arts in Primary Education, accredited by the Higher Education and Training Awards Council (HETAC), is provided by Hibernia College, a privately-owned organisation. This is a part-time blended learning course which takes place over two years and is recognised by the Teaching Council for the purposes of primary teaching.

After their first appointment all primary teachers serve a probationary period.

Entry and Training

Applicants must be at least 17 years old on 15 January in the year following their entry to a College of Education. A Leaving Certificate with 3 subjects at minimum grade C3 on Higher Level papers and 3 other subjects at minimum grade D3. These must include at least grade C3 on a Higher Level paper in Irish (including the equivalent of grade C3 at the Leaving Certificate Oral Irish examination), grade C3 or an Ordinary Level or D3 on a Higher Level paper in English and grade D3 in mathematics at either Ordinary or Higher level.

All teacher training students in Colleges of Education must be proficient in spoken Irish and are required to attend a three-week course in the Gaeltacht at the end of their first year in training. It should be noted that this is a compulsory part of the course of training. In addition, students are subject to an oral Irish test at the end of their first year in training, a pass in which is necessary in order to continue to the second year of the course. Students who fail this oral Irish test may, at the discretion of the College, be allowed to repeat the test following attendance at the Gaeltacht course.

Secondary Teacher Training

Post-primary Initial Teacher Education (ITE) is provided through programmes of a consecutive or a concurrent nature, available at many universities and colleges throughout the country.

The most common route to qualification is the consecutive route, which comprises a suitable degree and teacher education qualification. A suitable degree is defined as an award from a state-recognised university or similar third-level college, which enables the holder to teach at least one curricular subject to the highest level within the post-primary schools curriculum. For most subjects, this means to Leaving Certificate Higher Level.

A suitable ITE qualification is defined as a qualification from a state-recognised university or similar third-level college, incorporating three specific elements (Foundation Studies, Professional Studies and School Placement) and which is directed towards the 12 to 18 age range (first year to sixth year). The programme must extend over at least one year of full-time study or equivalent. With effect from September 2014, postgraduate programmes of ITE accredited by the Teaching Council have been extended to two years full time study or 120 ECTS credits.

The Teaching Council website provides details of the individual subject requirements (subject criteria) for all post-primary curricular subjects. The Teaching Council website also provides a list of degrees which have in the past been deemed to meet the requirements for named curricular subjects. Given that degree programmes and elective modules within degrees can change over time, it is important that this list should only be considered as a guide.

Other routes

If you are a primary or post-primary school teacher who qualified outside Ireland and you wish to teach in a recognised school in Ireland, you must apply for recognition of your qualifications prior to registration. However, you must be fully qualified in the country in which you did your training. Once your qualifications have been recognised, you may then apply for registration.

Primary teachers trained in another Member State of the European Union, whose qualifications have been assessed and accepted by the Department of Education and Skills, but who do not possess an appropriate Irish language qualification, will be granted a five year period of provisional recognition to teach in national schools.

At Secondary level, there are aptitude tests/exams in areas where there is a shortfall between qualifications gained abroad and gained in Ireland. You are allowed 15 months after registration to take the appropriate test. The most common one necessary is the History and Structure of the Irish Education System, a knowledge of which is considered essential in the training of a teacher in Ireland.

Suggested Reading

How to Survive your First Year in Teaching
- Sue Cowley, Bloomsbury, 2013

Teaching Uncovered
- Karen Holmes, Trotman, 2010

The Newly Qualified Teacher's Handbook
- Elizabeth Holmes, Routledge, 2008

Get Ready to Teach
- Verity Lush, Longman, 2009

Further Information

Department of Education and Skills
www.education.ie
Postgraduate Diploma in Education (NUI) Applications Centre
www.pac.ie/main.php?inst=pe&ln=e
Teaching Council
www.teachingcouncil.ie
Irish National Teachers' Organisation
www.into.ie
Association of Secondary Teachers, Ireland
www.asti.ie
Qualifax: National Learners' Database
www.qualifax.ie
Central Applications Office
www.cao.ie

Education (Scotland)

Original article adapted from material supplied by Teach in Scotland

Introduction

To work as a teacher in an education authority school in Scotland you must have a teaching qualification and be registered with the General Teaching Council for Scotland. This article gives details of the minimum qualifications you need to enter a teacher education course in Scotland and how to register when you qualify.

Primary Education

If you have the relevant Standard grades, Higher grades or other Higher level qualifications (e.g. HNC, HND), you could obtain a degree in any subject then do a one-year postgraduate Professional Graduate Diploma in Education (PGDE) teacher training course.

To follow the PGDE route, you must have at least:

- A degree from a UK university (or an equivalent degree from outside the UK)
- Higher English at Grade C or above (or equivalent)
- Standard Grade Maths at Credit level (or equivalent)

The universities will also want to see evidence that you have studied at least two of the following subjects: Science, Social Studies, Expressive Arts, Religious and Moral Education, Technology and Modern Languages.

It's also essential that you get as much experience as possible of working with children of primary school age. For example, this could be as a classroom assistant or as a Brownie or Cub Group leader. If you are able to gain experience at after-school clubs or sports coaching or music tuition, this is also good to mention on your application form. You'll need to demonstrate a good understanding of the Primary Education system in Scotland.

An alternative route would be to undertake a four-year undergraduate degree course in Primary Education. Entry requirements differ between universities depending on their admissions policy but are usually four Highers at BBBC or three Highers at ABB. You must have Higher English at level B and Credit level Standard Grade Maths (or equivalent). You should also try to show that you have experience working with children, perhaps through voluntary work with youth groups, sports clubs and so on.

Both PGDE and undergraduate Primary programmes are available at Aberdeen, Dundee, Edinburgh, Glasgow, West of Scotland and Strathclyde, while Stirling offers undergraduate only and Highlands and Islands PGDE only.

Secondary Education

Your first step, in most cases, is to obtain a degree in the subject you wish to teach in Scotland, followed by the one-year PGDE. Some teaching subjects have specific requirements for entry to the PGDE course, so it is advisable to check with the university you want to apply to that the degree course you are thinking about undertaking will be suitable for teaching that subject.

If you don't want to go down the PGDE route, you can complete a four-year combined degree course in a relevant subject at a Scottish university. The degree includes your main subject, study of education and some school experience.

The entry requirements for combined degree courses are set by individual universities and vary by course and by university. To find out more, simply contact the university in which you are interested.

Career opportunities

To teach in a school in Scotland you need to be registered with the General Teaching Council for Scotland (GTCS). You are guaranteed a teaching post with a Scottish local authority for a full school year, known as the Induction year, if you are a newly qualified teacher, who has graduated from a Scottish university and has been assessed as a home student for fees. You will be provisionally registered with the GTCS until you meet the Standard for Full Registration on successful completion of your Induction year.

You can choose five Scottish local authorities that you'd be willing to work for in your Induction year. At the same time, local authorities work out the number of posts they have for probationer teachers. The selection process then chooses students at random and allocates them to teaching posts, starting with your first preference local authority. Unfortunately, your personal circumstances won't be taken into account during the process.

Suggested Reading

Scottish Education: Post-devolution
- Tom Bryce and W Humes (Eds), Edinburgh University Press, 2003

How to Survive your First Year in Teaching
- Sue Cowley, Bloomsbury, 2013

Teaching Uncovered
- Karen Holmes, Trotman, 2010

Get Ready to Teach
- Verity Lush, Longman, 2009

Further Information

Teach in Scotland
www.teachinginscotland.com

General Teaching Council for Scotland
www.gtcs.org.uk

Education Scotland
www.educationscotland.gov.uk/index.asp

Electronic and Electrical Engineering

Original article by Dr R S Quayle, Manchester University School of Engineering

Introduction

Choosing a university can be difficult in areas such as electronic and electrical engineering, where there is a wide variety of courses available. It is important to consider the specialist interests of the department, as well as the structure of the courses and the topics covered to make sure that they meet your needs and interests. Various universities and colleges have set up one-year foundation and conversion courses for young people who, for example, may have passes in subjects other than mathematics and physics.

Degree Courses

Electronic engineering is often referred to as 'light current' engineering, and involves systems which use relatively low current and relatively low voltage. It embraces technologies such as communications, broadcasting, computers, control, medical systems and many more. Electrical engineering, or 'heavy current', is concerned with relatively high current and high voltage, including electrical power generation, power distribution by the national grid, electrical machines and so on.

BEng and MEng Degree Courses - Most universities offer both the BEng and the more demanding MEng first degree courses. BEng honours courses may be of three years duration (or four in Scotland) plus an additional year of industrial experience. The MEng course is generally of four or five years duration, depending upon the time spent in industry. In many universities the BEng and MEng courses have common first years and transfer is allowed.

What sort of courses are there? - There are narrower electronic and electrical programmes and there are broad programmes that cover light and heavy current topics in a single degree - highly suitable if you do not know where your eventual interests will lie. Later you may realise that you will find yourself concentrating on a narrow aspect but need to have knowledge over a wider field. Take a radar system, for example. You may be involved in designing the high power electronics that produce a very short pulse of high frequency energy and so you may be an expert in radio frequency electronics. But a radar system has many other electrical and electronic component parts such as the aerial that will transmit and receive the radio frequency pulses, wave guides to connect the transmitter/receiver to the aerial and so on. The system you are working on will influence all of the others and all of the others will influence yours.

Programme content, what will courses contain? - All electronic and electrical engineers must be able to analyse circuits, understand amplifiers, design analogue and digital systems, program computers and use computers as tools to aid other aspects of their work. Engineering is a practical subject, which requires work in laboratories to reinforce academic material, to provide expertise in the use of measuring and test equipment and to build confidence in your ability to design and construct working systems. This material is then enhanced with subjects such as power engineering, electrical machines, semiconductors and devices, software engineering and, for overseas programmes, tuition in a foreign language. Project work performed in groups or as individuals is undertaken in all years. In the final year, there is likely to be an individual design, development or research project, which forms a significant component of your final degree classification.

Career Opportunities

Graduates work at the forefront of modern technology and wealth creation. Most engineers are employed in research, development and design, often working with teams of scientists and other engineers. They also enter electronic communications, energy/power production, transport, (eg rail, shipping, aircraft fields), computing, automation, the NHS, the Ministry of Defence, marketing, sales of electrical equipment, teaching at college and university levels, or general commerce, banking and insurance.

Related Degrees

Electronic and Microelectronic Engineering; Telecommunications; Systems Engineering; Radio Frequency Engineering; Digital Systems Engineering; Broadcast Engineering; Communication Systems; Mobile Telecommunications; Instrumentation and Control Engineering; Electronic and Photonic Engineering; Electrical Power Engineering; Electronic Systems Control; Medical Electronic Engineering; Electronic Engineering with Music; Optoelectronic/Video Engineering; Electronics Manufacturing and Management; Mechanical Electronic Systems.

Suggested Reading

Electrical and Electronic Technology
- Edward Hughes, John Hiley, Keith Brown and Ian McKenzie - Smith, Pearson, 2012

Electrical Circuit Theory and Technology
- John Bird, Routledge, 2013

Electronics: a Systems Approach
- Neil Storey, Pearson, 2013

Electronics for Today and Tomorrow
- Tom Duncan, BPB Publications. 2008

Getting into Engineering Courses
- James Burnett, Trotman, 2013

Further Information

Engineering Council UK
www.engc.org.uk

Institution of Engineering and Technology
www.theiet.org

Electro-Technical Council of Ireland
www.etci.ie

Engineers Ireland
www.engineersireland.ie

Energy Engineering

Original article by Dr John Staggs, School of Process, Environmental and Materials Engineering, University of Leeds

Introduction

Energy engineers are concerned with the uses and economic combustion of fuels, with atomic energy and developments in the use of water, wind, tide and sun as sources of energy. They study the relative costs of producing energy in industry, comparing the economic advantages of using fuels such as coal, oil, natural gas, nuclear- or wind- generated electric power. They also look at methods to conserve energy and reduce heat loss from buildings.

If you are concerned about our environment and fuel poverty and want to be part of realising a sustainable energy future, then energy engineering may be the course for you. Look for a degree accredited by the Energy Institute, which will train you to apply and design processes that reduce environmental damage. Courses may lead to a BEng or MEng qualification.

Degree Courses

Many universities now have all degree courses organised in a modular structure, with each year split into two semesters. In the energy engineering example below, 12 equally weighted modules are completed each year and each module consists of lectures, practical and associated course work.

Year one core engineering topics include fluid mechanics and heat transfer, and thermodynamics. Specialist topics include energy and the environment, renewable sources of energy, and combustion. There are options to study management and/or language subjects.

Year two core engineering topics include management and economics, design, measurement and control, and laboratory techniques. Specialist topics include waste processing, advanced renewables, managing aqueous effluents, and combustion-generated pollution.

In year three of the BEng degree, core engineering topics include industrial finance, safety management and hazard protection. Specialist topics include efficient use of energy, control of air pollution, advanced energy systems, wastewater engineering, law and the environment. You would also undertake a research project related to the field of energy and the environment.

In year three of the MEng Degree, core engineering topics include industrial finance, safety management and hazard protection, computational aerodynamics, plant engineering and design. Specialist topics include advanced energy systems, efficient use of energy, and an industrially related research project with an associated business plan. You would continue this research project in more depth in year four.

In year four of the MEng Degree, you would extend your breadth of knowledge and undertake a considerable industrially related group project. You can choose from a range of intensively taught courses with industrial participation in their delivery. Other specialist modules offered include atmospheric process, control of air pollution, flames, explosions, and hazards.

Recent projects include engine emissions under real driving conditions, diesel particulate emissions and their effect on the urban atmosphere, and biomass combustion in a fluidised bed.

Career Opportunities

There are good career prospects in industries such as energy production, waste management, chemicals, sustainable design and development as well as with environmental agencies and consultancies. The fuel and energy supply and utilisation industry in the UK alone is worth over £40 billion and has wide ranging career opportunities. Examples of career paths of former students include assessment of environmental impact of energy production, improvement of efficiency of energy utilisation, energy equipment manufacturing, energy conservation and pollution consultancy. The broad-based nature of the degree also allows the student to pursue careers outside the energy sector.

Related Degrees

Energy Systems with Industrial Studies in Europe; Energy and Environmental Engineering; Fuel/Fire/Energy Engineering.

Suggested Reading

The Bottomless Well: The Twilight of Fuel, the Virtue of Waste, and Why We Will Never Run Out of Energy
- Peter Huber, Mark P Mills, Basic Books, 2006

A Brighter Tomorrow: Fulfilling the Promise of Nuclear Energy
- Pete V Domenici, Rowman and Littlefield, 2006

Power Struggle: World Energy in the Twenty first Century
- John Moroney, Greenwood Press, 2008

Ten Technologies to fix Energy and Climate
- Chris Goodall, Profile Books, 2009

Tomorrow's Energy: Hydrogen, Fuel Cells and the Prospects for a Cleaner Planet
- Peter Hoffman, MIT Press, 2012

Sustainable Energy: Without the Hot Air
- David J C MacKay, UIT, 2008

Energy Systems and Sustainability: Power for a Sustainable Future
- Bob Everett et al, OUP, 2011

Further Information

Energy Institute
www.energyinst.org

Energy Information Centre
www.eic.co.uk

Centre for Alternative Technology
www.cat.org.uk

Association of Energy Engineers Ireland
www.aee.ie

Engineers Ireland
www.engineersireland.ie

Engineering

Original article by Dr A M Price BSc, PhD, CEng, MIMM, University of Warwick

Introduction

The range of available engineering degrees encompasses everything from Aeromechanics to Water Engineering; from very specialised degrees to those with a broader mandate. Virtually all programmes require A level/Higher/IB or equivalent mathematics or equivalent, many (but by no means all) require A level/Higher/IB or equivalent physics. Engineering degrees also recruit from a broad range of other qualifications.

The major disciplines are Mechanical, Civil, Electronic, Aeronautical, Production/ Manufacturing Systems, Chemical and General. It is not possible to give detailed descriptions of each programme within this article but there are already individual articles on each of these major branches of engineering elsewhere in the Degree Course Descriptions.

- **Mechanical Engineering**
- **Civil Engineering**
- **Electronic and Electrical Engineering**
- **Aeronautical Engineering**
- **Manufacturing Engineering**
- **Chemical Engineering**

We can identify a number of generic features, such as design, science and engineering principles, analytical techniques, management and communication skills

Degree Courses

In general, accredited engineering degree programmes will award either a BEng or MEng qualification. The BEng degree is normally awarded after three years of full-time study (four in Scotland), whilst the MEng is awarded after four years (five in Scotland). The MEng degree is normally an enhanced or broader-based degree than the BEng, and increasingly includes modules equivalent to postgraduate standard. Some programmes may also offer an exchange year abroad or sandwich programme, combining academic study with periods of employment. Under the criteria for accreditation, known as UK-SPEC, the Engineering Council has set the MEng degree as the normal route for those intending to apply for Chartered Engineer status. Many BEng degree programmes are accredited as suitable for meeting the academic requirements of Chartered Engineer status when combined with a one-year 'matching section', such as an approved MSc. Other degree programmes may set their objectives as meeting the academic requirements for Incorporated Engineer status and you should check the university prospectus to determine the level of accreditation granted to the degree.

With so many specialist degrees to choose from, it may seem odd that some universities also offer general engineering degrees. For some departments these represent a foundation year or 'Year 0'. For others, the different engineering disciplines exist within one unified department. These departments allow students to obtain specialist degrees, founded on common principles. This common material may extend for one or two years before specialisation is invited. Frequently there is also provision for studying a degree programme in general engineering for the full period.

In unified departments it is usually a mistake to equate the entry code with the degree at graduation, since the act of specialisation effectively moves students from one degree programme to another. Students use the common year to make their final choice of specialisation. This offers a clear advantage to the student who wants to read engineering, but cannot decide between the different branches. A good engineer has the knowledge and flexibility to work in the 'grey areas' found at each boundary between specialisations. Such an engineer has the capacity to apply basic engineering principles and concepts to a wide range of problems. General engineering degrees and unified departments seek to deliver these skills by careful development of the curriculum. Students learn how to model engineering problems across the spectrum. This gives the student the skills necessary to work effectively with other engineers on multi-disciplinary projects.

Career Opportunities

Whilst the expected post-recession upturn has not yet materialised to any significant level, either within the UK or the European Union, future trends paint a very different and more optimistic picture. Reports project that annual global output will more than double in two decades, from $78 trillion to $176 trillion. The UK does not have the capability or the resources to succeed in every emerging technology, but it can excel in such areas as energy-efficient computing, energy harvesting (from the environment), graphene (the thinnest material possible), nanotechnology and digital technologies.

Related Degrees

Integrated Engineering; Engineering Foundation; Engineering with Business Management; Engineering with Overseas Study; Design Engineering; Forensic Engineering; Agricultural Engineering; Mathematical Engineering; Engineering/ Economics/Management; Medical Engineering; Engineering with Product Design; Environmental Engineering; Railway Infrastructure Engineering.

Suggested Reading

Higher Engineering Science
- W Bolton, Routledge, 2004

Engineering Mathematics
- John Bird, Routledge, 2014

Getting into Engineering Courses
- James Burnett, Trotman, 2013

Higher Engineering Mathematics
- J O Bird, Routledge, 2010

Further Information

Royal Academy of Engineering
www.raeng.org.uk

Tomorrow's Engineers
www.tomorrowsengineers.org.uk/16-19

Institution of Engineering and Technology
www.theiet.org

Engineering Council UK
www.engc.org.uk

UK Standard for Professional Engineering Competence
www.engc.org.uk/professional-qualifications/standards/uk-spec

Engineers Ireland
www.engineersireland.ie

English

Original article by Professor Patrick Parrinder, University of Reading

Introduction

The initial attraction of an English course is likely to be the opportunity to immerse oneself in some of the most exciting works of poetry, fiction and drama in the language. Some of our motives for studying literature are quite properly introspective - a desire to know ourselves and to explore our cultural and psychic identity. But literary study is outward- as well as inward-looking. Literary criticism, as developed in the writings of such intellectual precursors as S T Coleridge, Matthew Arnold, T S Eliot and F R Leavis, combines formal analysis with the belief that literature offers a key to the nature of human experience. The separation of literature from entertainment is central to the traditional justification of literary studies. Until recently, the need to demonstrate that literary students were not wasting their time on trivia led to a heavy emphasis on the intellectual and moral benefits of 'high culture'. Nowadays, it is acknowledged that all social life involves feelings and attitudes which are reflected in the culture's systems of symbolic expression. 'High' and 'Low' culture serve much the same functions in this respect. The notion of symbolic systems has permitted the extension of English studies beyond the canon of recognised major literary works to other texts including advertisements, popular romantic fiction and TV soap operas. Some teachers argue for a still broader redefinition of the subject. But the subtlety and complexity of the verbal creations of the greatest writers, from Chaucer to the Nobel Prize winning Caribbean poet Derek Walcott, remains the raison d'être of most English courses.

The reason why some kinds of writing are considered more literary than others is a question of language and form. Yet most varieties of current criticism give pride of place to the multiple meanings of literary texts, including below-the-surface meanings, the different meanings attached to them in different historical periods, and the meanings they may have for different readers. Since virtually every literary text contains moral, psychological, religious, political and philosophical layers of significance as well as evoking an aesthetic response, the number of valid critical approaches is very considerable. You are likely to be introduced to several approaches and you will have the opportunity to find out others for yourself.

Degree Courses

Which authors and texts will you be expected to study? Shakespeare is no longer invariably compulsory. You will meet a selection from the other canonical writers such as Chaucer, Donne, Milton, Pope, Swift, the Romantic poets, the Victorian novelists and the early twentieth-century Modernists. Such works as the *Canterbury Tales*, Spenser's *Faerie Queene*, Milton's *Paradise Lost*, Wordsworth's *Prelude* or the major novels of Dickens, George Eliot or Virginia Woolf may be studied in depth. The analysis of short unseen passages may be used to teach the skills of attentive reading and to develop versatility of response. In the final year, you are likely to be given the opportunity of writing a dissertation or series of extended essays on subjects of your own choice. Occasionally the study of some literature in another language is required.

The range of specialist options offered in many departments makes 'From Beowulf to Virginia Woolf' sound narrow. Anglo-Saxon, *Piers Plowman* and the Elizabethan sonnet sequences and verse romances continue to attract some of the best students, but the majority opt for the more modern subjects, which are likely to include American and post-colonial literatures, women's literature, 'minority' literatures, contemporary popular fiction, aspects of film and television studies, and literary theory. Broad intellectual movements such as feminism, structuralism and semiotics (ie theories of sign and symbol), hermeneutics (ie theories of interpretation), post-modernism and post-colonialism have had a marked impact on the teaching of many degree courses. Current linguistic theories are probably less influential.

Many departments allow students to take part of their degree abroad. A possibility is a placement with a local firm. Creative writing and literary composition as such are very rarely part of the syllabus, though a number of departments run voluntary writing workshops. The creative atmosphere which a good English department can succeed in nurturing is a precious asset, but an English degree is only one course of study open to a future novelist or poet. English, like history and philosophy, is usually regarded as a humanities rather than a creative arts discipline, but even this generalisation is open to challenge, since the subject remains vigorous, argumentative and self-critical.

Career Opportunities

The skills you can gain through studying English are useful in a wide variety of career areas. Perhaps the major strength of all English graduates is communication skills, both in speech and in writing. However, you also learn to organise your workload, work to tight deadlines, convey meaning precisely, pick out the essential points from texts, interpret, assess and evaluate sources, lead and participate in discussions, work independently, think critically and develop opinions, propose ideas and theories, persuade others of your point of view, think and act creatively, and develop IT skills. Many English students write for student newspapers and magazines, get involved with student radio or film societies or volunteer in the community or local schools. Given that English is generally seen as a non-vocational course, the skills you develop outside your study could be critical in developing a rounded CV.

A large number of graduates choose to work in a creative field, like writing, publishing, PR or acting. However, there is a huge amount of variety in English-graduate career choices: legal, financial, and sales positions are also popular. Statistics about employment after graduation can be misleading. Immediately after their degree, many English graduates choose to take temporary jobs or to travel rather than entering a career. Because these choices show up in the charts as unemployment or low-level employment, it can look like it's harder to get a good job than it really is.

Related Degrees

English Language; English Studies; English Literature; Literary Studies; English Language and Literature; Creative Writing; Script Writing.

Suggested Reading

The English Studies Book
- Rob Pope, Routledge, 2002
The Common Pursuit
- F R Leavis, Faber and Faber, 2008
Doing English: a Guide for Literature Students
- Robert Eaglestone, Routledge, 2009
A Reader's Guide to Contemporary Literary Theory
- Raman Selden, Peter Widdowson and Peter Brooker, Routledge, 2005
The Norton Anthology of English Literature (Vols 1 and 2)
- S Greenblatt et al, Norton, 2012
Beginning theory: an introduction to literary and cultural theory
- Peter Barry, Manchester University Press, 2009

Further Information

Why Study English?
www.whystudyenglish.ac.uk
Society of Authors
www.societyofauthors.org
Irish Writers' Centre
www.writerscentre.ie

Environmental Health

Original article by Catherine Gairn, Faculty of Health and Environment, Leeds Metropolitan University

Introduction

Accredited environmental health courses all cover the same basic syllabus, although the emphasis varies from one university to another. Essentially, all involve accumulating operational skills and a fundamental knowledge of legal and organisational issues, understanding environmental and public health stressors and linking these with the principal realms of environmental health including food, housing, occupational health, environmental protection and public health.

As the course progresses, you will also acquire the qualities of confidence, independent critical judgement and leadership, and the ability to work as part of a team. These are all essential prerequisites for a career as an environmental health practitioner (EHP).

Degree Courses

When you apply for an accredited course, it is advisable to look for work-based learning opportunities as soon as possible. If you can find a placement before you begin the course, you will be able to complete a sandwich route and become qualified within four years (or in two years if you already have an appropriate science degree and have enrolled on an MSc course).

Work-based learning opportunities are available within a wide range of organisations including local councils, private sector companies, government departments and the NHS and its related agencies.

Universities offering accredited courses may be able to assist with finding work-based experiential learning places. Employers may notify universities of such vacancies. Newspapers, too, are a good source of information.

If you cannot find a placement, you will still be able to enrol on the course and look for a placement whilst you are a student. If you still find it difficult to find a placement, you can complete your full-time accredited degree and then complete your work-based learning after graduation.

The five main subject areas on accredited courses are: food safety, environmental protection, occupational health, public health and housing. These subjects involve both theory and practical (laboratory) work and a variety of visits to such places as power stations, water sewage and water treatment plants and docks. You will also develop additional skills such as numeracy, literacy, IT, research, communication and other transferable skills.

A 12-month placement of structured, practical training is required, usually integrated into the third year of the course, although it can be undertaken on completion of the three years of academic study. Work-based learning is an essential element towards professional qualification and this may be undertaken without time limits in any organisation that delivers an environmental health service. An opportunity to spend up to 12 weeks in another European country is available to students in their placement year, although a sound knowledge of the appropriate language is usually required. Throughout the placement year you'll also produce an experiential learning portfolio, which will be assessed as the precursor to the professional examinations, when you must satisfy the Chartered Institute of Environmental Health (CIEH) assessment prior to registration for professional practice as an EHP.

Career Opportunities

Local authorities, as the agencies concerned with the protection of public health (including food, housing, health and safety, environmental/pollution control) employ environmental health practitioners but there are plenty of other possibilities including: central government and its agencies, such as the Food Standards Agency, the Environment Agency and the Health and Safety Executive; the armed services; holiday companies (checking out foreign hotels etc); shipping and flight companies (ensuring passengers' on-board health and safety, for example); the National Health Service.

Beyond that, many EHPs work abroad. For example, the European Commission employs some, whilst others travel further afield to work in Australia, Canada, New Zealand and the US. A wide range of opportunities exists for EHPs in a world where pollution and danger to health have become vital international issues.

Related Degrees

Public Health; Trading Standards.

Suggested Reading

Essentials of Environmental Health
- Robert Friis, Jones and Barlett, 2011

Clay's Handbook of Environmental Health
- Stephen Battersby (Ed), Routledge, 2011

Environmental Health Procedures
- W H Bassett, Routledge, 2007

Environmental Health News
- View the current issue at: **www.ehn-online.com**

Further Information

Environmental Health Careers
www.ehcareers.org

Institution of Occupational Safety and Health
www.iosh.co.uk

Charted Institute of Environmental Health
www.cieh.org

Health Service Executive, Ireland
www.hse.ie/eng/staff/jobs

Environmental Protection Agency, Ireland
www.epa.ie

Environmental Health Association of Ireland
www.ehai.ie

Environmental Sciences

Original article by Malcolm Hudson, Senior Tutor, Centre for Environmental Sciences, University of Southampton, based on a previous contribution by Professor Ian F Spellerberg, Lincoln University, New Zealand (visiting Professor, University of Southampton)

Introduction

Environmental Sciences is a comparatively new approach to interdisciplinary science, based on various aspects of the traditional science subjects such as biology, geography, chemistry, geology and oceanography. Environmental sciences and environmental studies are concerned with both the natural and human environments but, whereas environmental sciences has a science component, environmental studies incorporates more aspects of social sciences and the arts. In reality, there is quite a bit of overlap between the two, depending on the interests of the university department and the choices available to the student.

In all the traditional science subjects there are topics of practical relevance to our understanding of the environment and the processes which take place in the environment. Such topics can be brought together in an integrated fashion and so provide the all-important interdisciplinary basis for informed and integrated management. For instance, academically valid studies of water pollution in rivers and estuaries require an interdisciplinary approach, incorporating relevant aspects of environmental biology, physical geography, environmental chemistry and marine ecology.

Environmental sciences deal with current issues about the natural and the human environment, and as a result attract students with a wide range of interests, but clearly any such interdisciplinary studies and training are not a soft option or an easy way to get a degree. Although the component parts of environmental sciences are generally the same as those taken by students specialising in single subject degree courses, environmental sciences students have to think about the links between subjects and have to draw upon resources provided by more than one subject when tackling interdisciplinary assignments.

A major attraction is that you can either specialise in any one of the many areas or retain a more general approach. You might specialise, for example, in nature conservation, waste resource management, economic geology, coastal management, hydrology or irrigation, public health engineering, urban planning, ecological chemistry, land management, pollution control or sustainable development. Alternatively, many students choose environmental sciences because they simply want a good grounding in a broad variety of environmental topics. Many students come to the degree with a general interest in the area, and develop their own specialisms as their studies progress.

An interdisciplinary approach to the study of the environment has increasing practical relevance because of the growing concern for human activities upon the world we live in. There is an awareness now that 'everything links together'; for example, use of fossil fuels in the developed world can affect the climate thousands of miles away, or lead to the destruction of low-lying coasts or islands. Thus concern about many environmental issues (such as climate change, deforestation, desertification, disposal of toxic wastes and loss of biodiversity) has prompted the need for more research and better ways of managing our resources. The increasing awareness of environmental problems is resulting in a greater participation in environmental pressure groups and in the creation of more environmental legislation, which must be based on sound knowledge of environmental processes. At the same time, industry has begun to embrace the environmental agenda, with international corporations now routinely reporting on their environmental effects and setting targets for long-term improvement. Furthermore, environmental impact assessment of proposed major developments (eg motorways, marinas or chemical works) is now a comparatively new legislative requirement but has already stimulated the need for more people to be trained to manage interdisciplinary problems.

Degree Courses

Environmental sciences as a degree subject has a common core but, depending on where you study, there are different and unique components to the way that it is taught because the bias or structure will, in part, reflect the research interests of the teaching staff. This provides an added bonus of choice but it makes it essential that you find out all you can about the different courses. Checking out university web pages is a good place to start. All course admission tutors offer a friendly information service about teaching, research projects, field-courses, entry requirements and the careers of their graduates. Ask them for a reading list and in addition note the books mentioned below.

Career Opportunities

There is no single career path for an environmental sciences graduate, but recent years have seen a major expansion in the potential job market as employers have begun to recognise the value of interdisciplinary expertise. Pollution control (eg with the Environment Agency) or conservation management are two of the commonest areas for graduates to work in. There are increasing opportunities in consultancy, which may require some specialist knowledge (eg on contaminated land treatment or ecology) or interdisciplinary skills (in environmental impact assessment or planning). While traditionally the water companies, along with the biotechnology and agrochemical industry, have provided vacancies, other major industries now need environmental specialists for their sustainability programmes. International initiatives and the increasing challenges of managing our waste have produced many career opportunities in local government. There are even opportunities in unexpected areas, such as ecotourism. Some graduates enter teaching or take postgraduate courses, and some go on to an academic or research career after completing a PhD.

Related Degrees

Environmental Pollution/Protection; Environmental Conservation; Agriculture of the Environment; Environmental Biology; Environmental Chemistry; Environmental Technology; Environmental Physics; Environmental Archaeology; Marine Environmental Studies; Environmental Resources; Aquatic Science.

Suggested Reading

The Human Impact on the Natural Environment
- Andrew Goudie, Wiley-Blackwell, 2013
The Global Casino: an Introduction to Environmental Issues
- Nick Middleton, Routledge, 2013
The Environment: Principles and Applications
- Chris Park, Routledge, 2001

Further Information

Natural Environment Research Council
www.nerc.ac.uk
Chartered Institution of Water and Environmental Management
www.ciwem.org
Institution of Environmental Sciences
www.the-ies.org
Environmental Sciences Association of Ireland
www.esaiweb.org

Equine Science

Original article by Dr Jeremy F Burn, University of Bristol

Introduction

Equine science is the study of horses from a scientific perspective. If you enjoy science and horses, then perhaps this could be the ideal subject for you. Since horses are animals, the areas of science that relate to them are broadly described as biological or biomedical sciences. These include such diverse subjects as anatomy (the study of the relationship between structural form and function), physiology (how body systems work), biomechanics (how the principles of mechanics such as Newton's laws can be applied to the animal body) and biochemistry (how chemical reactions are involved in everything from metabolism to muscle contraction). These are only a few examples of the way in which science helps us to understand horses and the way they work. If you are interested in horses and have read books on them, much of the information you will have learned has been passed down through generations of horsemen and women. Some of this information has a scientific basis, even though in most cases the originators of the information were not scientists. Some of the things you might have learned about horses do not have any scientific basis. An equine science degree course will allow you to differentiate between the two. You will learn the basic scientific principles that underlie, for example, behaviour, nutrition, reproduction, structural form, function, movement and husbandry of the horse. Hopefully, this will increase your appreciation and enjoyment of horses and may lead to a graduate career in horses either in industry or in research.

Degree Courses

The content of equine science courses varies widely between institutions so the first and important point to note is to shop around for the one that best suits your requirements. The reasons for the variation are firstly that, because equine science is a relatively new subject to be offered at degree level, there is not yet a consistent view of what an equine science course should contain. Secondly, the various institutions specialise in different areas of equine-related science and tend to focus their course around their internal expertise. Aspects of the courses that vary are typically (a) the amount of contact with live horses (which can vary from none at all to the opportunity to manage and ride horses) (b) the amount of business management in the course (which can range from none to several modules) (c) the areas of science covered (for example some courses might not cover genetics or biomechanics) (d) the significance and scope of the final year research project. Final year research projects will usually involve you working independently or in a small group on a piece of equine-related research. This is one of the most enjoyable parts of the degree course, as you are able to put the knowledge and skills you have learned during the course into practice. If you are particularly interested in an area of equine research, it might be worthwhile checking that your chosen institution is able to support a research project in that area.

Career Opportunities

A science degree is a general academic qualification that allows you to follow 'graduate entry' paths into finance, media, management, marketing, etc. In many cases there are specialist jobs in these areas relating to horses, for example within finance, you might work for a company that provides horse insurance, or in media, you might work for the natural history unit of a television company or an equine specialist magazine. Although the equine industry in the UK is large in both financial and employment terms, it relies predominantly on non-graduate employment and it is worth considering that a degree in equine science is not the best qualification for working with horses at a practical level. There are also specialist careers such as equine physiotherapy, chiropractic and osteopathy that have their own training programmes, and a degree in equine science is not usually the fastest route to qualification in these areas.

Related Degrees
Animal Science; Horse Management and Equitation; Equine Studies.

Suggested Reading
Horse Behaviour Exposed
- Abigail Hogg, David and Charles, 2009

The Nature of Horses: their Evolution, Intelligence and Behaviour
- Stephen Budiansky, Phoenix, 2009

Whole Heart, Whole Horse: Building Trust between Horse and Rider
- Mark Rashid, Skyhorse Publishing, 2014

The Athletic Horse: Principles and Practice of Equine Sports Medicine
- David R Hodgson and Reuben J Rose, Saunders, 2013

Equitation Science
- Paul McGreevy and Andrew McLean, Wiley-Blackwell, 2010

Equine Locomotion
- Willem Back and Hilary Clayton, Saunders, 2013

Equine Behaviour: a Guide for Veterinarians and Equine Scientists
- Paul McGreevy, Saunders, 2004

Equine Nutrition and Feeding
- David Frape, Wiley-Blackwell, 2010

The Domestic Horse: the Origins, Development and Management of Its Behaviour
- D S Mills and S M McDonnell, Cambridge University Press, 2005

Further Information
Equine Science Update
www.equinescienceupdate.com

British Horse Society
www.bhs.org.uk

Irish Horse Society
www.irishhorsesociety.com

European Studies

Original article by Professor Juliet Lodge, Jean Monnet European Centre of Excellence, University of Leeds

Introduction

European studies exposes you to the many facets of life that have gone into producing the Europe of today and involves a broad examination of Europe's history, geography, culture, economics, philosophies, literature, politics and society. European Studies normally involves gaining fluency in at least one and usually two European languages besides your mother tongue. French, German and Spanish are the most popular but it is also possible to study Italian, Dutch, Russian etc. Language courses that form part of European studies degrees are increasingly practical in their orientation. Modern languages rather than linguistics or the literature of the 17th century are stressed, although you would also gain an appreciation of the literature of the country(ies) whose language(s) you were acquiring.

Comparative politics and political economy or economic history often form components of European studies degrees. The states most often studied include: Germany, France, Russia, the UK and possibly Italy, Spain and Sweden. You would normally learn about American and international politics as well. European studies degrees also normally involve a study of political philosophy from Plato, Machiavelli and Hobbes to Locke, Marx and Marcuse, for example. Major contemporary political trends - liberalism, socialism, communism, totalitarianism, fascism, feminism, etc - may also be studied from a variety of perspectives: literary, philosophical, historical, economic or political, for example.

Degree Courses

It is now possible to take degree courses in subjects like chemistry or maths, for instance, that have a European studies component in them. You can also combine European studies with languages, or with law, history, art history, environmental studies, business studies, management, sociology, economics or politics.

Normally, you would also spend a period of time in Europe either at a European university or working. Some courses sandwich two periods abroad into a four-year programme. During this time, you would be expected to write a dissertation of around 8,000 words (in English or one of your other European languages) on a topic relevant to your studies. Departments in the field of social science now offer some of the most exciting courses in European studies. If you are keen on politics, lobbying, trade, international affairs and business, for example, you can now take courses which build in a 'stage' at the European Parliament. (A 'stage' is the European term commonly used to refer to a period of unpaid internship.) This means that, while continuing your studies in Brussels, you may also have working links with Members of the European Parliament. You get to see how Europe ticks. Periods working in Europe or as 'stages' or in partner European universities are highly illuminating, socially and personally rewarding. In addition, they are fun. As you become an active part of the trans-European student community, your circle of friends will grow, your intellectual horizons will alter and your experiences will challenge your preconceptions daily!

If you want such a course, make sure that you look beyond language departments. The social sciences, business and law, and increasingly English and science departments, provide rich hunting grounds. If your main interest is language you would do well to choose a course that has a high European studies component and one which does not restrict you to the study of European literature. Many departments now offer the chance to study commercial language alongside literature, culture and politics. Many allow you to study in another European university and gain an extra qualification or diploma. European studies courses offer you numerous options and they often benefit from excellent schemes such as the European Union (EU) Erasmus+ programme, which offers funding to enable young people in the UK to study, train, gain work experience and volunteer across the EU and further afield.

In short, European studies is predominantly about understanding Europe today; how and why Europe is shaped as it is; what its role and place is in the world; where it is going; what problems it confronts; how it resolves them, whether they are economic, political, environmental, social, cultural, scientific, commercial or technical. Europe encroaches on all aspects of our lives and all aspects of education.

Career Opportunities

These courses develop interest and awareness of trends in overseas markets which are of value to employers with overseas interests. Graduates tend to favour jobs in the Fast Stream of the Civil Service, buying, selling, marketing, trading/retailing and banking organisations. Journalism, public relations, broadcasting, lobbying and EU consultancies in the private and public sectors are also popular. Increasing numbers of graduates enter law, accountancy, teaching and computing.

Related Degrees

European Law; Culture and Language; Contemporary Europe; European Studies with Languages; European Studies (History); Viking Studies; East European Studies; Welsh Studies; Celtic Studies; Irish Studies.

Suggested Reading

The SAGE Handbook of European Studies
- Chris Rumford, Sage Publications, 2009

The Penguin Companion to European Union
- Timothy Bainbridge and Anthony Teasdale, Penguin, 2012

The European Union: A very short Introduction
- John Pinder and Simon Usherwood, Oxford, 2013

Understanding the European Union
- John McCormick, Palgrave Macmillan, 2014

Further Information

Europa (Official website of the European Union)
http://europa.eu

Erasmus+
www.erasmusplus.org.uk

Jean Monnet European Centre of Excellence
www.leeds.ac.uk/jmce

European Commission - representation in the United Kingdom
http://ec.europa.eu/unitedkingdom

European Commission - representation in Ireland
http://ec.europa.eu/ireland

Fashion Design

Original article written with help from Central St Martins College of Art and Design, now part of the University of the Arts, London

Introduction

A degree in fashion design should encourage you to explore your talents and individuality, helping you to develop the combination of innovation and design skills, technical ability and awareness of current trends and business objectives that you will need to succeed as a fashion professional in design, retail or production.

Many courses offer you a choice of subject routes to suit your career ambition, usually starting with a broad base in Year One and becoming increasingly specialised as you progress through Year Two.

In most cases, you would apply via UCAS after completing a foundation or access course. This would give you the opportunity both to explore a variety of creative options and to build a suitable portfolio. For fashion design, your portfolio should contain life, objective and fashion drawing. Admissions staff look for colour work, creative design ideas and development as well as evidence of how you have answered set briefs or initiated work for yourself. You would be encouraged to bring to interview sketchbooks, made-up garments and written work (essay and reports). In general, evidence of 3D work is more important than huge 'pieces' or folders full of patterns. A good tip is to set up your own fashion shoot - complete with accessories, hair and make-up - and present photographs rather than including too many completed garments.

Degree Courses

Fashion design studies are normally based on a mixture of studio and workshop practice, lectures, seminars, visits and personal study, with a typical ratio of approximately 80% practical work and 20% theoretical and historical study. You should have the opportunity to meet visiting designers and specialists, to take part in sponsored projects with major fashion companies and to gain experience in work-based placements. Many courses arrange overseas study trips for students, usually to international fashion centres such as New York, Paris or Milan.

Level 1 (first year) modules typically introduce the subject and are concerned with experimentation and the exploration of design language and process, while

Level 2 (second year) modules emphasise technical knowledge and creative development and include collaboration with designers and industry. During this level you may be asked to make your choice of subject route for Level 3, on some courses, while on others you may be asked to make this choice on entry.

For example, you may focus exclusively on fashion design or you may prefer to develop your business skills by combining fashion with marketing or retail management. If you are more technically inclined, you may choose to link fashion with product development.

During Level 3 study you will certainly be asked to undertake a self-directed project of your own choice that focuses your work in the direction of your intended career

Career Opportunities

As a fashion design graduate, you should be able to work across a very wide spectrum. While you may not become the next Donna Karan, Stella McCartney or Tommy Hilfiger, you can still work successfully and influentially as a company designer, freelancer or consultant. Alternatively, you may pursue a fashion-related career as a journalist, stylist, photographer, illustrator, public relations consultant, pattern cutter, buyer or retailer. Career opportunities may depend to a certain extent on the pathway you choose.

Related Degrees

Depending on your interests, you may wish to consider courses in: *Textile Design, Interior Design, Industrial Product Design, Jewellery Design, Graphic Design.*

Alternatively, you might look at *Photography, Journalism* or *Retail Management.*

Suggested Reading

Getting into Art and Design Courses
- James Burnett, Trotman Education, 2014

Fashion Design Workshop: Stylish Step-by-step Projects and Drawing Tips for Up-and-coming Designers
- Samantha Rei, Walter Foster Publishing, 2011

Fashion Sketchpad
- Tamar Daniel, Chronicle Books, 2011

Fashion Design Course: Principles, Practice and Techniques
- Stephen Fearm, Thames and Hudson, 2010

Fashion Design
- Sue Jenkyn Jones, Laurence King, 2011

200 Projects to Get You into Fashion Design
- Adrian Grandon and Tracy Fitzgerald, A & C Black, 2009

Fairchild Dictionary of Fashion
- Sandra Keiser and Phyllis Tortora, Fairchild Books, 2014

Patternmaking for Fashion Design
- Helen Joseph Armstrong, Pearson Education, 2013

Women's Wear Daily
- access online at the WWD website address below

Le Book: international meeting point for fashion and photography
- access online at the website address below

Further Information

Fashion United
www.fashionunited.co.uk

Creative Skillset
http://creativeskillset.org/creative_industries/fashion_and_textiles

Laurence King Publishing
www.laurenceking.com

Women's Wear Daily
www.wwd.com

Le Book
www.lebook.com

Fashion Net
www.fashion.net

Style Bible
www.stylebible.ph

Institute of Designers in Ireland
http://idi-design.ie

Film Studies

Original article written with material supplied by the University of East Anglia

Introduction

Cinema was arguably the most exciting art form to emerge in the 20th century. Now, in the early years of the 21st century, film is surrounded and challenged by an array of new media. A degree in Film Studies offers the critical, historical and theoretical tools needed to understand and appreciate the creative potential of cinematic and electronic images and to assess critically how they mediate our experience of the world.

Programmes usually cover subjects ranging from the history of cinema to the close analysis of film texts. Studying film requires you to investigate both visual and written materials, to master approaches from diverse disciplines and to apply ideas adopted from various intellectual perspectives. You might also have the opportunity to engage in practical film-making activities such as script-writing and video production.

Film Studies combines insights drawn from a range of disciplines - history, sociology, art history, comparative studies and aesthetics. The subject usually incorporates concepts from major theoretical perspectives such as semiotics, feminism, Marxism, psychoanalysis and post-colonial theory.

Degree Courses

Courses are usually modular in structure and often adopt broad topics such as:

- Aspects of film theory, examining the fascinating approaches that have been developed in order to think about, study and analyse films;

- Hollywood cinema, investigating the world's dominant system of film production;

- National cinemas - in particular, those of Britain, India, France, Germany and Spain - placing films within the broader contexts of the societies producing them.

Further modules might extend the scope to cover early cinema, experimental work, aspects of 'world cinema' and exploitation and cult films.

As you are unlikely to have any prior experience of film studies, Level 1 modules typically introduce the analytical terms and perspectives that would enable you to engage effectively with the programme. When you progress to Levels 2 and 3, you should be able to choose study options to tailor the course to your own developing interests. An 'extended essay' at Level 2 and dissertation at Level 3 would enable you to explore individually chosen topics of study under staff supervision.

Teaching normally comprises a mix of lectures, seminars, workshops, film presentations and tutorial support. You would be expected to develop your own programme of reading and film study and you would be assessed by essay, seminar presentation, study logs, dissertation and examination.

Career Opportunities

As a Film Studies graduate, you should be able to show a well-informed awareness of many of the cultural and social issues under debate in contemporary Britain as well as being able to demonstrate an in-depth knowledge of film. Your degree should give you advanced transferable skills in areas such as analysis and communication and could serve as a useful preparation for a wide variety of posts in media or other cultural industries. It could also lead on to postgraduate study. It is not, however, a vocational course providing technical skills.

Related Degrees
You might also consider Media and Cultural Studies or you could combine Film Studies with a related subject such as English, Drama, American Studies, History, French, Spanish, Art or Sociology.

Suggested Reading
Film Art: An Introduction
- David Bordwell and Kristin Thompson-McGraw-Hill, 2012

Film History: An Introduction
- Kristin Thompson and David Bordwell, McGraw-Hill Higher Education, 2009

The Oxford Guide to Film Studies
- John Hill and Pamela Church Gibson (Eds), OUP, 1998

The Cinema Book
- Pam Cook, BFI Publishing, 2008

How to Read a Film
- James Monaco, OUP USA, 2009

A Dictionary of Film Studies
- Annette Kuhn and Guy Westwell, OUP, 2012

Further Information
British Film Institute
www.bfi.org.uk

UK Film Network
http://ukfilmnetwork.com

Film-Philosophy: International Salon-Journal
www.film-philosophy.com

Irish Film Institute
www.ifi.ie

Irish Film and Television Network
www.iftn.ie

Finance

Original article by David J. Collison, University of Dundee

Introduction

The terms 'finance' and 'accountancy' mean much the same thing to many people and are often used interchangeably. However, there are important distinctions between them, especially in the context of choosing a university course. The term 'finance' relates to the ways in which organisations raise money to fund their operations and also to ways in which money is invested: the focus may be on individual organisations or on investments made in many organisations through financial markets (eg the stock exchange).

In contrast, 'accountancy' includes the preparation and communication of financial information about an organisation's operations (which could be in the private or public sector). Accounting information is needed to help manage an organisation and accountants are often part of the management team: accounting information is also needed by a variety of other users (eg employees, suppliers, bankers and other investors, tax authorities and other government agencies).

While there is a distinction between these two main areas of activity, there is also much overlap and people with an accounting background may work in finance and vice versa.

Degree Courses

The purpose of a finance degree is to provide an undergraduate education in an area in which the UK is, in many respects, a world leader. The financial intermediation sector is one of the largest industrial employers in the UK; the sector is also remarkable for its adaptability to changing economic conditions and hence for the flexibility required from its professional employees. The UK financial intermediation sector - banking, building societies, insurance and pension funding - employs just over one million people, and many more financial experts work in other industries. A finance degree will not only furnish an array of skills, techniques, knowledge of institutions and understanding of the often turbulent macroeconomics environment, but will also examine the theoretical and practical limitations of financial techniques.

The UK financial sector's development has been continued for decades and so there is no reason to think that the market for specialist finance graduates will not be sustained.

A distinctive feature of a typical finance course is the blending of financial economics-based and business finance-based courses to produce a course combination specifically tailored to the requirements of financial institutions. Potential employers among the financial institutions and the former UK Society of Investment Professionals (now the CFA Society of the UK), for example, were consulted about the content of the Bachelor of Finance degree at Dundee University.

The aim of a finance degree is to produce graduates with a deep understanding of the operations of financial institutions and a knowledge of the relevant techniques that will enable them to analyse operations at both microeconomic and macroeconomic level.

Career Opportunities

The global economic crisis of 2008 was blamed by most commentators on reckless investment in high-risk sectors by professionals who should have known better. Consequently, careers in finance, normally one of the most sought-after sectors by the most ambitious graduates, lost much of their allure. The return of sustained market confidence in 2014 means that many firms are keen to restore their recruitment levels and regain their traditional appeal.

Graduates enter such areas as accountancy, retail and investment banking, insurance, financial services, pension investment organisations, HM Revenue and Customs, building societies, stock and commodity markets. The scope is enormous in industry, commerce, central and local government.

Related Degrees

Banking and Finance; Business Finance; Financial Management; Insurance; International Finance and Trade; Investment, Finance and Risk; Accounting and Finance; Business and Finance (Marketing); European International Financial Management; Insurance/Banking; Economics.

Suggested Reading

Look at the financial sections of quality newspapers such as the *Financial Times* and specialist journals such as *Accountancy* or *The Economist*.

Getting into Business and Economics Courses
- Carly Roberts, Trotman, 2013

Business Accounting and Finance
- Catherine Gowthorpe, Cengace Learning EMEA, 2011

Economics for Business and Management
- Alan Griffiths and Stuart Wall, Prentice Hall, 2011

The New Psychology of Money
- Adrian Furnham, Routledge, 2014

Quantitative Methods for Business and Economics
- Glyn Burton et al, Prentice Hall, 2001

Business Finance: Theory and Practice
- Eddie McLaney, Financial Times/Prentice Hall, 2011

Further Information

CFA Society of the UK
https://secure.cfauk.org

International Institute of Public Finance
www.iipf.org

Biz/Ed
www.bized.co.uk

Chartered Insurance Institute
www.cii.co.uk

Directions
www.directions.org.uk

Institute of Bankers in Ireland
www.bankers.ie

Business and Finance Ireland
http://businessandfinance.com

Food Science

Professor Nazlin Howell, Professor of Food Biochemistry, University of Surrey

Introduction
'Food Science' is a multidisciplinary subject involving the application of sciences such as chemistry, biology, biochemistry, nutrition, physiology, mathematics and physics to the study of food. This broad-based curriculum provides an understanding of how raw materials become food and how food components interact with each other during processing to have a major impact on texture and colour as well as on health and safety. Courses with the title 'Food Technology' have a strong emphasis on the unit processes involved in the production of food in the factory; this is likely to appeal to students interested in the engineering aspects of production. 'Nutrition and Food Science' degrees focus on both Food Science subjects and how nutrients in food influence human health and disease. 'Food Science and Microbiology' degrees deal with major aspects of Food Science combined with Food Microbiology that covers beneficial and harmful microrganisms and Food Safety. There are also other courses bearing the names 'Food Catering' or 'Food Management' that are mainly aimed at students seeking careers in catering and in the handling and distribution of food after production.

Degree Courses
Food Science topics or areas listed above make up several unique degree programmes that are on offer in UK universities, allowing students to choose the subjects that interest them the most. Most Food Science courses cover the chemistry of food components, the detailed analysis of nutrients such as proteins, lipids, carbohydrates and vitamins in food commodities including dairy, meat, bakery products; the effect of processing (heating, freezing and drying) on the physical and chemical properties of food components and their nutritional value; and the role of food additives in food manufacture.

Specialisations like nutrition deal with the role of nutrients in health and disease states; nutritional requirements for infants and the elderly, and a detailed understanding of the effect of diet on obesity, cardiovascular disease, diabetes, cancer and other diseases. There are interactions between Food Science and Nutrition like the manufacture of dietetic products and sports drinks. Food Technology is an essential element for producing food and covers engineering aspects of unit processes such as refrigeration and freezing, filtration, centrifugation and heating. In Food Microbiology students learn about the beneficial aspects of microorganisms like the science of brewing, fermented foods like cheese and yoghurt; and probiotic and prebiotic functional foods, as well as undesirable microorganisms that cause food poisoning and threaten health and safety. Food Safety not only includes microbiological safety but also chemical safety, for example, the formation of toxic acrylamide in certain processed foods, the presence of natural toxins in plant foods and ways of minimising these dangers to health. It is essential to learn about food analysis and quality control of food to produce products that comply with food legislation and that are nutritious, safe and tasty to eat. The provision of adequate food in the face of a predicted rise in population, climate change and reduced energy and water supplies is a major challenge faced by all governments and the role of the food scientist to meet this challenge is very important.

Most university courses, including vocational Food Science courses, emphasise their transferable skills. Students will have analytical skills that will be useful in the food and pharmaceutical industries as well as IT, presentation and writing and communications skills developed throughout their course.

100

Some universities offer a professional or placement year in the food and related industries, regulatory bodies or research institutes. Students enrol on a four-year degree programme and spend twelve or six months of the third year in the food industry or research institute. They gain valuable experience related to the application to industry of knowledge gained on the degree course. In addition, they improve teamwork and inter-personal skills. The students are supervised at the placement and by visiting university tutors. This experience is invaluable for future job applications and when they return to the university for their final year.

A number of universities offer a European Erasmus year out to enable students to study at a different university within the EU as part of their degree course. These courses may require language training prior to the placements.

Career Opportunities

Food Science degree courses are vocational and offer a wide range of skills and opportunities to work in food manufacture, product development, research, teaching, food legislation, food quality assurance and quality control. Having an understanding of how to produce safe and nutritious food is a key attribute for graduates seeking to enter the food sector. Most universities, particularly the ones that offer the professional year placements, have excellent contacts with potential employers who look favourably on their graduates.

Related Degrees

Food Biosciences; Food Production and Quality; Food and Consumer Science; Food Science with Business; Food Biology; Food Technology Management; Food Manufacture and Management.

Suggested Reading

Food: the Chemistry of its Components
- T P Coultate, Royal Society of Chemistry, 2008

Fox and Cameron's Food Science, Nutrition and Health
- Michael E J Lean, Hodder Arnold, 2006

Introduction to Human Nutrition
- M Gibney, S Lanham-New, A Cassidy and H Vorster (Eds), Wiley-Blackwell, 2009

Food Microbiology
- M R Adams and M O Moss, New Age Publications, 2008

A Sociology of Food and Nutrition: the Social Appetite
- John Germov and Lauren Williams, OUP, 2008

Further Information

Institute of Food Science and Technology
www.ifst.org

Food Navigator
www.foodnavigator.com

Food Standards Agency
www.food.gov.uk

Food Safety Authority of Ireland
www.fsai.ie

Institute of Food Science and Technology of Ireland
www.ifsti.ie

Forensic Science

Original article by Dr Lee Chatfield, Department of Forensic and Investigative Science, University of Central Lancashire

Introduction

Forensic science is the application of scientific techniques and principles to matters pertaining to the law. It is primarily concerned with the scientific analysis of evidence from crime scenes and also provides an opportunity to place scientific principles and techniques within a vocational framework. The evidence criminal investigators collect varies depending on the case but it might consist of minute traces of paint or glass fragments, human hairs, footwear impressions, small samples of vegetation on footwear, fingerprints, different inks or handwriting, body fluids or chemicals or human remains. The analysis of these samples requires the application of scientific methods from different scientific disciplines.

Degree Courses

There is no one academic route recommended by the Forensic Science Society, nor one that will guarantee you a job in this heavily oversubscribed field. The Society's website lists courses that have undergone its accreditation process, and this could be a good starting point for your research.

The accreditation process focuses on the three essential elements of a forensic case: crime scene investigation, laboratory analysis and interpretation of the scene/laboratory results.

All accredited courses must meet the Interpretation, Evaluation and Presentation of Evidence (IEPE) component standard. For *General Forensic* courses, such as the BSc (Hons) Forensic Investigation, all three areas are assessed, although it is possible to be accredited for only two elements should the course be more focused. The BSc (Hons) Forensic Biology, for example, may not contain Crime Scene components.

For *Digital Forensics* courses, the accreditation process focuses on the three essential elements of a digital forensic case: IEPE plus Computer Network Evidence Recovery and Analysis and Digital Evidence Analysis, Recovery and Preservation of the information in forensic context. Although there are exceptions, it is generally expected that accreditation will be against all three areas in courses with titles such as BSc (Hons) Digital Forensics.

There are further specialist component standards for degrees in *Forensic Anthropology* and *Forensic Archaeology*. Forensic archaeologists are employed by police and other agencies to help locate evidence at a crime scene using the skills normally used on archaeological sites to uncover evidence from the past. The work may involve locating, excavating and recording buried remains, or unearthing evidence, such as weapons, drugs, money or mobile phones, buried by a perpetrator of a crime to hide their involvement. A forensic anthropologist may assist in the identification of deceased individuals whose remains are decomposed, burned, mutilated or otherwise unrecognisable.

Forensic Pathology is also part of Forensic Science but applicants should note that a career as a forensic pathologist requires a medical degree and applicants interested in pursuing this as a career need to enter via a medical school rather than a forensic science degree.

Broadly speaking, certain forensic science degrees have evolved in university science departments, building on existing expertise in chemistry or biology. These courses tend to focus primarily on these scientific aspects of the subject. A second type of course is more likely to blend these aspects equally with scenes of crime investigation. Some courses will have specialist teaching from experts working in forensic science, most notably from one of the suppliers of primary services.

The Royal Society of Chemistry (RSC) also accredits a range of science degrees. Look for courses recognised as suitable for admission to Associate Membership of the Society (AMRSC).

Career Opportunities

This is a fiercely competitive area of work. Employment in the sector has grown at an unprecedented rate over the past ten years, due largely to advances in technology such as the National DNA Database, and an increased reliance on forensic techniques by police forces. While there are about 5,000 people working in the UK forensic science industry, there are currently some 1,500 forensic science graduates being produced each year by UK universities, chasing around 200 vacancies.

The majority of forensic scientists in England were employed by the Forensic Science Service (in England and Wales), by specific police forces (in Scotland) and by regional government (in Northern Ireland). However, the government controversially closed the Forensic Science Service in March 2012 and its work is now contracted to private companies. These may specialise in providing primary forensic science services to the police, or focus on specific areas of forensic science such as fire investigation. Check the Chartered Society of Forensic Sciences and Skills for Justice websites for news of the latest developments.

Related Degrees

Forensic Psychology; Forensic Analysis; Forensic Biology; Forensic Engineering; Forensic Technology; Forensic Investigation with Law; Chemistry with Forensic Analysis; Chemistry with Forensic Chemistry; Forensic, Fibre and Colour Science; Forensic Studies; Forensic Psychobiology; Forensic Science and Toxicology.

Suggested Reading

Forensic Science: an Introduction to Scientific and Investigative Techniques
- Stuart James; Jon Nordby and Suzanne Bell (Eds); CRC Press; 2014

Forensic Science
- Andrew and Julie Jackson; Prentice Hall; 2011

Criminalistics: an Introduction to Forensic Science
- Richard Saferstein; Pearson Education; 2013

Crime Scene to Court: the essentials of Forensic Science
- Peter White (Ed); Royal Society of Chemistry; 2010

Fundamentals of Forensic DNA Typing
- John M Butler; Academic Press; 2009

Further Information

Chartered Society of Forensic Sciences
www.forensic-science-society.org.uk
Forensic Science Northern Ireland
www.dojni.gov.uk/fsni
LGC Forensics
www.lgcgroup.com/sectors/forensic-science
Orchid Cellmark
www.orchidcellmark.co.uk
Skills for Justice
www.sfjuk.com/sectors/forensic-science/working-in-forensic-science/careers
All about forensic science
www.all-about-forensic-science.com
Eolaíocht Fhóiréinseach Éireann (Former Forensic Science Laboratory)
www.forensicscience.ie

Forestry

Original article by Ken Reynolds, specialist writer on careers and higher education

Introduction

Forest ecosystems are important components of the life-support system of the planet. Trees and forests not only provide us with many of our most important raw materials such as timber and paper, but also supply much of the oxygen we breathe, contribute to our most precious landscapes, act as habitats for much of the world's wildlife and provide welcome resources for recreation, particularly in and around urban areas. Increasingly, we are also recognising their vital contribution to the regulation of the world's climate. Many people take these benefits for granted but it is the job of the forester to manage these precious natural resources in such a way that they provide the maximum benefits to society. Today's forestry is therefore concerned with environmental protection, conservation of habitat for wildlife and meeting recreational needs as well as the traditional use of forests for the production of domestic and industrial raw materials. The benefits provided by forests include the conservation of biodiversity, the protection of soils and water and the production of wood and other marketable goods. Forests play an important part in the landscape of many countries and are used for formal and informal recreation, with beneficial effects on the emotional and physical health of visitors. Modern foresters need a wide range of skills such as plant identification, knowledge of how trees grow and develop, conservation issues, computer literacy, planning and management skills and an ability to work with many different groups of people.

Degree Courses

The main subjects for starting the study of forestry include the science of renewable resources, geology and sustainable land management, moving on to soil science, community ecology, plant physiology and diversity and economics. From these roots, students can branch into silviculture, forest measurement, forest planning, wood science, harvesting and wood use, forest ecology, social forestry and research skills, together with the opportunity to take a year out with the Forestry Commission or another forestry organisation. There may also be the possibility of spending a year on an overseas project. The final year usually involves the preparation of a forest management plan that allows the skills and knowledge acquired during the earlier years to be put into practice. An individual research project is also completed. Successful completion of the course should give you exemption from the Institute of Chartered Foresters Part I examinations.

Career Opportunities

Traditionally, there has been a strong demand for well-motivated and educated individuals in all aspects of forestry. The predicted doubling of wood production in Britain over the next 15 years can only make career prospects brighter. Presently, about half of forestry graduates become foresters within the state and private sectors in Britain; the remainder progress to urban, environmental or social forestry, timber processing, forest management overseas or research. Forestry professionals are employed in most parts of the world, perhaps protecting delicate ecosystems in the tropical rainforests, managing large productive areas of plantations, creating attractive urban forests from industrial wasteland, caring for individual trees in towns and cities or managing natural tree cover in National Parks and nature reserves.

Related Degrees
You might also consider: Agriculture; Arboriculture; Biology; Ecology; Landscape Architecture or Surveying.

Suggested Reading
Woodland Management: a Practical Guide
- Christopher Starr, Crowood Press, 2013

The Woodland Way: a Permaculture Approach to Sustainable Woodland Management
- Ben Law, Permanent Publications, 2013

Trees: their Use, Management, Cultivation and Biology, a Comprehensive Guide
- Bob Watson, Crowood Press, 2007

Collins Tree Guide
- Owen Johnson, Collins, 2006

Forestry: the International Journal of Forestry Research
- Five issues per year. Subscribe via the Institute of Chartered Foresters website below

Further Information
Royal Forestry Society
www.rfs.org.uk

Forestry Commission
www.forestry.gov.uk

Institute of Chartered Foresters
www.charteredforesters.org

Royal Scottish Forestry Society
www.rsfs.org

Society of Irish Foresters
www.societyofirishforesters.ie

French

Original article by Professor Alison Saunders, University of Aberdeen

Introduction

French can be studied as a single honours subject in its own right; as half a joint honours degree with another language, or with a non-language subject like history, philosophy or politics; as the major component of a major-minor combination like French with film studies or as the minor component, like law or chemistry or business studies with French.

In cases where French is an adjunct to the main subject, usually only the language is studied, but in other cases, while the language component is obviously very important, it is only a part of the degree programme. Equally important are the 'content' courses, which form the other part of a French degree. Traditionally language degrees used to be described in terms of 'lang. and lit', but nowadays 'content courses' mean something much more wide ranging than just the study of French literature, although this is usually still an important feature. French culture, politics, institutions, film, linguistics - to name only some areas - may also figure in the range of topics available for study. In some universities francophone African or Caribbean literature and culture may also be studied. The division between language and content is, of course, an artificial one, since the two complement each other. Linguistic ability is necessary in order to read and understand works in French, but equally the more widely we read, the more we enrich our linguistic awareness and increase our own communication skills. Cultural awareness and understanding is vital to anyone contemplating a career in translation or interpreting, or any career which involves working closely with French-speaking people. Whilst most Honours degrees in French will require an A level (or equivalent) pass in the subject, a number of universities now also offer Honours courses in French to beginners or to people who have not studied the subject beyond GCSE (or equivalent).

Degree Courses

Language is usually taught in smallish groups, and an important feature of most French departments is the presence of young French native speakers who take responsibility for oral work. Accuracy in the use of language is very important at university level, but so also is the ability to select the appropriate register of language according to circumstances (the language used in casual conversation with friends is different from the more formal language used, for example, to impress a potential employer at interview). So, as well as traditional translation and composition work, students learn to write letters, summaries or reports, to use the telephone, to make speeches and presentations, all of which have their own conventions. Students also exploit a range of other aids to language learning: magazines and periodicals; video and television; computer packages.

Content courses are taught differently. Like language courses they may or may not be taught in French: practice varies from university to university; from level to level; from course to course. Some parts of the content courses will often be taught in big lectures. These are backed up by work in smaller groups in tutorials and seminars, with the focus on student presentations and in-depth informal discussion on pre-arranged topics; the material covered in lectures provides a starting point.

While language study is normally a compulsory core course throughout the degree programme, this is less often the case with the content courses. Sometimes a common core is compulsory in the earlier stages, but normally thereafter a range of optional courses is available, from among which students select those which most interest them. Very often a dissertation forms an important part of the course, and for this students usually have considerable freedom in their choice of topic.

Most honours degrees in a language require a period of residence in France itself, or French-speaking Belgium or Switzerland or even francophone Africa or Caribbean. The time may vary from as little as one month to nine months, but it is best to spend as much time as possible in a French-speaking country, whether as part of the course or during the vacation. Students frequently seek employment in France during the summer vacation to supplement their official period of residence. The most common ways of carrying out the official period of residence are by spending a year as a language assistant in a French school, spending a year or less studying in a French university, or going on a work placement.

Career Opportunities

Modern languages currently enjoy one of the highest employment rates of all degree programmes. According to the latest statistics only 5% of modern languages graduates were unemployed six months after graduating. The majority went straight into employment - often abroad - rather than undertaking further training. Many went into business, and particularly popular areas of employment included finance, advertising, media, marketing, management, commerce and public relations. Fewer than 10% went into teaching.

Suggested Reading

The best way to prepare for a course is to spend as much time as possible in a French-speaking country, to read French novels, poetry, plays, newspapers, journals, and to listen to the radio, watch television, films, plays and so on.

For a more general approach towards Modern Languages, see *Degree Course Descriptions*: **Modern Languages**.

The French Language Today: a Linguistic Introduction
- Adrian Battye, Marie-Anne Hintze and Paul Rowlett, Routledge, 2000

Using French: a Guide to Contemporary Usage
- R. E. Batchelor and M. H. Offord, Cambridge University Press, 2000

Mot à Mot: New Advanced French Vocabulary
- Paul Humberstone, Hodder Education, 2010

101 French Idioms
- Jean-Marie Cassagne and Luc Nisset, McGraw-Hill Contemporary, 2009

Further Information

CILT - the national centre for languages
www.cilt.org.uk

Alliance Française de Londres
www.alliancefrancaise.london

Fédération des Associations Françaises en Grande-Bretagne
www.fafgb.org

Franco-British Council
www.francobritishcouncil.org.uk

Alliance Française Irish Network
http://alliance-francaise.ie/network

Genetics and Molecular Genetics

Original article by Dr John Kay, School of Biological Sciences, University of Sussex

Introduction

Molecular genetics is the study and manipulation at the molecular level of the DNA sequences that encode the genetic potential of all living things and allow the transmission of inherited characteristics from one generation to the next. The genetic information for a simple bacterium resides in a thousand or so different genes, averaging about a thousand base pairs each, laid out along a single giant DNA molecule - a huge encoded message written using just four letters. The instructions to form a human are more complex still, requiring several thousand different genes, spread along 23 pairs of chromosomes (and interspersed with ten times the amount of what appears to be meaningless non-coding DNA). Complete DNA sequences are now known for many types of viruses and bacteria and several small nucleated organisms - yeasts, insects and a nematode worm. The Human Genome Project - to identify all the 20,000-25,000 genes in human DNA and determine the sequences of the 3 billion chemical base pairs - was completed in 2003, with most of the sequencing performed in universities and research centres from the United Kingdom, United States and Canada. The mapping of human genes, an important step in the development of medicines and other aspects of healthcare, remains one of the largest single investigational projects in modern science.

The knowledge gained is of real practical value. Just one wrong letter in this huge mass of information present in the germ cells from which we develop can cause crippling disease, and tiny alterations in the DNA occurring in just one of our billions of cells can lead to a cancer that destroys the whole individual. Every week there are reports of new discoveries of the defects responsible for one or another of the thousand-plus inherited human genetic disorders known or those that underlie one of the multitude of cancers that may afflict us. We then at least know what has to be done to correct the problem, though gene therapy is still in its infancy. Discovery of features in the genome that vary from one individual to another has led to genetic fingerprinting, with applications ranging from fighting crime to investigating breeding patterns in frogs and blue tits. In every field of biology the ability to sequence genes and characterise the nature and function of their protein products after expression in laboratory bacteria or tissue culture cells has had enormous impact.

The molecular genetic techniques that have enabled this astonishing expansion of our knowledge (to the extent that huge computers accessed via the internet are required to store and analyse the mass of information obtained) are surprisingly simple in principle, encompassed in degrees in biochemistry or related biological sciences. However, most biochemistry students will have little opportunity to learn to use them at the practical level. Molecular genetics as a degree creates numerous employment opportunities for a new group of specialists in a whole range of large-scale projects, ranging from basic medical and agricultural research to the biotechnology industry, developing discoveries into novel treatments and products.

As well as the required academic grades, enthusiasm for the biological and chemical sciences, an active and inquiring mind, self-discipline and commitment to your studies are far more important than any specific formal qualifications.

Degree Courses

Most university genetics courses are of three or four years duration. In the *earlier years*, you would probably study core modules in Genetics, Biochemistry, Ecology, Evolution, Molecular Engineering, Molecular evolution and Ecological Genetics.

The *final year* is likely to include a Project and Coursework. The Project would be original work carried out under the supervision of a member of the university department.

In all years, expect to be offered other modules, some of them optional and even modules from other departments, which may be related or unrelated ones.

Career Opportunities

Work in the expanding field of genetic engineering is growing rapidly and many opportunities exist in the NHS and in medical research. General graduate opportunities in finance, manufacturing and commerce are also available.

Related Degrees

Medical Genetics; Human Genetics; Genome Science; Molecular Biology.

Suggested Reading

The Selfish Gene
- Richard Dawkins, Oxford University Press, 2006

The Double Helix
- James D Watson, Phoenix, 2010

Genome: The Autobiography of a Species in 23 Chapters
- Matt Ridley, Fourth Estate, 2000

Concepts of Genetics
- William Klug, Michael Cummings et al, Pearson, 2013

The Language of the Genes
- Steve Jones, Flamingo, 2000

Further Information

British Society for Genetic Medicine
www.bsgm.org.uk

Association for Clinical Genetic Science
www.acgs.uk.com

Irish Society of Human Genetics
http://irishsocietyofhumangenetics.blogspot.com

Geographic Information Systems (Cartography)

Original article by Giles Darkes, Oxford Brookes University

Introduction

The traditional, patient, painstaking world of the cartographer or map maker - where a single map sheet could take many weeks or months to prepare - has been totally transformed by the development of Geographic Information Systems (GIS).

GIS are computer systems that handle maps and geographical information in digital form. They link maps, remotely-sensed images, statistics and other information about the world around us. Once combined in computer format, a GIS can be used to analyse the human and natural world. For example, a GIS may combine a detailed map with statistics on health, allowing us to discover patterns of the incidence of disease.

Remote sensing and digital terrain modelling are subjects related to GIS and you would normally study both as part of your course. Remote sensing is the science of observation of the Earth's surface using images obtained from sensors on board aircraft and satellites. Examples of remote sensing range from weather satellite images to low altitude air photos used in ecological mapping or urban planning.

Using remote sensing technology, you would learn to map and monitor both local and remote areas and to further your understanding of our natural environment and human impact upon it.

Remote sensing has been used to map deforestation, to measure the extent of the ozone hole, to monitor the tracks of hurricanes and even to map movements of icebergs to assist shipping.

Digital terrain modelling uses computer systems and graphics to represent the Earth's surface, often using 3D display.

To use a GIS effectively, you need to understand something of the nature of geography and of the patterns of the natural and human worlds, and there is a large element of applied geography in this discipline. As part of a combined honours degree, GIS can be combined with any one of a wide range of subjects. It combines especially well, for example, with Physical Geography, Geography, Computing and Business.

You should note that many universities offer GIS only at postgraduate level and you may wish to consider this option while researching undergraduate degrees.

Degree Courses

The aim of a typical GIS course would be to produce graduates who are skilled in using GIS and understand how to apply and interpret the results of a GIS query. Such an approach focuses on applying GIS, rather than being based on computer science or programming, although you would be introduced to the computing environment.

Year 1 would give you an introduction to GIS, looking at how maps reflect the human and natural landscapes, and would familiarise you with basic skills of data measurement and analysis. In Years 2 and 3, core modules would further advance your knowledge of analysis using GIS. They would also look at the applications of GIS and the practical issues surrounding setting up and using GIS. A GIS project would give you the opportunity to apply your skills to a major study. In addition, optional modules would explore how to present GIS data and design good GIS maps, 3-D visualisation in GIS, and would give an introduction to remote sensing.

Career Opportunities
Opportunities for graduates with skills in GIS are continuing to grow around the world. Areas of local and national government (planning, education and health departments, for instance) are a good source of vacancies, together with the utilities, environmental monitoring, insurance, cartography and digital map management, not to mention other areas where the geographical nature of information is important.

The **British Cartographic Society** publishes a useful booklet entitled *Careers in Cartography*. You can download a copy of the sixth edition (2008) from the BCS website given below. You can also order from the same address: Cartography - an introduction.

Related Degrees
Surveying and Mapping Science; Hydrography; Geomatics; Surveying; Topographical Science.

Suggested Reading
Mapping: Ways of Representing the World
- Daniel Dorling and David Fairbairn, Routledge, 2013

Introduction to Geographical Information Systems
- Ian Heywood et al, Prentice Hall, 2011

Geographic Information Science and Systems
- Paul Longley et al, John Wiley, 2015

Principles of Geographical Information Systems
- Peter Burrough et al, OUP Oxford, 2015

Further Information
British Cartographic Society
www.cartography.org.uk

International Cartographic Association
http://icaci.org

Environmental Systems Research Institute UK
www.esriuk.com

Copernicus Masters
www.copernicus-masters.com

ESRI Ireland
www.esri-ireland.ie

Ireland Organisation for Geographic Information
www.irlogi.ie

Geography

Original article by Dr Alex Gibson, Exeter University

Introduction

Geography constitutes one of the more popular undergraduate degrees and can be studied at most UK and Irish universities, although the precise nature of the degree does vary significantly. Entry requirements tend to be quite high, and competition for some degree programmes can be fierce. For many students, and indeed employers, geography's particular attraction lies with its breadth. Most degree programmes will cover a wide range of topics, from hydrology and coastal geomorphology through to tourism and economic geography, and successful students will have had to demonstrate high levels of numeracy and literacy.

Degree Courses

Degree programmes in geography vary enormously from one institution to the next, and applicants should take care to ensure that their particular strengths and interests match both the content and structure of the programmes on which they wish to enrol. Most degree programmes are built upon compulsory first year courses, which seek to provide a broad introduction to the full range of geographical enquiry. Thereafter, students are usually permitted to select from a range of options those which they find most stimulating or relevant. Sometimes this specialisation is postponed until the final year, and sometimes choice may only be available between predetermined 'study routes', but the courses available in the second and third years will usually reflect the particular research interests of academics in the department. Geography covers such a diversity of topics that few departments can cover the entire subject at an advanced level. Many, in fact, have chosen to focus in particular on relatively few 'themed areas' for the purpose of research and this, given the relationship between research and teaching, tends to have an impact on the nature of second- and, in particular, final-year courses. At Exeter, for instance, we have particular research strengths in hydrology, Quaternary geomorphology, historical geography, contemporary social geography and tourism studies. Whilst a wide range of second and third year option courses is offered, a significant number are influenced by these particular research foci. Careful attention to the detailed course descriptions provided by departmental prospectuses is essential for applicants with established interests in particular aspects of geography.

This attention to detail is also required to distinguish between the wide variety of degree structures that are available, both within and between institutions. One university may offer more than one degree course in geography. BA and BSc courses could both be available and will often be subject to different entry requirements and regulations.

Courses can be assessed by a variety of mechanisms; most incorporate tutorial support for students from arrival through to the final examinations, and most include compulsory fieldwork. Differences between institutions in these areas can be marked. The emphasis placed on tutorials, practicals and fieldwork varies significantly from place to place. Similarly, many departments require students to undertake personal research by means of a dissertation. This often contributes very significantly to a student's final assessment profile, but different departments take different views on how dissertations should be supported and assessed.

It should be clear that there is no 'standard' curriculum that underpins the study of geography at university. In terms of both content and structure, there is enormous variation between institutions and the only way to ensure that you end up with a course which suits you is through careful preliminary research. It is only through a careful study of departmental prospectuses, websites and other publications that the sometimes subtle but always important differences between departments will become apparent. It is also always worth attending the open days put on by departments in which you are seriously interested.

Career Opportunities

Geography is not a vocational subject - indeed, a substantial minority of students find it necessary to undertake a further year's postgraduate training to prepare them for particular vocations (such as teaching or planning) - but it is widely acknowledged by employers to impart the broad range of transferable skills that is required of today's graduates.

The skills you develop include analysing and problem solving, decision making, critically interpreting data and text, developing a reasoned argument, number skills (interpreting and presenting relevant numerical information), team working, planning, presenting oral and written arguments, and information, communication and technology skills (ICT).

A study of 2013 geography graduates shows that, six months after graduating, they had the lowest rate of unemployment among the social sciences at just 5.8%, which is below the unemployment rate of graduates from all subjects (7.3%). A fifth (20.3%) of geography graduates were in further study. While the spread of types of work is very broad, nine of the top ten Masters courses studied by those in further study remain closely linked to geography. Many organisations are interested in the analytical and research skills developed by geographers during their degrees.

Examples of employers include local government, the armed forces, private companies, environmental consultancies, environmental protection agencies, utilities, charities, information systems organisations, education authorities, further and higher education institutions, commerce, industry, transport, tourism and the civil service.

Related Degrees

Physical Geography; Human Geography; Marine Geography; Environmental Geography; Development Geography; Topographical Science; Social Geography; Geographical Science; Population Studies.

Suggested Reading

Geography @ University
- Gordon Clark and Terry Wareham, Sage, 2003

The Student's Companion to Geography
- Alisdair Rogers and Heather Viles, Wiley-Blackwell, 2003

A Dictionary of Human Geography
- Alisdair Rogers et al, OUP Oxford, 2013

An Introduction to Human Geography
- Peter Daniels, Michael Bradshaw, Denis Shaw and James Sidaway, Pearson, 2012

An Introduction to Physical Geography and the Environment
- Joseph Holden, Pearson, 2012

Key Methods in Geography
- Nicholas Clifford, Shaun French and Gill Valentine, Sage Publications, 2010

Further Information

Royal Geographical Society
www.rgs.org

Geographical Society of Ireland
www.geographicalsocietyireland.ie

Geology and Earth Sciences

Original article by Dr R Gayer, Department of Earth Sciences, Cardiff University (with contributions from Oxford Brookes University)

Introduction

Geology and the Earth Sciences are courses that study the planet Earth; its composition, structure, internal and surface processes and history. It is difficult to generalise about these courses since each course will have many unique features. Careful study of prospectuses, departmental brochures and websites is therefore essential.

Degree Courses

Many courses offer a holistic view of the Earth, basing some of the modules on 'Earth System' and major global processes and issues. Some courses are research-led, so that major new initiatives or research findings can be introduced rapidly into the course by active researchers to stimulate enthusiasm. The first year subjects aim to introduce you to the main aspects of a study of the Earth and in particular bring students who have not previously studied the subject at A Level or H grade into alignment with those who have. Where more than one degree scheme is offered in the Earth Sciences it is usual for the first year of these schemes to be common. Modules might include:

- *Planet Earth* (the structure and composition of the planet and of its origins, evolution and principal internal processes), *Introduction to Rocks, Geological History of the British Isles, The Fossil Record, Geological Structure and Maps, Sediments and Sedimentary Rocks*. In addition a range of optional modules is usually offered. These might include *Geological Chemistry, Geophysics, Computing for Geologists, Geology of Natural Resources, Oceanography* or *Global Change*.

In later years, modules are usually designed to reinforce those which you took in the first year, allowing you to gain an in-depth understanding of the different aspects of the subject. This is the 'power house' year. Modules are introduced which separate the various degree schemes, so that progressively you will diverge from students taking one of the other schemes. For example, several modules could be included in the field of:

- *Environmental Geoscience, Exploration Geology* and *Geology*.

In the last year a typical scheme could include:

- *Geochemistry and Petrogenesis, Sedimentology, Tectonics and Structural Analysis, Palaeobiology* and *Macroevolution*.

There is a greater emphasis on project work, with certain individual modules consisting entirely of projects. As an example, modules in Exploration Geology include an Industrial Placement Project where you could carry out a carefully supervised study in the work place of an industrial sponsor.

Throughout any Earth Sciences degree scheme there is a major emphasis on field training, which is important not only for the study of Geology but is required by many potential employers. Most Earth Sciences degree schemes include at least a week's residential field course in year one, two weeks in year two and a period of at least four weeks independent field project work in the vacation between years two and three.

Many universities offer a 4-year Master of Geology (MGeol) or Earth Sciences (MESci) first degree for students who aim to enter a career in research geology, whether in industry or as an academic. These courses usually follow the first two years of the

BSc degree before diverging into specialist areas that normally incorporate a major research project in the fourth year.

Some departments encourage students to spend one or two semesters in a partner European University. You can study a European language before taking part in the exchange.

Career Opportunities

Many degree schemes are accredited by the Geological Society or other professional bodies, so that your degree will lead to a further qualification after a period of professional work (e.g. Chartered Geologist). A significant number of graduates go on to higher degrees, which are needed in some areas; others undertake postgraduate teacher training. Opportunities exist for geologists in the public services, including the British Geological Survey, local government and water companies. The oil industry is a major employer. Graduates may work for oil companies or for contractors who undertake well-logging, seismic interpretation and other tasks. The mining industry employs geologists as exploration and mine geologists, while expanding areas of employment for Geology graduates exist in the civil engineering, construction and water industries.

Related Degrees

Geoscience; Exploration Geology; Geophysics; Applied Geology; Environmental Geology; Earth and Planetary Science; Geological Oceanography; Engineering Geology; Geochemistry; Exploration Geophysics; Earth System Science; Palaeobiology.

Suggested Reading

Understanding Earth
- John Grotzinger and Tom Jordan, W H Freeman, 2014

Earth Systems: Processes and Issues
- edited by W G Ernst, Cambridge University Press, 2000

A Dictionary of Geology and Earth Sciences
- Michael Allaby, OUP Oxford, 2013

Earth Science
- Edward Tarbuck, Frederick Lutgens and Dennis Tasa, Pearson, 2013

The Geology of Britain
- Peter Toghill, Crowood Press, 2002

Further Information

British Geological Survey
www.bgs.ac.uk

Geological Society
www.geolsoc.org.uk

Institute of Geologists of Ireland
www.igi.ie

History

Original article by Dr Maurice Keen, Balliol College, Oxford University

Introduction

History opens at the moment when the person studying the past can establish contact with statements that come direct from an articulate individual who lived in a past period and who can tell us of his or her internal reactions to the contemporary external environment. History is not just about man's experience as a species, but also about the experience of individuals with inner feelings and opinions and ambitions which are still communicable, even across major barriers of time.

Your first duty as a historian, therefore, will be to learn to listen critically since you will hear a great many people talking, and people in the past were just as divided as they are now by differences of status, situation and attitude. They were often the victims of their own prejudices, and they were prone to handling the truth carelessly. This is as true of historians themselves as it is of the people who made history, which is why in the study of history there is no substitute for the original sources. Naturally it is important to read what historians have said about their own fields, but history books are not infallible. They are valuable as interpreters, to put you in touch with the past to form your own judgement about it. The final test of a history book is whether what the author says rings true when his or her words are set alongside those of the people about whom he or she is writing.

Languages will be important to you as an historian. This is obviously true in the superficial sense: to specialise in French or Spanish history, for example, you must be able to catch the special nuances of people's words. But an historian must also learn to speak the 'language of the past'. The different environments of past ages and the differences in the range of possibilities in social, economic and technological terms caused people to value different priorities and to talk and think about their situation in ways that are different from those natural to us. The historian must be able to grasp these differences imaginatively in order to understand what the people that he or she studies are saying.

This is what makes history an educational subject in the best sense of the term. Many problems in any age arise from people's inability to appreciate and to make allowance for differences of opinion and attitude that stem from differences in upbringing, in physical and economic environment, in cultural background and in individual reactions. The study of history cannot solve the problems that arise thus, but it should teach us to approach them in an intelligent way. The study of long past history can be highly relevant and educational: seeking to understand the ways of those remote in time is a useful introduction to understanding modern people who are divided from us, by barriers of distance and culture. The process is a two-way one: what anthropologists can tell us about primitive societies of our own time may illuminate, for example, the thought-world of the early Anglo-Saxons.

Listening and looking imaginatively with a critical ear and eye are the keys to understanding **how** things happened in the past. Just how different that is from understanding **why** things happened remains debatable. You have to form your own judgement about it. Does history have an inner logic of its own? To what extent do such impersonal factors as physical environment, technological development and economic relations allow individual endeavour and action to have a decisive impact? In the past 100 years, a powerful school of historians, influenced by Marx, has believed and taught that we can perceive a coherence in history, based in the dynamic working out of impersonal factors, and that in the understanding of this lies the key to the improvement of the human condition. Other historians, as I myself, do not believe that history shows as efficient a measure of coherence as this, and claim simply that its study is a humanising exercise. These are only two lines of approach, around which a lot of debate has focused: there is an infinity of alternative approaches. History is a very broad and important subject and it is bound to raise controversy. History is a subject that requires a lot of patient work, and there are a number of ancillary skills which are very helpful. In terms of A levels (or Scottish Higher, or the IB), you will be wise to offer history and, if at all possible, a modern language (or Latin). Mathematics or economics can be very useful: historians nowadays are much more statistically minded than they once used to be. Geography is another subject that can directly cross-fertilise with history. Classical studies or classical civilisation can be helpful, especially if the degree course covers ancient history.

Degree Courses

Degree courses vary enormously in their subject matter and approach, so it is essential to study prospectuses with great attention to detail to ensure you select a course which will suit your own needs and interests.

Career Opportunities

Historians develop valuable skills in the balanced assessment of historical evidence, which are of great value to them in their ultimate careers. History graduates are more likely to undertake further study (21%) than any other graduates within the Arts and Humanities. Over half of those in further study (53.7%) pursue a Masters, with many studying history. When compared with graduates from all subjects, a high proportion of history graduates who enter employment in the UK work in business, HR and finance professions (12.3%) and marketing, PR and sales professions (12.7%).

Related Degrees

Modern History; Contemporary History; Victorian Studies and Church History; History with Study in North America; Ancient History; European History with year abroad; Economic and Social History; American History; Scottish History; Jewish History; Economic History; Political History; Social History; Cultural History; Welsh History; Intellectual History; Ancient and Medieval History; History Philosophy and Politics; Historical Studies; Irish History; History and Philosophy of Science; Mediaeval History.

Suggested Reading

The Hedgehog and the Fox: Essay on Tolstoy's View of History
- I Berlin, Phoenix, 2014

A Concise History of Modern Europe: Liberty, Equality, Solidarity
- David Mason, Rowman and Littlefield, 2015

The Penguin History of the World
- J M Roberts and Odd Arne Westad, Penguin, 2014

Further Information

Institute of Historical Research
www.history.ac.uk

Historical Association
www.history.org.uk

Archives Ireland
www.archives.ie/prof_body.html

History Teachers' Association of Ireland
www.htai.ie

History of Art

Original article by Professor W H T Vaughan, Birkbeck College, London

Introduction

Because it emphasises art as an historical product, art history is to be distinguished from art appreciation - which has as its object the closer knowledge of individual works for the edification of the individual and is concerned with evaluation. History of art is not concerned with making value judgements about works of art - although it has to take into account the value judgements that have been made and are still being made by others. History of art is also to be distinguished firmly from the practice of studio art. While many courses do combine the two, they are not dependent on each other, and the premier sites for history of art teach the subject on its own. While historians of art are not expected to practise an art form themselves, they do have to pay special and minute attention to the processes whereby works of art are made. They also have to develop their visual awareness of how effects are achieved. This is the side of the subject that has traditionally been known as 'connoisseurship'. Although such a name might imply it was a skill that was only of use for collectors and in the salesroom, it does mean the close critical reading of pictures in a manner similar to that of the close reading of texts in literary studies.

What, then, do art historians do? They must first become aware of how works of art are made and the different ways in which images and other artefacts have been used over the centuries. This involves close looking and note taking. There should be a constant habit of going to museums and art galleries as well as visiting sites. Above all, you must keep your eyes open as relevant objects might be seen at any place.

It has already been remarked that close reading and knowledge of objects is important. But equally important is a knowledge of the ways in which pictorial language has developed and changed. While we always feel we 'know' what is in a picture because we can see it, we have frequently lost the knowledge that enables us to interpret it. In a society where there are rapid cultural changes, this knowledge can quickly become lost. We are no longer in a society that would immediately recognise a woman holding a child as a 'Madonna and Child' - and we have long passed the time when people could read the subject matter in Greek sculptures. But changes can be more subtle than this. Pictures of daily life of the past - Dutch seventeenth century pictures of interiors, for example - might look as though they were simple pictures of people at home. But in fact, they depict elaborate moralities. They would have been evident as such to people of the time, but no longer to us. When we think of the visual imagery that we also interpret from our own culture (think, for example, of advertising and how incomprehensible much of it would be to people outside our society) one can see how much of the job of the historian of art is to reconstruct the visual culture of a society as well as the physical reconstruction of objects.

Traditionally in this country the history of art has largely covered Western art. This comes from the time when it was supposed that great art was primarily a Western achievement. We have a very different perspective on this now, and there is an increasing tendency to include the art of other cultures - particularly those of the East. But it is still the case that most specialist courses of this kind are taught within institutions that specialise in the language and culture of the West.

Degree Courses

Traditionally, the history of art has involved the study of 'high art', with painting, sculpture and architecture taking pride of place. Over the last two decades, however, there has been a great expansion of new areas of study. Perhaps the most notable of these is design history. This can now be studied as a separate subject, but it is also being incorporated far more into history of art courses. An area which has only been explored patchily is that of popular and folk art. Here there has been a tendency to expand into areas which involve mass production (such as prints and photographs), but not into painting. Photography and film history are now studied far more than they were and often within an art historical context.

History of art is now seen familiarly as an aspect of cultural history and is therefore studied more and more as a symptom of a whole social structure rather than as a practice on its own. This can have the disadvantage of taking students away from the object and undermining their capability to make fine judgements and analyses of artefacts. On the other hand, it makes clear the extent to which aesthetic valuations are related to the wider values of a society and thereby presents a more exciting and challenging context within which to study. Issues of gender and race are amongst the important ones that have been coming into courses increasingly in recent years.

History of art is only offered in a minority of schools so candidates are rarely expected to have a detailed knowledge of the subject when they apply to university. They are of course expected to show an interest in history and art, and these tend to be the areas explored when candidates are called for interview.

While not being essential, it is an advantage to have done some historical studies at school before, and also to have knowledge of at least one other language. Not much of the art studied will be from English-speaking countries (traditionally French and Italian art have been studied most, and these languages are particularly useful, as is German).

Career Opportunities
As with other arts subjects, employment opportunities in areas directly related to the study are limited. It does nevertheless open the way to careers in teaching (at all levels), working in art galleries and museums, working in the trade with dealers and auctioneers, in publishing and in various forms of arts administration as well as leading to careers in general management, administration, commerce, finance, public relations, advertising, and so on.

Related Degrees
Art, History and Culture; History of Decorative Arts; History of Art and Design.

Suggested Reading
Art and Illusion: A Study in the Psychology of Pictorial Representation
- E H Gombrich, Phaidon Press, 2002

The Story of Art
- E H Gombrich, Phaidon Press, 2006

Critical Terms for Art History
- Robert Nelson and Richard Shiff, University of Chicago Press, 2003

Careers in Art History
- Association of Art Historians, 2006, downloadable from their website below

Further Information
Association of Art Historians
www.aah.org.uk
National Gallery
www.nationalgallery.org.uk
Arts Council England
www.artscouncil.org.uk
Irish Antique Dealers' Association
www.iada.ie
History of Irish Art
www.visual-arts-cork.com/irish-art.htm

Horticulture

Original article by Dr Eunice Simmons, Nottingham Trent University, with additional material from the Institute of Horticulture

Introduction

Horticulture is the science of plant production, not only for food but also for recreational purposes. In addition to the commercial production of fruit, vegetables and flowers, horticulturists are engaged in the establishment of parks and gardens and in the conservation of the countryside. Horticulture impinges on the lives of everyone. Beyond the science, it's a huge industry encompassing both the commercial production of vegetables, fruit, flowers and plants, and the establishment and maintenance of vast areas of parks, sports grounds, open spaces, amenity and roadside plantings, private estates and botanical gardens. It also supports and services one of the nation's main leisure pursuits - gardening.

Loosely, there two main branches of horticulture, but there is no precise division:

Environmental (or Amenity) *Horticulture* embraces the establishment and management not only of our parks and open spaces but also the vast areas of recreational turf from county cricket grounds to the local bowling club. And, of course, some sectors of it are highly commercialised such as landscape design and construction, interior plant displays, etc.

Commercial Horticulture on the other hand, embraces the actual production of vegetables and fruit both outdoors and under the protection of glass and plastic, flowers (for cutting), bedding and pot plants and nursery stock. All the aspects of horticulture have many basic features in common.

Degree Courses

Several universities or colleges offer degree courses involving horticulture and it would be wise to consult prospectuses before making your choice. Several of the universities offer straightforward horticulture as a three-year course, with an alternative of a four-year course involving a year of work experience. Another possibility is a four-year course 'Horticulture with Studies in Europe'.

Here is an example of a degree course in Horticulture. The **foundation** courses form a vital introduction to the international nature of the industry. They include principles of plant propagation, an introduction to ecology, design and analysis of experiments and surveys, principles of marketing management, horticultural biology, microbiology and genetics. Lectures are complemented by practical work and visits.

In the **second and/or third year**, courses in amenity horticulture and crop production form the core of the teaching: plant growth in relation to the environment, crop pests and diseases, soils, horticultural crop production, landscape and ornamental plants, and hardy ornamental nursery stock production. Practical work and visits to horticultural enterprises and gardens form an integral part of the teaching, and an overseas tour is arranged in the Easter vacation, often to the Netherlands or to the Loire Valley in France. The option is available to all students to do a 'sandwich' year between the second and final year in College. Such students have to produce a report on the work undertaken during their year away and this is taken into account in assessing their overall performance.

Students decide whether they want to specialise during their **final year** in amenity horticulture or horticultural crop production. Nevertheless, the opportunity exists for students with broad horticultural interests to study both. All students have to produce a comprehensive report, which could be a literature review or a research project involving experimental work. Current work at many universities involves links with countries in all the continents.

Career Opportunities

Opportunities are forecast to increase in commercial horticulture. Ever-growing technological demands are creating a need for high-level skills in information and production technologies as well as the ability to understand and operate complex production systems. There is also a demand for graduates with business management and marketing abilities. The amenity side is slightly less positive, with local authorities in particular cutting back staffing levels. Specialised skills associated with historic gardens, restoration and environmental conservation are, however, in increasing demand.

Related Degrees

Crop Management; International Horticulture; Floriculture; Environmental Horticulture Management; Commercial Horticulture Management; Turf Science.

Suggested Reading

Fundamentals of Horticulture
- Chris Bird (Ed), Cambridge University Press, 2014

Principles of Horticulture: Level 3
- C R Adams et al, Routledge, 2014

A Handbook for Horticultural Students
- Peter Dawson, Dawson, 2011

Further Information

Chartered Institute of Horticulture
www.horticulture.org.uk

Grow Careers
www.growcareers.info

Land-based and Environmental Careers
www.lantra.co.uk/careers

Royal Horticultural Society
www.rhs.org.uk

Royal Botanic Gardens Kew
www.kew.org

Royal Botanic Garden Edinburgh
www.rbge.org.uk

Royal Horticultural Society of Ireland
www.rhsi.ie

Hospitality Management

Original article by Clive Robertson, Head of the School of Hotel and Restaurant Management, Oxford Brookes University

Introduction

The provision of hospitality to the traveller has always been important and can be traced back at least as far as ancient Rome. Today, the hospitality industry is enormous and diverse, providing accommodation and food and drink for millions of people each day - from a local pub to complex leisure resorts, from bed and breakfast to luxury five star hotels, from large international conferences to weekend breaks, from catering for students to catering for company chief executives, from patients in hospital to up-market restaurants. It is a truly international industry, whether in terms of the customers it serves or the opportunities for travel and career development internationally which it offers.

Successful hospitality businesses are concerned with meeting the needs of consumers. Managers must harness and develop the skills of their staff and use all the resources at their disposal (buildings, equipment, technology and finance) to provide the hospitality expected by customers.

Degree Courses

More than 70 universities and colleges offer degrees, foundation degrees and higher national diplomas in hospitality management across the UK. Most of the degrees are four-year sandwich programmes, including a year spent in industry. Some degree programmes are linked to specific areas of the hospitality industry, such as event management and licensed retail, but the majority provide a broad vocationally oriented business education leading to a wide range of career opportunities. A common core of most degree programmes is operational experience and the development of operational management skills. Thus, students have 'hands-on' experience of information technology systems and software used in industry, and they work in training kitchens and restaurants within the university or college and spend a year working outside in hotels and restaurants, with opportunities to work overseas. Many students also work part-time in the hospitality industry to extend their range of experience and develop a wide perspective of the industry.

Feeding into the operational core, and drawing from it in terms of examples of current practice and contemporary issues, programmes include studies in financial management, human resource management, marketing, information systems, legal aspects and strategic management. To capitalise on career opportunities internationally, students should ideally have fluency in a second language, and many degree programmes are designed to enable students to study a second language.

To be successful on a programme which includes a wide range of subject areas requires enthusiasm and motivation, important attributes of a hospitality manager. At the same time, working in training kitchens and restaurants and work experience in the hospitality industry requires other important attributes, a desire to work effectively with other people and a passion to provide hospitality of the highest quality. The hospitality industry is a people industry, you will be working with people and for people. You also need to be prepared to be working at times when others are enjoying the hospitality you provide: weekends, evenings and holiday time!

Career Opportunities
Vacancies in the hospitality industry outnumber the supply of graduates each year and hospitality management graduates are in great demand. You might decide to work for an international hotel company, or in contract catering, where you could be involved in anything from restaurants for city executives to supplying an oil rig, or feeding university students. You could work in a chain of high street restaurants, or in a country house hotel. In all cases, your education and development doesn't end with your degree. You will normally be offered a company graduate training scheme and should expect to continue your professional development as your career progresses. This could include studying for an MBA or another masters degree from those now available in hospitality management. You could also register with a university to undertake research, full-time or part-time, towards a PhD. A complex, diverse and growing industry needs research evidence to underpin its future development and approaches to providing hospitality.

Related Degrees
Food Industry Management; International Hospitality Management; Catering Management.

Suggested Reading
Successful Event Management
- Anton Shone and Bryn Parry, Cengage Learning, 2013

An introduction to the UK Hospitality Industry: A Comparative Approach
- Bob Brotherton, Routledge, 2000

Hospitality Management and Organisational Behaviour
- Laurie Mullins and Penny Dossor, Pearson, 2013

Food and Beverage Management
- Bernard Davis et al, Routledge, 2012

Introduction to Management in the Hospitality Industry
- Clayton Barrows, Tom Powers and Dennis Reynolds, John Wiley, 2011

Further Information
Hospitality Guild
www.hospitalityguild.co.uk

Institute of Hospitality
www.instituteofhospitality.org

Springboard: Hospitality, Leisure, Tourism
www.springboard.uk.net

Irish Hospitality Institute
www.ihi.ie

Human Resource Management

Original article by Sharon Herkes, Aston Business School

Introduction

Understanding the human side of organisations is central to their performance and effectiveness. As organisations change, grow, divide, develop and operate internationally, professional knowledge of the part played by their people is essential at both operational and Board levels.

Human Resource Management considers how people, processes and structures inter-relate. It focuses on the crucial part played by individuals and groups in organisation processes, such as decision making, planning and managing new technology. On a degree course in this area, you would develop an appreciation of the central importance for all organisations of effective human resource strategies, set within the legal, institutional, national and international contexts within which organisations operate. You would also gain a sound understanding of employee development, relations, resourcing and reward and of how these specialisms are integrated into wider corporate strategies.

You should seek out a course that will give you exemption from the Core Management exams of the Chartered Institute of Personnel and Development (CIPD).

Degree Courses

Your first year might be shared with students intending to follow other specialisms in business and management. You would study a range of subjects to ensure that you have a broad foundation of management awareness, considering the economic, financial, human and legal issues managers deal with, together with the tools and techniques they use. You would be introduced to the key areas of business as well as carrying out project work to help draw together the subjects you have studied.

First year modules could therefore include such topics as: Foundations of Management; Introduction to Economics; Business Computing; Business Decision Analysis; Organisational Behaviour; Contract Law; Economic Environment of Business; International Perspectives in Organisations; Principles of Operations Management; Quantitative Techniques.

In your second year, you would concentrate on developing critical, vocational and analytical skills, focusing more on the management of people and the strategies of human resource management. At the same time, you would develop sound theoretical bases for considering the ways in which people behave and can contribute to organisations.

In your final year, you would typically explore how organisations relate to their wider context, from both a socio-psychological and socio-economic perspective. You might examine, in particular, how changes in the external environment (social, financial, competitive and legislative) relate to the processes of management.

You may opt to benefit from a four-year sandwich programme, incorporating a full year in a paid professional placement in a relevant role, gaining valuable practical experience. This usually comes at the end of the second year of your studies.

Teaching and learning methods would include lectures, seminars, workshops, group work, computer-assisted learning, case studies, video and other multimedia presentations. Self-directed study and independent learning materials are also used in some modules. Assessment would be by a combination of written assignments, group presentations, poster sessions and time-constrained examinations.

Career Opportunities

Entry to careers in human resource management is highly competitive, a message which reinforces the importance both of the sandwich year and of gaining CiPD recognition. If you can demonstrate that you have a thorough understanding of organisations and of issues related to change and development, that you possess advanced literacy, numeracy and IT skills, and that you can work in teams and groups, you should be particularly well suited to today's rapidly evolving employment market.

Related Degrees

Personnel Management; Business Studies/Entrepreneurship/Marketing/Finance/ Psychology with Human Resource Management; Computer Networks with Human Resource Management.

Suggested Reading

Human Resource Management: Theory and Practice
- John Bratton and Jeffrey Gold, Palgrave Macmillan, 2012

Human Resource Management at Work: People Management and Development
- Mick Marchington and Adrian Wilkinson, CIPD, 2012

Human Resource Management
- Derek Torrington et al, Pearson, 2014

Further Information

Chartered Institute of Personnel and Development
www.cipd.co.uk

International Journal of Human Resource Management
www.tandfonline.com/toc/rijh20/current

Irish Management Institute
www.imi.ie

CIPD Ireland
www.cipd.co.uk/global/europe/ireland

Information and Library Studies

Original article by Dr Anthony Booth, Loughborough University and Dr Chris Baggs, Aberystwyth University

Introduction

What do courses in information and library studies offer students today? First, they provide a sound professional education that enables students to take up posts in the wide range of information careers now available. Information professionals are eagerly sought by all kinds of organisations, including libraries and information services, in the public and private sectors, as well as all those organisations developing the management of their information resources, in such wide-ranging fields as marketing, charity and welfare education or commerce. The market for information professionals is expanding rapidly, as the significance of information increases in our society, and the young information worker can anticipate a challenging and varied career.

Degree Courses

The emphasis in most courses today is on developments in information management, made possible by the increasing sophistication of technology. This means that computer literacy is essential for students: IT skills are developed in students from the very beginning of courses.

Knowing how to organise information is one of the key skills to be developed (and expected by employers), but equally important is knowing how to manage that information in the context of a library or information service. The kinds of management skills developed in students are therefore very similar to those you would find on a business studies course, as all libraries today are in the business of information provision. Many libraries or information services are also engaged in selling their services: university libraries, for example, are being encouraged to market their business information services to local industries. Courses include a considerable element on the basic management skills needed to achieve this: resource management, managing people and marketing.

Inevitably, information professionals will spend a great deal of their time in communicating to users, to other information services through the extensive national and international information networks, and also to information providers such as publishers or database producers. It is therefore essential to learn how to communicate effectively, whether verbally or in writing. Report writing and abstracting, and presenting skills, feature considerably, as do languages.

So far, we have concentrated on the development of the various necessary skills. There are as well huge areas of knowledge that you will gain. The history of knowledge and of information transfer is intrinsically fascinating and you will be introduced to the contribution made to our culture by authors, publishers, libraries and other learned institutions. In addition to the 'core' areas of study, such as organising information, and managing libraries and information services, there is also a range of optional elements for specialist study, which caters for students' particular subject and career interests.

Students are encouraged to take up work placements during the long vacations; to take a sandwich year out, either in the UK or in institutions overseas; and to undertake project work in libraries and information services as part of their course assessment.

Career Opportunities

CILIP (see below) accredits undergraduate and postgraduate library and information courses in England, Wales, Scotland and Northern Ireland. Successful completion of an accredited course will help you secure professional posts in the UK and elsewhere in the world. It will also enable you to register for progression to Chartered status with CILIP.

As a librarian/information professional, you would be at the heart of the information revolution. This does not necessarily indicate a huge shortage of suitably qualified people but it does acknowledge that library work is changing rapidly. Indeed, your career development may depend on how willing you are to embrace new methods of storing and accessing information and to move between different employment sectors in order to broaden your experience. There is a particular shortage of librarians with scientific or technical backgrounds.

In the current climate of spending cuts, there is a concern that local authorities may seek to close a substantial number of public libraries.

Related Degrees

Museum and Galleries Studies; Communication and Information Studies; Media Technology; Information Management; Business Information Management.

Suggested Reading

An Introduction to Library and Information Work
- Ann Totterdell, Facet Publishing, 2005

The Enduring Library: Technology, Tradition and the Quest for Balance
- Michael Gorman, ALA Editions, 2003

The Library in the 21st Century
- Peter Brophy, Facet Publishing, 2007

Your Essential Guide to Career Success
- Sheila Pantry and Peter Griffiths, Facet Publishing, 2003

Successful Enquiry Answering Every Time
- Tim Buckley Owen, Facet Publishing, 2012

Further Information

Chartered Institute of Library and Information Professionals (CILIP)
www.cilip.org.uk

Society of College, National and University Libraries
www.sconul.ac.uk

Association for Information Management
http://aslib.com

Library Association of Ireland
https://libraryassociation.ie

International Relations

Original article by Professor Trevor C Salmon, Department of Politics and International Relations University of Aberdeen

Introduction

International relations is concerned with issues involving life and death for individuals and nations. Traditionally, the focus has been on the great issues of war and peace. Indeed, for much of the twentieth century, certainly from the end of World War 1 (1918) to the end of the Cold War (1989-1991) war and peace were the issue of international relations. Increasingly, however, there has been a recognition that issues such as world poverty, hunger and the environment also require co-operative or collective action by states or groups of individuals acting across state boundaries.

The main preparation for the study of international relations is not particular courses at school but a genuine interest in the world and what makes it tick. Similarly, it would be wrong to study international relations just because you desire to work for the United Nations (UN), European Union (EU) or the Foreign and Commonwealth Office. In today's world a wide range of careers require an awareness of the European or international dimension. It is also true that many believe that, given the nature and complexity of today's world, international relations is best studied in conjunction with a range of other subjects.

Typical international relations courses focus upon the relations between states, nations, political systems, organised groups or multinational corporations and even individuals as they try to deal with the issues confronting humanity. Most of the discipline focuses on international politics (and in most cases departments or units are entitled International Politics or Relations regardless of focus). International politics is concerned with the nature, distribution and use of power to resolve disagreements. Those disagreements can cover a range of issues: territorial or ethnic disputes, tariff or quota disputes, or perceived threats to peace and security; but most importantly they require power in one form or another to resolve them. That may involve fighting a war, threatening to use force, the use of economic sanctions or embargoes, or just persuasion - i.e. diplomacy. The resolution of such disputes may only involve the parties involved, but it may also involve international institutions, international courts and law, or mediation. Indeed, states may often seek to obviate disputes by coming together in voluntary organisations to discuss pressing matters. Most of these organisations exist to defend the interests of the members and to help them resolve the tensions between an insistence on sovereignty and independence and having to survive in an inter-dependent, shrinking world environment. Some of the organisations are heavily institutionalised, others may be largely ad hoc, even informal.

Degree Courses

Different courses increasingly tend to focus on different aspects of the subject, or even to diverge on the whole approach they take to the teaching and study of international relations.

Some courses, reflecting the influence of political philosophy, diplomatic history and law in the development of the discipline, put an emphasis on seeking to analyse developments, institutions, policies and concepts such as war in an empirical or descriptive manner. This is not to be equated with 'current affairs' since the prime motivation is to look beyond, say, the day-to-day events in Israel or Iraq to extrapolate what these events tell us about the role of the UN, NATO or EU; the nature of alliances; the utility of military power or economic sanctions, and the issue of when it is legitimate to intervene or not etc. Other courses take this extrapolation much further and treat international relations as a social science. Some courses fall somewhere in between these two ends of the spectrum. Students should, therefore, take care to determine what the actual content and focus of each degree programme is.

However, there is no one truth. Explore, enquire, experiment and enjoy - that is the motto of international relations.

Career Opportunities
Very few careers are available in related political and international organisations. Approximately 50% of international relations graduates enter the general graduate employment market and 25% go on to professional careers as teachers or lawyers, after further specialist training.

Related Degrees
International Studies; International Politics; Peace Studies.

Suggested Reading
International Relations: the Key Concepts
- Martin Griffiths, Terry O'Callaghan and Steven Roach, Routledge, 2013

International Relations Theories: Discipline and Diversity
- Tim Dunne, Milja Kurki and Steve Smith, OUP Oxford, 2013

The Globalisation of World Politics
- John Baylis, Steve Smith and Patricia Owens, OUP, 2013

Introduction to International Relations: Theories and Approaches
- Robert Jackson and Georg Sorensen, OUP Oxford, 2012

Key Research Concepts in Politics and International Relations
- Lisa Harrison and Theresa Callan, Sage Publications, 2013

Further Information
Political Studies Association
www.psa.ac.uk

Foreign and Commonwealth Office
www.gov.uk/government/organisations/foreign-commonwealth-office

European Union
http://europa.eu

United Nations
www.un.org

Political Studies Association of Ireland
www.psai.ie

Department of Foreign Affairs and Trade, Republic of Ireland
www.dfa.ie

Journalism

Original article by Ken Reynolds, specialist writer on careers and higher education

Introduction

Learning about journalism is like working as a journalist: both offer an experience that is varied, fast-moving and challenging. A vocationally oriented degree course should give you the chance to learn about and practise the core journalism skills of writing, reporting and researching, underpinning these practical elements with factors such as the development of news organisations, news values, sources, language, regulation, ethics and the uses and influences of news. Look for a department with a long history of journalism teaching, close links with the media industries - including guest lectures by leading national media figures - and staff with experience of working as professional journalists.

It is important that you research courses carefully and consider why you want to take a degree in journalism. Some courses, for example, focus exclusively on journalism and are accredited by bodies such as the National Council for the Training of Journalists and the Broadcast Journalism Training Council. Other courses may be less vocationally specific, combining the study of journalism with another subject, such as English, a foreign language, economics, psychology or sociology.

You may be invited, as part of the admission process to some of the more popular courses, to submit a 500-word typed essay and up to three examples of your written work, published or unpublished. If you are successful at this stage, you could be invited to visit the university for practical tests and an interview.

Degree Courses

During the first two years of a vocational course, you would learn the basic skills of reporting and writing for all the main news media. This would involve news gathering, reporting, editing and production for newspapers, online sites, radio and television. In your third year, you should have the opportunity to specialise and pursue routes that reflect your interests or career aspirations. Third year options usually include newspapers, radio, television or online journalism or a dissertation. You must also learn about media law, regulation and ethics and public administration. News both reflects and contributes to society and culture, and you would study these relationships from historical, political, economic and organisational perspectives.

If you are pursuing a vocational option, seek out a course offering work placements in the media industries.

Much of your learning should take place in specially equipped newsrooms and digital radio and TV studios, where you would undertake realistic projects, reporting events and issues for your own newspaper, online sites and radio and television bulletins.

Many of the combined honours courses have a stronger academic emphasis, especially on your other subject in the first year, leaving you significantly less time to develop your skills in practical journalism.

Career Opportunities

Journalists are trained to research complex issues, pick out the main threads quickly and explain them in a straightforward way. Studying journalism as a combined honours subject could be suitable if you want to acquire valuable communication skills in preparation for careers in areas such as information dissemination, book production or magazine journalism. This is a less suitable route, however, if you intend to start a journalism career in the traditional way through news reporting. Should this be your intention, you might prefer to consider a single-subject journalism programme, although the combined honours route could lead to various forms of specialist journalism or to a place on a postgraduate course. There is an argument that learning to write as a good journalist is helped by reading both widely and critically. This is one of the reasons that, say, journalism and English literature provide a popular combination of subjects.

It should be said that most journalism graduates seek careers in the professional media and many succeed in gaining employment with national and regional newspapers and magazines, radio and TV stations.

Related Degrees
Multimedia Journalism; Broadcast Journalism; Writing for Media Arts; International Journalism.

Suggested Reading
Journalism: a Career Handbook
- Anna McKane, A and C Black, 2009

The NCTJ Essential Guide to Careers in Journalism
- Andy Bull, Sage Publications, 2007

A Career Handbook for TV, Radio, Film, Video & Interactive Media
- Shiona Llewellyn and Sue Walker, Skillset/Methuen, 2003

Getting into Films and Television
- Robert Angell, How To Books, 2009

Journalism: Critical Issues
- Stuart Allan, Open University Press, 2005

The Universal Journalist
- David Randall, Pluto Press, 2011

My Trade: A Short History of British Journalism
- Andrew Marr, Pan Books, 2005

Tell Me No Lies: Investigative Journalism and its Triumphs
- John Pilger, Vintage Books, 2005

Further Information
Creative Skillset
www.creativeskillset.org

Broadcast Journalism Training Council
www.bjtc.org.uk

National Council for the Training of Journalists
www.nctj.com

National Union of Journalists (UK and Ireland)
www.nuj.org.uk

Landscape Architecture

Original article by Alistair Taylor BSc DipLD ALI, Head of Landscape Architecture, Leeds Metropolitan University

Introduction

Landscape Architecture is a design-based discipline concerned with promoting, designing and conserving the external environment. It seeks to achieve a balance between human needs and a respect for the earth's natural systems.

Historically, landscape architecture was concerned with the design of parks and gardens born out of the traditions of the great families and houses of Europe. The garden of Louis XIV at Versailles and the 18th century landscape style parks in Britain are examples of this art. The park designers of these eras altered the configuration of the land form, created lakes and used plants and structures to define space and delight the eye of the beholder. Today, landscape designers are still designing parks but the people who use them have different demands and values from the privileged aristocratic patrons of Versailles and the English parkland. The notion of landscape now covers all scales of outdoor space, from courtyard to countryside and from rural locations to city centres. The emphasis now includes landscape assessment, landscape planning and the environmental and land arts.

David Lowenthal sums up the demands a landscape architect has to meet: *"To do this well they (landscape architects) must command an awesome sweep of subjects: art, architecture, engineering, sociology, politics - perhaps alchemy and magic as well."* He might have added *ecology*. In an increasingly environmentally conscious world, the relationship between development and environment presents man with a great challenge. The landscape architect works at the interface between development and the environment.

Degree Courses

Most landscape architects begin by completing an undergraduate or postgraduate course accredited by the Landscape Institute. Successful completion of the course leads to Licentiate Membership of the Landscape Institute, the first step on the path towards becoming a chartered landscape architect.

The next step is to undertake a period of mentored experience as part of the Pathway to Chartership (P2C). The Pathway is about developing the knowledge, understanding and professionalism required to practise as a chartered landscape architect in the UK. Individuals can progress at their own pace and previous learning and experience is also taken into account - but most people will need two to three years on the Pathway in professional practice before they are ready to go forward to the final stage of the Pathway, the oral examination.

Successful completion of the Pathway means you are eligible to become a full Member of the Landscape Institute and may use the initials CMLI after your name. A CMLI is allowed to use the title Chartered Landscape Architect, a designation which is protected by law.

Becoming an MLI is a milestone rather than the end of a landscape professional's learning and development. As with other chartered professions, being a chartered landscape architect involves making a commitment to keeping one's skills up to date. All landscape architects are required to complete at least 20 hours continuing professional development each year.

The curriculum design and content of landscape architecture courses will vary from school to school and will usually reflect the discipline of the parent school (i.e. Schools of Art, Architecture and Design, Town and Country Planning or one of the Environmental disciplines).

Landscape Architecture is typically taught as an art and design based discipline within the context of producing socially and environmentally responsive landscapes. Most

Landscape Architecture courses are studio based and use landscape design projects as the principal learning focus.

The degree begins by developing a student's critical awareness and understanding of landscape and introducing landscape design processes and skills. Students acquire an appreciation of the principles and theories underlying the historical development of landscape architecture and of the natural processes affecting the landscape. A basic understanding of the potentials and constraints of landscape materials and technologies is also introduced.

In the second year, students will further develop creativity and technical abilities through a range of landscape design projects which focus on site planning and engineering, site design and design with hard (construction) and soft (plants) materials. This work is undertaken in the context of exploring the contribution of landscape to urban and rural locations. Students also develop their understanding of the relationship between cultural and natural processes. Techniques of landscape and environmental assessment are introduced.

The final year emphasises self-direction and the application of design skills to real situations.

Career Opportunities

Around half of landscape architects work in private practices - others are employed by the public sector, for local authorities or government agencies such as Natural England, Scottish Natural Heritage and Natural Resources Wales or environmental charities such as Groundwork. There are also numerous opportunities to work overseas.

The increased emphasis at local and national level on the importance of the environment, green spaces, sympathetic and aesthetically pleasing development means that landscape architecture is a profession in demand. Like the construction industry generally, however, landscape architecture has highs and lows reflecting the state of the national economy.

Related Degrees

Landscape Design and Conservation; Garden Design; Landscape Planning; Exterior Spatial Design; Marine Resource Management

Suggested Reading

Landscape Architect's Pocket Book
- Siobhan Vernon, Nicola Garmory and Rachel Tennant, Routledge, 2013

Professional Practice for Landscape Architects
- Nicola Garmory, Clare Winsch and Rachel Tennant, Routledge, 2007

Cities and Natural Process: a Basis for Sustainability
- Michael Hough, Routledge, 2004

The Landscape of Man: Shaping the Environment from Prehistory to the Present Day
- Geoffrey and Susan Jellicoe, Thames and Hudson, 1998

Further Information

I want to be a landscape architect
www.iwanttobealandscapearchitect.com
Landscape Institute
www.landscapeinstitute.org
British Association of Landscape Industries
www.bali.co.uk
International Federation of Landscape Architects
http://iflaonline.org
Irish Landscape Institute
www.irishlandscapeinstitute.com

Law

Original article by Professor Geoffrey Wilson, Warwick University

Introduction

The common reason for reading law is that students are thinking of becoming solicitors or barristers. For those who eventually decide to practise as lawyers, a law degree has the advantage of providing them with the opportunity of getting exemption from the First Part of the professional examinations as well as giving them a better idea of what might be involved in practice, and laying a foundation of legal knowledge that should stand them in good stead as lawyers in future years. One does not have to take a law degree to be a lawyer, but three or four years on a law degree does provide the chance of a more thoughtful and grounded introduction to the way the law works than can readily be acquired by practising it; taking the first part of the professional examinations after leaving university means more time and money. An alternative for those who do not wish to spend three years reading law is to look for a mixed degree, providing that it is the right law to secure an exemption from the first part of the professional examination. Each law department will know if this is the case.

Degree Courses

Most law schools would agree that the study of law has advantages for students who do not intend to practise. They would point to the intellectual training involved in the close reading of texts, statutes and the judgements in decided cases, in the isolation of the relevant from the irrelevant and the identification and disposal of the main issues in complex problems and situations, and in the practice of rational argument according to the ground rules of English legal reasoning. They would emphasise too the special characteristics of legal reasoning that it is not simply abstract and academic, not simply logical, but reasoning with a view to reaching a decision; that even though it is conducted in an academic environment, it is dealing with real-world problems, real legislation, real cases, real facts, real judgements. It is reasoning of a practical kind. In this respect, law as a degree subject can provide a convenient halfway house between school and the real world.

To the arguments that law is a suitable subject of study for future lawyers and when done well provides a good general training in rational analysis, discussion and decision, most law schools would probably add the importance of law and the legal profession in the community. Here it stands with other subjects which study important aspects of society, such as economics or politics, looking at society from one important perspective, that of the part law plays in it. Along with law go the legal profession and the machinery of justice, criminal and civil. Individuals, companies and groups cannot avoid the impact of law and lawyers, which extends into family life, labour relations, the organisation of companies, commercial and business relationships, taxation, social security, the environment, consumer questions, the business of buying, selling and renting houses, and all the millions of contacts between them and public authorities of one kind or another. In other words the study of law is as important as the law itself.

The growing interest in foreign legal systems has been accompanied by the creation of formal links between UK law schools and law departments in foreign universities and the introduction of special degree courses which include a year abroad. For students with modern language skills, a law course with a year abroad is one of the best legal courses at present, subject to proper preparation beforehand and good provision for supervision by the host university when abroad.

Law schools vary in their strengths and weaknesses. Different schools emphasise different aspects of legal study and, as with other subjects, one needs to follow up a general interest in the prospect of studying law with a closer look at what each has to offer. It is important for those who want variety to see what options are available.

Courses in international and comparative human rights, the environment, media, medicine, women and the law and even sport can add a bit of excitement to the hard core.

Competition for places to read law is exceptionally strong and university admissions tutors expect high grades at A level/Advanced Higher, Higher or equivalent. No particular subjects are specified. You will have to take the National Admissions Test for Law (LNAT) to secure a place on a Law degree at nine of the most prestigious UK universities (plus, in some circumstances, NUI Maynooth in Ireland and IE Law School in Spain).

Equally important to what is offered is the spirit of the place and here one is pretty well bound to be dependent on rumour and reputation, but even a day's visit may help and this goes for the question of studying law itself. Although there is a lot of law around for those still at school, it is largely invisible, but although it is invisible it is not inaccessible. All courts are open to the public. Many solicitors' firms welcome inquiries and some even offer opportunities for part-time work. Visits of this kind can help to give some idea at least of the atmosphere in which the professional lawyer works.

Career Opportunities

In addition to the legal professions, law degrees open doors to a wide range of careers in the Civil Service, police, social services, community legal services, accountancy, industrial and commercial management, teaching/lecturing, local government, politics etc.

Related Degrees

European Law; Business Law; Taxation and Revenue Law; Criminal Justice; Legal Studies; American Legal Systems; Conveyancing and Executive Law; Law with French or German or Italian Law; Law with Legal Practice Management; Politics, Economics and Law; Law with Criminology.

Suggested Reading

Law in Modern Society
- Denis Galligan, Oxford University Press, 2006
Learning the Law
- Glanville Williams and A T H Smith, Sweet and Maxwell, 2013
The Law Machine
- Marcel Berlins and Clare Dyer, Penguin, 2000
What About Law? Studying Law at University
- Catherine Barnard, Janet O'Sullivan and Graham Virgo, Hart Publishing, 2011
Letters to a Law Student: A Guide to Studying Law at University
- Nicholas McBride, Longman, 2010

Further Information

Law Careers
www.lawcareers.net
National Admissions Test for Law (LNAT)
www.lnat.ac.uk
Law Society of Scotland
www.lawscot.org.uk
Faculty of Advocates
www.advocates.org.uk
Law Society of Ireland
www.lawsociety.ie
Bar Council, Ireland
www.lawlibrary.ie

Leisure and Sport Studies/Management

Original article by Gill Lines, University of Brighton

Introduction

During the last decade there has been an increase in leisure and sports related university courses. These come from a variety of academic disciplines such as Recreation Studies or Maritime Leisure Management. The type of course selected is likely to be determined by the student's interests, expertise and career aspirations. See also our separate article on Sport and Exercise Science.

Degree Courses

It is essential to study course information with great care. Here, for example, are two distinct programmes within the same department at one university:

The *Sport and Leisure Management* degree combines academic study with work experience, ensuring that you gain a broad understanding of the sport and leisure industry and the management skills sought after by employers. The course responds to demands from both students and the sport and leisure industries for graduates with management skills and abilities.

You put your university learning into practice on a 10-week work placement and in a final year project. Typical examples of work placements include managing sporting opportunities for young people at local schools and colleges, working with a leisure trust, or gaining experience with professional sports clubs and other organisations. Your placement experience gives you a competitive edge at interviews and allows you to make useful contacts for the future.

Sport topics include: the role of sport and leisure in people's lives; policy and funding; and the influence of politics, economics, legal and social issues. You will develop management skills such as: project management; strategy and planning; employment law; financial documentation, funding sources and budgets; staffing (skill identification, motivation, retention) and marketing. Personal skills such as time management, communication, career planning, research and public speaking are also covered.

If you are interested in understanding sport and leisure from a social science viewpoint, the *Sports Studies* course may be more appropriate. The course takes a cross-disciplinary approach to explore the social, political and cultural roles of sport in today's society.

You are encouraged to take account of issues as diverse as inequality, nationalism, gender, celebrity, commercialisation, exclusion, and to reflect on major sporting events such as the Olympic Games and the football, rugby and cricket World Cups. You will develop a broad understanding of the place of sport in society, preparing you for a wide range of sport-related careers.

The degree allows you to engage with a range of academic disciplines including cultural studies, media studies, history, politics, sociology, philosophy and policy analysis, as well as applied interests including sport and leisure management, sport development, physical education, coach education, outdoor education and sport journalism.

At the beginning of year 2 you may apply for an alternative route, the *Sport Studies with Physical Education* degree. This prepares you for the PGCE PE course - an additional year's study that leads to Qualified Teacher Status (QTS). Choosing the 'with PE' route opens up opportunities in teaching as well as coaching and sport development.

Topics within this area of study include the role of sport and leisure in people's lives; debates over the purpose and roles of sport in society, the ethics of sport, questions of governance and media representation, and how politics, economics, legal and social issues influence sport.

Career Opportunities

With high levels of investment planned by government and employers; and more people actively taking part in sport and leisure activities, opportunities for graduates with the required skill set continue to grow.

Key areas for graduates are in management roles within the leisure sector and sport performance or development roles within the sport sector. The sport sector is particularly popular and relevant work experience and specific postgraduate study is in some cases essential to gain entry.

Opportunities exist within the public and private sectors - the main areas being local authorities, sports councils and commercial leisure groups.

Related Degrees

Leisure and Tourism; Leisure Management; Golf Management; Events Management; Leisure Studies.

Suggested Reading

Researching Leisure, Sport and Tourism: The Essential Guide
- Jonathan A Long, Sage Publications, 2007

Research Methods for Sports Studies
- Chris Gratton and Ian Jones, Routledge, 2014

Sports in Society: Issues and Controversies
- Jay Coakley and Elizabeth Pike, McGraw-Hill Higher Education, 2009

The Comprehensive Guide to Careers in Sports
- Glenn M Wong, Jones and Bartlett, 2012

Working in Sport: How to Find a Sports Related Job in the UK or Abroad
- James Masters, How To Books, 2011

Career Opportunities in the Sports Industry
- Shelly Field, Checkmark Books, 2010

Further Information

SkillsActive
www.skillsactive.com

Chartered Institute for the Management of Sport and Physical Activity
www.cimspa.co.uk

Sport and Recreation Alliance
www.sportandrecreation.org.uk

UK Active
http://ukactive.com

Irish Sports Council
www.irishsportscouncil.ie

Linguistics

Original article by Professor Richard Hudson, University College London

Introduction

Linguistics is the scientific study of language. People are often surprised to hear that there's anything in language to study, and are even more surprised to hear that it can be studied 'scientifically' but there is actually a wide range of researchable topics and of active research. The topics range from physics (How does a 'd' sound move through the air?), through physiology (How do we make a 'd' sound?), to psychology (How do we plan a 'd' sound?), and then through grammar (How do we use 'd' sounds to show tense, as in 'walked'?), and lexicology (Which verbs use 'd' to form past tenses?), to history (How long have we been using 'd' to form past tenses?) and philosophy (What do we mean by 'past tense'?), not to mention sociology (How do we use past tenses to show politeness?) and, of course, other languages (How do other languages mark, and use, past tenses?).

Degree Courses

It is impossible to generalise too widely about linguistics courses. However, one course in Linguistics goes as follows:

Early Years:

- **Pronunciation** (Phonetics and Phonology) - Speech sounds - how to classify and transcribe them, how we make them, how they affect each other when combined in words.

- **Sentence-structure** (Syntax) - Word-patterns in sentences - how to diagram them, how to write a grammar to explain them.

- **Meaning** (Semantics and Pragmatics) - The nature of meaning - how to use the notation of logic, how we extract information from what we hear and read.

- **Principles of linguistics** - The aims, methods and discoveries of linguistics.

Later in the course:

A choice of courses on other parts of linguistics:

- **Sociolinguistics**: socially significant variation, politeness, prejudices.

- **Language Acquisition**: child language and how it grows: nature or nurture?

- **Applied Linguistics**: how to teach (and learn) a foreign language.

- **Computational Linguistics**: how to program a computer to analyse sentences.

- **Language Structures**: the structure of some language (e.g. Esperanto) as viewed by a linguist.

In the Final Year:

As above, plus a project, e.g. the accent or dialect of your home town; a study of a child's language; differences between a few male and female speakers; a survey of ideas on the meaning of tense.

In other departments you may find other optional subjects. Even the following list is incomplete:

- **Language Processing**: how we plan, produce and understand speech and writing.

- **Morphology**: patterns of roots and affixes within words.

- **Discourse Analysis**: how we organise speech beyond the sentence.
- **Historical Linguistics**: how languages change, and the history of particular languages.
- **Typology**: how do the world's 5,000-odd languages vary?
- **Language and Gender**: differences between men and women.
- **Language and Ideology**: how language transmits ideologies.

Career Opportunities

Linguistics graduates are well equipped to teach languages but also have skills of communication, analysis, logic and debate, which can be valuable in many careers. Some train as lawyers, librarians, social workers - others enter commerce, the Civil Service, management services, computing, finance, public relations, marketing, etc.

Related Degrees

Linguistic Science; Psycholinguistics.

Suggested Reading

Invitation to Linguistics
- R Hudson, Wiley-Blackwell, 1993 - What's it like to be a linguistics student?

The Language Instinct: How the Mind Creates Language (MP3 CD)
- Steven Pinker, Brilliance Audio, 2014 - A superbly written guide to some big issues

The Stuff of Thought: Language as a Window into Human Nature
- Steven Pinker, Penguin, 2008

Aitchison's Linguistics
- Jean Aitchison, Teach Yourself Books, 2010 - A clear and helpful introduction

The Cambridge Encyclopaedia of Language
- David Crystal, CUP, 2010 - A marvellous collection

Internet Linguistics: a Student Guide
- David Crystal, Routledge, 2011

Further Information

Linguistics Association of Great Britain
www.lagb.org.uk

International Association of Applied Linguistics
www.aila.info

Irish Association for Applied Linguistics
www.iraal.ie

School of Linguistic, Speech and Communication Sciences, Trinity College, Dublin
www.tcd.ie/slscs

Logistics

Original article by Ken Reynolds, specialist writer on careers and higher education

Introduction

Getting the right product to the right place in the correct quantity at the appropriate time, in the best condition and at an acceptable cost, is the challenge of logistics. It is the strategic management of the total supply chain, which goes from raw material via the resulting product and its availability to the consumer and ultimately to its recycling. When new products are in the development stage, logistics professionals are often involved in helping to ensure that the product will have an efficient supply chain. The wide range of functions, each with its own challenges and associated skills are interdependent and logistics experts work together to manage, coordinate and continuously improve the total supply chain. Supply chains are often complex and their smooth operation depends on high-level managerial skills, coupled with effective communication systems utilising information technology. The latest developments in e-commerce demand extremely effective supply chains and, in addition today, professionals working in the logistics field are required to combine business development with a sustainable approach to the environment.

Degree Courses

There are different types of courses in logistics: some cover all aspects whilst others may concentrate on core topics and incorporate aspects of a European language programme. There are also courses which enable you to specialise in a specific area such as transport management, maritime or even e-logistics. There are both three- and four-year courses, with the longer ones incorporating a paid professional placement or study abroad. In addition it is possible to do a one-year course in Logistics as a top-up to a relevant Foundation Degree or Higher National Diploma. Some of these courses are fully accredited by the Chartered Institute of Logistics and Transport, so that in completing the course you will qualify for Corporate Membership. Following relevant practical experience, you will be eligible to become a full member of the profession. In a logistics course, you study human resource management, financial management, systems analysis and information technology. You will also develop a wide range of managerial skills to enable you to meet the challenges facing manufacturing organisations as well as learning about transport planning and economics and studying different forms of freight transport operations, including rail, air and sea.

The first year at one university, offering a range of Logistics degrees, gives you a broad grounding in core business subjects. Logistics is a cross-functional subject and draws from marketing, operations, finance, accounting and corporate strategy. You develop knowledge of a range of business issues and academic skills that provide the foundation for more specialist study.

In the second-year core modules, your study focuses on the principles and practices of logistics and supply chain management and of distribution and warehouse management. Supply chain managers need a comprehensive grounding in the foundations of the discipline so that they can make informed decisions about future strategic developments.

All the Logistics programmes at this university provide the opportunity either to spend your third year abroad (at an institution where the teaching is in English) studying your specialist subject in an international context, or to enhance the value of your programme by taking a work placement year before returning to your final-year studies.

In the final year, you focus on global freight movement and international collaboration, on how e-business influences supply chain integration and on the modelling of supply chains. A choice of optional modules also allows you to specialise further in logistics or broaden your studies with related subjects.

Career Opportunities

There is currently a shortage of appropriately qualified logistics graduates in the UK. Graduates can follow careers in logistics and supply chain management with a variety of companies, including specialist providers of logistics and distribution services, airlines, major industries and retail management. They often join management training schemes and quickly take on managerial roles. They work in Local and Central Government as well as in the Health Service and the Armed Forces.

Related Degrees

Transport Management; Transport and Logistics Management; E-logistics; Business (Logistics); Purchasing and Logistics; Maritime Business with Logistics; European Logistics Management; Logistics and Supply Chain Management; Logistics with French/ German.

Suggested Reading

Logistics and Supply Chain Management
- Martin Christopher, Financial Times/Prentice Hall, 2011

Green Logistics: Improving the Environmental Sustainability of Logistics
- Alan McKinnon et al, Kogan Page, 2015

The Handbook of Logistics and Distribution Management
- Alan Rushton et al, Kogan Page, 2014

Global Logistics and Transport News
- view the very latest information live at: **www.transportnews.itn.co.uk/Logistics/All**

Graduate Career Guide to Logistics and Transport Management
- downloadable from the Chartered Institute of Logistics and Transport website below

The Dictionary of Transport and Logistics
- David Lowe, Kogan Page, 2002

Further Information

Chartered Institute of Logistics and Transport (UK)
www.ciltuk.org.uk

Skills for Logistics
www.skillsforlogistics.org

Careers in Logistics
www.careersinlogistics.co.uk

National Institute for Transport and Logistics, Ireland
www.nitl.ie

Supply Chain Management Institute, Ireland
www.ipics.ie

Manufacturing Engineering

Original article by Dr Ian Pillinger, School of Manufacturing and Mechanical Engineering, University of Birmingham

Introduction

To study Manufacturing Engineering at University, you will normally be expected to obtain high grades at A level/Higher/IB or equivalent in Mathematics and two other subjects. If you have achieved good grades, but have not studied Mathematics, you may still be able study Manufacturing Engineering by undertaking a preliminary Foundation Year. This year will be designed to bring you up to the required level in this subject and so you would need to have good GCSE, SCE Standard or equivalent passes in Mathematics and Physics (or Double Science).

Degree Courses

Accredited university degree programmes in Manufacturing Engineering are now often of four years duration, at the end of which you obtain a Master of Engineering (MEng) degree. During the first two years, you study the fundamental subjects of Engineering Science, Manufacturing Processes and Technology, Manufacturing Systems (the organisation of manufacturing installations), Industrial Automation, Operations Management (controlling the flow of products and materials) and Metrology (measurement techniques and methods). Underpinning all these subjects will be the study of Mathematics. You may take various other subjects that Manufacturing Engineers need to know about such as Ergonomics, Economics and Accounting. Some of the time you will be attending lectures, but you will also be carrying out laboratory work and computer exercises, and undertaking personal study such as working through quizzes set by the lecturer or researching a topic in the library. There will also be the opportunity to develop professional skills like report writing, making presentations, working in teams and time management, through various mini-projects and assignments.

After your first two years, you may choose to take a year out to work in industry in order to gain some of the experience you need to become a Chartered Engineer.

During the final two years of your degree programme the core subjects you studied during your first two years are continued at a more advanced level, and in addition you will be able to choose from a range of specialised topics such as Experimental Design, Statistical Process Control, and Computer Aided Production Management. An important element of the final part of your degree studies will be the undertaking of a major project. The subject of this may well be related to the research your lecturers are doing, and you could find yourself working alongside a research team. Alternatively, it may be a problem you have brought back from a placement in industry.

There are many variations to this basic outline. For example, many universities allow you to study a foreign language or business-related topics in addition to the Manufacturing Engineering subjects. In some places, the mid-course year out is compulsory; in others it is optional. (Most universities would, however, be happy for you to work for a year in industry before starting your degree programme, and you would be encouraged to find industrial placements during the summer vacation.) Part-time study is also possible, generally by interspersing blocks of time (a term or a year) at university with similar periods in industry.

Career Opportunities
Graduates are well qualified for work in industrial production/management, in analysing the performance and efficiency of companies, in solving operational problems and establishing good working practices. These skills can also be used in banking, accountancy, insurance, commerce, local/central government, marketing, purchasing and in a wide range of businesses or management consultancies.

Related Degrees
Industrial Engineering; Product Design Engineering; Manufacturing Engineering and Management; Food Manufacture and Management; Mechanical Engineering.

Suggested Reading
Engineering Mathematics
- K A Stroud with Dexter Booth, Palgrave Macmillan, 2013

Mechatronics Principles and Applications
- Dr Godfrey Onwubolu, Butterworth-Heinemann, 2005

Getting into Engineering Courses
- James Burnett, Trotman, 2013

Manufacturing Engineering and Technology
- Serope Kalpakjian and Steven Schmid, Pearson, 2013

Further Information
Institution of Mechanical Engineers
www.imeche.org

Engineering Employer's Federation - EEF: the Manufacturers' Organisation
www.eef.org.uk

Engineering Council UK
www.engc.org.uk

Institute of Industrial Engineers, Ireland
www.iieireland.net

Engineers Ireland
www.engineersireland.ie

Marine Biology

Original article by Dr David N. Thomas, School of Ocean Sciences, Bangor University

Introduction

Marine biology encompasses many biological disciplines covering the range of organisms found from viruses through to blue whales: microbiologists study bacteria and fungi; botanists look at plants of the ocean that range from unicellular algae to giant kelps 60m long. Zoologists look at everything from microscopic organisms to crustaceans, molluscs, fish and marine mammals. Some choose to concentrate on a group of organisms, although others look at systems as a whole studying the ecology and the interaction between groups of organisms and the factors that influence long- and short-term changes.

Marine biologists increasingly rely on sophisticated technology to carry out their investigations. Modern molecular and biochemical techniques are common in most established marine laboratories. Chemical analysers and light and electron microscopes are all tools commonly used. Marine biologists are often required to span several biological disciplines, and even several scientific disciplines. The biologist has to understand the chemistry and physics of the system marine organisms find themselves in. In turn, the biology affects the chemical properties of the seas.

It is not just an academic curiosity that drives this search but a realisation that the biology of the oceans may be the source we have to turn to in order to feed the world's increasing population; to find novel chemicals for the pharmaceutical industry; and as a buffer to combat the global warming induced by increasing levels of carbon dioxide.

Marine biologists have a key role in deciding how to manage fish stocks around the world. This involves long-term monitoring work and liaising with both politicians and fishermen. The oceans are no longer a place that we can indiscriminately use as a dumping ground. Marine biologists monitor the effects of previous dumping of waste.

Degree Courses

Most marine biology degrees in the UK are based on a modular system. During the course of a three- or four-year study, a degree will provide experience in many of the major biological disciplines, including genetics, ecology, zoology, botany, microbiology and biochemistry. Often in the first year there are more general modules to cover the basics in these disciplines, which can be built upon in second and third year modules. In addition to the different biological aspects, there will be modules designed to give the necessary background in marine chemistry and oceanography, where details will be given of the forces dictating the tides, waves, optical properties of water and circulation patterns. Modules are designed to describe how the physics, chemistry and biology interact to determine what is found in the various seas and coastlines.

Most marine laboratories are near or at the coast, and so many courses have a large fieldwork component involving working on rocky shores, beaches, salt marshes, mudflats and estuaries. If the facilities include a research vessel, this is used to collect water samples and marine organisms to analyse during field trips and laboratory practical classes.

Increasingly, there is the need to acquire skills in information technology, together with the skills required to enable scientists to interact as part of a team. So, as well as learning the basics of marine science, varied transferable skills will be learnt and honed during the degree. This is one of the clear advantages of studying such a multifaceted subject as marine biology.

Courses are generally based on a lecture series plus practical classes and fieldwork. In most cases assessment is by continuous assessment of practical and course exercises as well as end-of-course examinations. Frequently, final year students are expected to carry out an independent piece of research under supervision. This is a highlight of the degree course, giving the opportunity to express ideas, derive hypotheses and test them in experiments. Normally this work has to be written up as a small thesis, and an oral presentation of the project is also part of the assessment.

Marine biology is a degree in which there are plenty of opportunities to get your hands dirty. In many cases it also means getting wet, and at times cold. But that does not seem to matter so much when you are able to get to grips with understanding the overwhelming diversity and sheer fascination of the plants and animals that live on our shores, in coral reefs, in salt marshes and mangroves and of course in the vast expanses of ocean that stretch from the poles to the tropics.

Career Opportunities

There are few careers opportunities directly related this biological specialism, but the transferable skills that you will acquire – including research, analysis, problem-solving and reporting - mean that you will be very employable both within the field and in the business world. Marine biologists can be employed by government and conservation agencies, environmental laboratories, the water industry, coastal authorities, pressure groups and within the leisure and tourism industry. Eco-tourism is becoming particularly popular and creating an increasing number of career opportunities. There are also postgraduate study options.

Related Degrees

Marine and Freshwater Biology; Marine Biotechnology; Coastal Marine Biology; Aquatic Biology; Aquaculture; Marine Zoology.

Suggested Reading

Mapping the Deep - The Extraordinary story of Ocean Science
- Robert Kunzig, Sort Of Books, 2000

Introduction to the Biology of Marine Life
- John Morrissey and James Sumich, Jones and Bartlett, 2011 (plus free elearning area at: **http://biology.jbpub.com/marine10e**)

Oceanography and Marine Biology: An Introduction to Marine Science
- David Townsend, Sinauer Associates, 2012

Cod - A Biography of the Fish that Changed the World
- Mark Kurlansky, Vintage, 1999

Marine Biology: Function, Biodiversity, Ecology
- Jeffrey S Levinton, OUP USA, 2013

Further Information

Marine Biology
www.marinebiology.co.uk

MarineBio
http://marinebio.org

Society of Biology
www.societyofbiology.org

Marine Biological Association of the UK
www.mba.ac.uk

Institute of Biology of Ireland
www.ibioli.net

Marine Institute
www.marine.ie

Marine Technology

Original article by Emeritus Professor J. B. Caldwell, Newcastle University

Introduction

This study area is about the sea, and mainly about designing and building things that go to sea. Ships, of course, but other things too; from boats and barges to the large structures and systems which will be needed as mankind looks increasingly to the sea for a multitude of purposes. The oceans have been described as our last resource, and the exploring and harvesting and preserving of this resource will pose some fascinating challenges to the marine technologists of the future.

Their work is a reflection of, and a response to, our need to use the sea. Throughout history the principal uses have been firstly to move people and goods and weapons around the globe, and secondly to harvest some of the many varieties of food which exist in the sea. The centrepiece of these activities is the ship in its multifarious forms, sizes and functions. Through many centuries the art of creating ships evolved by trial and error and experience, but with the Industrial Revolution came the need to design and build ships in new materials with new forms of propulsion, without the benefit of prior experience. And so there emerged the profession of naval architecture, signalled formally by the founding of the Institution of Naval Architects some 150 years ago. Since then the main task of the naval architect has been the designing and building of all kinds of ships and crafts for both civil and military uses, from ferries to frigates, tankers and trawlers, icebreakers and hydrofoils, containerships to cruisers. What is particularly fascinating is that, despite the antiquity of shipping, new concepts continue to appear. Wave-piercing catamarans and SWATH ships (small waterplane area twin hull) are recent examples.

Nor should we overlook the part played by naval architects in the growing business of leisure activities at sea, whether on luxury cruise ships, or just messing about in boats. The design of both types of vessel depends on the same basic principles of naval architecture.

The marine engineer - and this is where the definitions can get a little confusing - can have two fairly distinct roles. One is as an operator of the machinery and systems on board ship; the other, which is the real counterpart of the naval architect, is as the designer and builder of this equipment. Again, variety is a feature of this work: ships can be propelled by steam turbines, gas turbines, slow- or medium-speed diesel engines and electric motors, and many combinations of these are possible. The basic source of energy to push a ship along has changed through the centuries from wind, muscle-power, coal, oil and other special chemical fuels to nuclear fission. It is one of the fascinations typical of marine technology that the days of wind propulsion, or of coal used in new forms, may come again if technological developments and relative fuel costs make them feasible and economic. More futuristic ideas currently being researched include 'magnetohydrodynamic' propulsion, and even harnessing the energy in waves to push ships along!

Degree Courses

Marine engineers and naval architects work closely together, and the professional education and training they receive reflects their common interest in engineering for the sea. Mathematics and science - especially physics - provide the basis for degree-level education, not as ends in themselves, but for their usefulness when applied to solving the problems confronting the marine technologist. A foundation year of engineering science, mathematics, computing and some introductory work in marine technology is followed by an increasing emphasis through the second and third years on 'professional' studies. In the final year there may be a wide choice of specialised marine topics, and the student can begin to look forward to various career possibilities in choosing subjects for advanced study.

Career Opportunities

Employment opportunities are many and varied. This widening tapestry of marine activity now includes offshore, or ocean, engineering. This embraces a whole complex of engineering activities ranging from seabed technology (placing foundations for ocean structures, or pipes or cables) through underwater engineering (problems of submersible design, communication, visibility, life-support, safety etc.), up to engineering on the surface (mothering craft, production platforms, artificial islands, protective structures, wave-energy devices etc.).

Related Degrees

Marine Engineering; Naval Architecture; Marine Technology/Fisheries; Nautical Science; Marine Operations.

Suggested Reading

Careers in Naval Architecture
- at the Royal Institution of Naval Architects website:
www.rina.org.uk/hres/careersinnaleafletnew.pdf

Introduction to Naval Architecture
- E C Tupper, Butterworth-Heinemann, 2013

Sea your Future - a guide to Marine Careers
- downloadable from the Institute of Marine Engineering, Science and Technology website below

Introduction to Marine Engineering
- D A Taylor, Butterworth-Heinemann, 1996

Oceans of Opportunity
- careers information at the Society for Underwater Technology website below

Further Information

British Marine Federation
www.britishmarine.co.uk

Institute of Marine Engineering, Science and Technology
www.imarest.org

Society for Underwater Technology
www.sut.org

Royal Institution of Naval Architects
www.rina.org.uk

Maritime Ireland
www.imdo.ie

Maritime Studies

Original article by Dr Alston Kennerley, Plymouth University

Introduction

The development of undergraduate courses in Maritime Studies (at some universities called Marine Studies or Nautical Studies) has taken place in response to the increasing use of the seas for transportation, resource extraction (fish, energy, minerals), recreation and military purposes, and the growing awareness of the importance of their waters to the wellbeing of the planet Earth. Typically, course structures allow for the interdisciplinary study of marine subjects, spanning the sciences, technology and business. Though such courses bear titles not usually found in school curricula, admission tutors accept quite a wide selection of A level/Higher/ IB or equivalent subjects. Some of the Maritime Studies subject components have in recent years been developed as separate undergraduate degrees, which are highlighted below, but the ability to combine subjects suited to employment in many maritime industries is preserved through modular structures. Maritime undergraduate courses are designed taking account of the advice received from a wide variety of employers active in the maritime world. The courses are concerned with mankind's activity on and under the surface of the sea, and of necessity, with the interface between land and sea, the coastline and ports.

Degree Courses

Most established undergraduate courses in maritime studies have been built around the transportation use, having the ship as a focus. The range of marine subjects involved is surprisingly wide. The design, building and propulsion of ships and other marine structures such as offshore oil and gas rigs, is now grouped under *Marine Technology* or *Ship Science*, or *Ship Design*, though some courses still carry the titles *Naval Architecture* or *Marine Engineering*. In the engineering world they may be viewed as sub-specialisms of mechanical and electrical engineering, despite involving unique areas such as ship stability. Guiding a ship safely around the world involves the study of *Marine Navigation*. This broad scientific subject is equally important in recreational sailing. The core study involves positioning, using navigational charts, astro- and electronic navigation, together with navigation management and marine communications. It also involves aspects of oceanography (particularly tides and currents) and marine meteorology. A slightly different emphasis will be found in *Merchant Shipping Operations and Marine Operations*. The surveying and mapping of the oceans involves the specialist study of *Hydrography*. This is also a science-based subject, which ranges from the study of the shape of the earth and the principles of map projections to the practical business of marine surveying and marine chart production. *Oceanography*, the study of the chemical composition and physical movement of the waters of the world, including sedimentology, is important, for example, in the understanding of the impact of marine pollution. Some courses use the title *Ocean Science*, because they also cover aspects of fisheries and the legal regime, such as coastal zone management. Closely related is *Underwater Studies*. Courses in *Marine Biology*, also including elements of Oceanography, are concerned with the biological study of all forms of marine life. Because the progression from A level/Higher/IB or equivalent courses is so obvious, this tends to be a popular option. But the study of the commercial sea fisheries and fish farming or aquaculture, *Fisheries Science* or *Fisheries* or *Fisheries Science & Aquaculture*, although including Fish Biology, may also include Fishing Technology (the study of fishing equipment and boats), and Fisheries Business (the commercial and regulatory dimension of the fishing industry).

All the degree courses mentioned so far tend to draw on backgrounds in the sciences or mathematics, but applicants with other backgrounds are also catered for through courses in Maritime Business, Marine Law and Maritime Recreation. The finance, ownership and commercial operation of ships are topics at the heart of *Maritime Business*, with *Marine Law* as an essential component. Courses also include elements of economics, management and personnel, and variants deal with port operations. Marine Law is a specialism having ancient roots and international dimensions. Britain has a significant maritime past, and there is at least one degree in *Maritime History*.

The long established courses in Marine Navigation and Maritime Business have provided many students with a valuable foundation for careers in maritime recreation. But recent years have seen the design of degree courses tailored more closely to the needs of this important industry. Degrees in Maritime Recreation combine relevant maritime aspects of business, management, tourism, and sport. Even individual sports are beginning to be treated as degree course subjects. Examples include *Applied Marine Sports Science* and *Surf Science and Technology*, which both require a background in the sciences, and involve the study of selected elements from marine science and technology as well as the study of the sports and their equipment. For a non-science-based approach try *Maritime Leisure Management*.

Many of the degrees mentioned in this article can be found at Plymouth, Southampton Solent and Liverpool John Moores (Lairdside Maritime Centre) Universities.

Career Opportunities

Apart from the provision for seagoing careers, there are upwards of three thousand vacancies annually ashore in industries and businesses which in some way are connected with the maritime world. There are always opportunities in the commercial world of shipping, mainly in London, in ship operation, ship broking, chartering, marine lawyer practices and marine insurance. Ports also offer a range of jobs in management, conservancy, hydrographic survey and marine traffic management. Government and international agencies also have departments concerned with the maritime world and need suitable staff. Marine equipment suppliers need technical and sales staff versed in maritime affairs. Water companies employ marine scientists. Indeed, think of a field for employment and there will be a maritime dimension to it. Another option is postgraduate study. There are taught masters degrees in most of the subjects noted here. Examples include *Applied Marine Science* and *International Shipping*.

Related Degrees

Ocean Science; Oceanography; Hydrography; Marine Navigation; Ocean Studies.

Suggested Reading

To explore the content of maritime studies a little further, start with one of the few books providing something of an overview:

The Times Atlas of the Oceans
- edited by Alastair D Couper (Van Nostrand Reinhold, 1987), despite its date, is particularly useful and should be found in larger reference libraries. It has short articles on almost all subject areas noted here and provides suggestions for further reading.

The Oxford Companion to Ships and the Sea
- edited by Peter Kemp and I Dear, (OUP, 2006) also contains concise articles on most subjects.

Further Information

British Marine Federation
www.britishmarine.co.uk

Maritime Ireland
www.imdo.ie

Marketing

Original article by George Long, Lancaster University

Introduction

Marketing is concerned with one of the most fundamental human activities - exchange. In primitive societies, as soon as individuals produce more than they require, or make something better than anyone else, it pays them to exchange goods and services in order to have a richer variety of things to consume. As societies become more developed, and individuals more specialised, the requirements for sophisticated and complex exchange increase and markets emerge. So marketing management is not just advertising or public relations or selling. It is the management of the whole set of decisions which help to create successful exchanges between a firm and its customers. As examples, marketing involves decisions about market analysis, product development, market structuring, pricing, distribution channels, product features and promotion. You can take a single major degree in marketing or a degree in advertising and marketing. Degrees are offered in marketing with studies in a foreign language (e.g. French, German, Spanish, Italian). Whereas most degrees are three- or four-year courses, those in which marketing is combined with a foreign language often include an additional year spent abroad. You will find other courses in which marketing is combined with subjects such as economics, advertising, law, computer sciences and many others. Some courses involve a placement in industry or in North America.

Degree Courses

A typical degree course will teach skills as well as knowledge. General transferable skills would include problem solving, computing, data analysis, report writing, market research techniques, interviewing and case study analysis. Among the learning experiences would be computer-linked market research exercises, business games, live market research and consultancy exercises for industry and other organisations. A major object of these experiences is to bridge the gap between university and the world of work by working in small groups, developing teamwork and presentational skills.

Departments are likely to have close contacts with industry and commerce, partly due to their consultancy work and research. In choosing a university, it is worthwhile investigating the research interests of its staff and matching them with your own interests.

Career Opportunities

To develop your career, you would need to gain relevant experience and to develop key transferable skills. One way of achieving these is by moving between in-house departments or working in a marketing agency/consultancy for several different clients. It may also be advantageous to move companies to obtain more rapid career progression. Marketing is considered to be a good basis for moving into general management, so promotion could eventually lead to a post such as managing director or chief executive. Additional qualifications in marketing would enhance your chances. Marketing is recognised as one of the core activities in manufacturing and service industries, and vacancies are widely available throughout the country. Marketing is closely linked with advertising and public relations and a great deal of interchange between these sectors is possible.

Related Degrees

Marketing Management; Food Marketing; Leisure Marketing; Retail Marketing; International Marketing; Advertising and Marketing; Public Relations; American Studies and Business Economics with Marketing; Agricultural and Food Marketing.

Suggested Reading

Marketing Uncovered
- Andi Robertson, Trotman, 2009

The Marketing Plan Workbook
- John Westwood, Kogan Page, 2005

The Hidden Persuaders
- Vance Packard, Ig Publishing, 2007

New Marketing Practice: Rules for Success in a Changing World
- David Mercer, Penguin, 1997

Marketing in Today's Wired World
- Debbie Mayo-Smith, Michael Joseph, 2009

The New Rules of Marketing and PR: How to Use Social Media, Online Video, Mobile Applications, Blogs, News Releases, and Viral Marketing to Reach Buyers Directly
- David Meerman Scott, John Wiley, 2013

Further Information

Institute of Sales and Marketing Management
www.ismm.co.uk

Communication, Advertising and Marketing Foundation
www.camfoundation.com

Chartered Institute of Marketing
www.cim.co.uk

Enterprise Ireland
www.enterprise-ireland.com

Marketing Institute of Ireland
www.mii.ie

Materials Science, Materials Engineering and Metallurgy

Original article by Vernon John, formerly of City University

Introduction

Today the spectrum of engineering materials is very wide, comprising a large range of metals and alloys, a continually increasing number of polymer materials, ceramics (including many new industrial ceramics) and glasses, stone, concrete, bituminous materials and very many composite materials.

The pace of development in both materials and processing techniques is rapid and exciting. Some examples of developments in recent years include new materials for the electronics industry with impurity levels measured in parts per billion; single crystal turbine blades capable of operating at temperatures very close to their melting temperatures for high performance aero gas turbines; ceramics which may be formed into complex shapes using processes similar to those for polymer materials; polymers for high temperature service; and carbon fibre and other high performance composites.

Degree Courses

The subject matter of degree courses in Materials Science, Materials Engineering or Metallurgy develops from a knowledge of physics, chemistry and mathematics. Some of the degree courses are orientated more towards science while others lean more towards engineering. In the first year of many degree courses there are further studies in aspects of physics, chemistry and mathematics, together with specialist materials science studies and, in many cases, an introduction to engineering studies. Practical work forms an essential part of all the courses. In the later years the courses cover a wide range of topics: the structure of materials and the relationships between structure and properties, the production and fabrication of materials, and the behaviour of materials and components in a wide variety of service conditions. Other important topics are failure mechanisms and failure prevention, corrosion, chemical and microbial attack, joining technology, test and evaluation methods, selection criteria and quality assurance. Economics and management studies feature in courses with a major bias towards engineering. Many universities have links with institutions throughout Europe and in North America and there are possibilities to have a study period abroad. On many courses, there are opportunities to have industrial training periods either in the UK or abroad.

Before selecting a course you need to decide whether to practise as an engineer or to remain fairly firmly within the world of science. Most of the degree courses available are accredited by the Institute of Materials, Minerals and Mining for the Engineering Council. These are the 4-year MEng and the 3- or 4-year BEng but some BSc courses are not accredited and will not lead directly to the professional qualifications of CEng or MEng.

Career Opportunities

The possession of a degree in Materials and/or Metallurgy can lead to employment in industry, the public services or the armed forces. There is a wide range of career possibilities including research, development, manufacturing, management, marketing or teaching in spheres as diverse as microelectronics, aerospace, off-shore engineering and general manufacturing industry. Many graduates register with the Engineering Council for the professional qualifications of either Chartered Engineer (CEng) or Incorporated Engineer (IEng), after which they follow a period of monitored Initial Professional Development (IPD). This comprises training, learning from experience and taking responsibility in appropriate roles. When the IPD phase is completed, usually about four years after graduation, the final assessment for the young engineer is a Professional Review. This normally includes presentation of a written report and an interview with suitably qualified and experienced professional engineers and is the final hurdle before being registered as either a Chartered or Incorporated Engineer.

Related Degrees

Ceramics; Polymer Science and Technology; Ceramics Science and Engineering; Recycling Technology; Materials, Economics and Management.

Suggested Reading

Materials Science and Engineering: An Introduction
- William D Callister and David G Rethwisch, Wiley, 2013

Materials: Engineering, Science, Processing and Design
- Michael Ashby et al, Butterworth-Heinemann, 2013

Mechanics of Materials
- James M Gere and Barry J Goodno, Nelson Engineering, 2012

The New Science of Strong Materials or Why You Don't Fall Through the Floor
- J E Gordon, Princeton Science Library, 2006

Getting into Engineering Courses
- James Burnett, Trotman, 2013

Further Information

Engineering Council UK
www.engc.org.uk

UK Centre for Materials Education
www.materials.ac.uk

Cogent Science Career Pathways
www.sciencecareerpathways.com

Institute of Materials, Minerals and Mining
www.iom3.org

Engineers Ireland
www.engineersireland.ie

Materials Ireland – Polymer Research Centre
www.tcd.ie/Physics/Molecular_Electronics/mi.php

Mathematics

Original article by J C Ault, University of Leicester, with contributions by Louis Billington, University of Hull and by Sheffield Hallam University

Introduction

All university mathematics courses are based on a core of pure mathematics consisting of topics from mathematical analysis and abstract algebra. Broadly speaking, analysis is that part of the subject which deals with limiting processes and includes concepts such as differentiation, integration and continuity of functions, while algebra deals with finite processes such as addition and multiplication and the solution of polynomial and simultaneous linear equations. It is in this core that you will learn the rigour of formal proofs and the logical thinking needed for the rest of the course. You will also have the opportunity to study other topics from pure mathematics and from some or all of the other main areas of the subject: applied mathematics, numerical analysis, mathematical statistics and computation.

Degree Courses

Usually the first year is fairly prescribed and most departments will take the opportunity to provide courses to help with the transition to university. In the second, third and, where applicable, fourth years an increasing choice of modules is provided, allowing you to concentrate on the areas of the subject which interest you most (or perhaps to avoid those that appeal to you least). The range of modules on offer will vary from department to department and from time to time and will depend on the interests and strengths of the staff, but you can expect a wide range of topics from at least three of the main areas.

The teaching of mathematics is normally by a combination of lectures, tutorials, problem classes and workshops. The whole class attends lectures, while tutorials and problem classes are organised for smaller groups and there is more interaction between tutor and students. Most workshops in mathematics tend to be in a computer laboratory, where you would be learning to use a specialised mathematical package or a spreadsheet, but there are also situations where you could be working with a small group of fellow students to investigate a problem. You will be expected to work on your own as well and to hand in solutions to exercises for assessment on a weekly basis. Assessment is generally by written examination but most mathematics courses also include a certain amount of coursework (typically 10% or 20%) and some may be assessed entirely on written reports of project work.

A typical university course offers a choice of studying mathematics for three years for the BSc degree, or for four years to obtain the MMath/MSci (Master of Mathematics/ Science) degree and you can often add a year abroad, in Europe, Australia or the USA. It can also be combined with many other subjects, among which astronomy, computer science, physics, education and economics are the more obvious ones, but this is by no means an exhaustive list.

By varying the choice of modules, it is also possible to concentrate on pure or applied mathematics including statistics, computer modelling or a number of other fields. There are also four-year degrees that have been developed in collaboration with mathematics staff in neighbouring European states. These involve students spending a year abroad. In each of these mathematics/language degrees, the mathematics load is reduced in the first two years so that you can take language modules that will enable you to enjoy living abroad in your third year when you are taught mathematics in the foreign language.

At one of England's larger universities, there are 19 choices of course to follow, including French Studies with Mathematics, Mathematical Economics and Statistics, Mathematics and Computer Science (with an industrial year) and Mathematics and

Sports Science. A modular structure allows you a considerable amount of choice and the chance, to a certain extent, to reconsider your preferences as the programme progresses.

Career Opportunities

The completion of a degree course opens the door to a wide range of careers. As well as those open to holders of any non-specialised degree, there are opportunities in areas requiring numerical skills and a capacity for organised and logical thought.

Related Degrees

Mathematical Sciences; Pure Mathematics; Applied Mathematics; Business/Finance Mathematics; Computational Mathematics; Industrial Mathematics; Mathematics with Study Abroad; Actuarial Science/Studies; Statistics; Economics/Mathematics and Statistics; Foundation Mathematics; Mathematical Engineering; Mathematics and Theoretical Physics; Mathematics/Statistics and Computing; Operational Research.

Suggested Reading

Archimedes' Revenge: The Joys and Perils of Mathematics
- Paul Hoffman, Penguin Books, 1991

Mathematics: A Very Short Introduction
- Timothy Gowers, Oxford, 2002

What Is Mathematics?: An Elementary Approach to Ideas and Methods
- R Courant and H Robbins, OUP, 1996

How to Study for a Mathematics degree
- Lara Alcock, OUP Oxford, 2012

From Here to Infinity
- Ian Stewart, Oxford, 1996

Further Information

Maths Careers
www.mathscareers.org.uk

Enriching Mathematics
http://nrich.maths.org

London Mathematical Society
www.lms.ac.uk

Royal Statistical Society
www.rss.org.uk

Operational Research Society
www.theorsociety.com

Institute and Faculty of Actuaries
www.actuaries.org.uk

Institute of Mathematics and its Applications
www.ima.org.uk

Irish Statistical Association
www.istat.ie

Irish Mathematical Society
www.maths.tcd.ie/pub/ims

Mechanical Engineering

Original article by Dr Ian Pillinger, School of Manufacturing and Mechanical Engineering, University of Birmingham

Introduction

To study Mechanical Engineering at university, you will normally be expected to obtain high grades at A level/Higher/IB or equivalent in Mathematics, Physics and one other subject. If you have good grades, but have not studied both Mathematics and Physics, you may still be able to study Mechanical Engineering by undertaking a preliminary Foundation Year. This year will be designed to bring you up to the required level in these subjects and so you would need to have good GCSE/SCE Standard Grade or equivalent passes in Mathematics and Physics.

Degree Courses

Accredited university degree programmes in Mechanical Engineering are often of four years' duration, at the end of which you obtain a Master of Engineering (MEng) degree, or three years' for the Bachelor (BEng) qualification. During the first two years of the MEng, you study the fundamental subjects of Mechanics of Solids (how things deform under load), Statics and Dynamics of Structures (the behaviour of objects under balancing forces and when they are moving), Thermodynamics (the interaction between heat and movement) and Fluid Mechanics (the movement of gases and liquids in machinery).

Underpinning all these subjects will be Mathematics, and all the other subjects are drawn together by learning about design. You may take various other subjects that Mechanical Engineers need to know about, such as Electrical and Electronic Theory, Metrology, Computing and Information Technology and Manufacturing Processes. Some of the time you will be attending lectures, but you will also be carrying out laboratory work and computer exercises, and undertaking personal study researching a topic in the library. There will also be the opportunity to develop professional skills like report writing, making presentations, working through various mini-projects and assignments.

After your first two years, you may choose to take a year out to work in industry in order to gain some of the experience you need to become a Chartered Engineer. During the final years of your degree programme the core subjects you studied during your first two years are continued at a more advanced level, and in addition you will be able to choose from a range of specialised topics such as Automotive Engineering, Control of Machinery, Mechatronics (the integration of electrical and mechanical behaviour) and Thermal Power Systems. An important element of the final part of your degree studies will be the undertaking of a major project. The subject of this may well be related to the research your lecturers are doing, and you could find yourself working alongside a research team. Alternatively, it may be a topic you have brought back from a placement in industry.

There are many variations to this basic outline. For example, several universities allow you to study a foreign language, materials science or business-related topics in addition to the Mechanical Engineering subjects. In some places; the mid-course year-out is compulsory, in others, it is optional. (Most universities would, however, be happy for you to work for a year in industry before starting your degree programme, and you would be encouraged to find industrial placements during the summer vacation.) Part-time study is also possible, generally by interspersing blocks of time (a term or a year) at university with similar periods in industry.

Career Opportunities

It is difficult to imagine a major industry that does not use the skills of mechanical engineers. Indeed, mechanical engineering usually plays a part in producing almost all the products and services we see around us. Mechanical engineers are likely to be recruited into the aerospace and automotive industries; the armed forces and the Defence Engineering and Science Group; energy utilities, including nuclear; engineering construction companies; engineering consultancies; manufacturing industries; medical engineering; oil and gas industries, including the petro-chemical sector; process industries, including pharmaceuticals, food and cosmetics; the public sector, including the Civil Service, local authorities, hospitals, and educational institutions; research establishments, both academic and commercial; and transport, including roads and railways.

Related Degrees

Automotive Engineering; Aerospace Engineering; Transportation Engineering; Agricultural Engineering; Marine Engineering; Motor Sport Engineering; Mechanical Electronic Systems; Manufacturing Engineering.

Suggested Reading

Mechanical Engineering Principles
- John Bird and Carl Ross, Routledge, 2012

Engineering Mathematics
- K A Stroud with Dexter Booth, Palgrave Macmillan, 2013

Mechatronics Principles and Applications
- Dr Godfrey Onwubolu, Butterworth-Heinemann, 2005

Getting into Engineering Courses
- James Burnett, Trotman, 2013

Manufacturing Engineering and Technology
- Serope Kalpakjian and Steven Schmid, Pearson, 2013

IMechE Engineers Databook
- Clifford Matthews, Wiley-Blackwell, 2012

Further Information

Institution of Mechanical Engineers
www.imeche.org

Engineering Employer's Federation - EEF: The Manufacturers' Organisation
www.eef.org.uk

Engineering Council UK
www.engc.org.uk

Institute of Industrial Engineers Ireland
www.iieireland.net

Engineers Ireland
www.engineersireland.ie

Medical Engineering/Technology

Original article by Clive Beggs, Professor of Medical Technology, University of Bradford

Introduction

Engineering plays as much of a part in modern healthcare systems as pharmaceutical drugs, although few people are aware of it. Every year, millions of radiographs are taken of fractured bones, thousands of artificial hips are installed, and countless lives are saved through medical ventilation, and yet the massive contribution that engineering makes towards the diagnosis of disease and the treatment of patients goes largely unrecognised.

The fact is, however, that engineering in its various guises runs through the health service like writing through a stick of rock and engineering is responsible for many of the medical advances that we now take for granted. Prosthetic hip joints, pacemakers, magnetic resonance imaging (MRI), computed tomography (CT scanning) and image-guided surgery are just a few of the technologies that have revolutionised modern medicine and changed the lives of many for the better.

Advances such as those listed above are all examples of work pioneered by medical engineers, alternatively known as bioengineers or biomedical engineers. Such people combine their engineering expertise with biology to solve medical problems and improve the wellbeing of patients. Although lower in profile than the more traditional disciplines of civil, electrical and mechanical engineering, medical engineering is nonetheless a fast growing discipline, which is increasing in importance as more and more medical procedures rely on advanced technology.

Indeed, the US Department of Labor states that employment in biomedical engineering is expected to grow at a much faster rate than average (in excess of 27%) from 2012 to 2022[1], driven by the healthcare needs of an ageing population and increased demand for sophisticated medical equipment and procedures. Given that the healthcare industry is the world's largest sector, it is no surprise that opportunities for medical engineering graduates are huge. Indeed, it is one of the few areas in engineering that is predicted to continue to grow for many years to come.

Which course?

Compared with civil, mechanical and electrical engineering, medical engineering is a new and emerging discipline - in every way it is a discipline for the 21st century. The UK is a world leader in medical engineering research and a number of universities now offer undergraduate programmes in this discipline. The broad range of activities covered by the subject means that the focus of medical engineering degrees can vary greatly from institution to institution. Some focus on mechanical engineering, while others are more electrical in their approach. Still others focus on materials science and the development of new biomaterials.

The medical engineering degree offered by the University of Bradford, while being mechanically based, has a very strong biological/clinical component, which means that students on this programme study cell biology, genomics and tissue engineering as well as more traditional subjects such as biomechanics, fluid dynamics and rehabilitation engineering. It is therefore wise when choosing a degree programme to look carefully at the course content, to check that it is what you want.

Given that medical engineering is very much a research-led discipline, it is also important to enquire about research activities of the various institutions. Lecturers tend to focus their teaching on their research interests - the best lectures are given by enthusiasts, and active researchers are great enthusiasts! Direct links with

---

1 US Department of Labor, Bureau of Labor Statistics. Engineers.
www.bls.gov/ooh/architecture-and-engineering/biomedical-engineers.htm

local hospitals are also important and are essential if the course is to have clinical relevance. Such links are an invaluable resource when it comes to final year projects and may prove useful when seeking employment after graduation.

Career Opportunities

Job prospects for qualified medical engineers are excellent - salaries are above average, with top engineers paid the same as hospital consultants. Opportunities exist in a wide variety of roles. Many are employed in commercial organisations designing and developing medical devices, some specialise in sales and marketing, while others are employed by hospitals where they work with clinicians to provide care for patients. Guidance on opportunities in the NHS is complicated as we go to press because of the implementation of the Department of Health Modernising Scientific Careers (MSC) programme. Career prospects should become clearer when the MSC programme is fully established. In the meantime, check the IPEM website for the very latest statements on discussions to maintain the professional status of medical engineers.

Opportunities also exist in research facilities, pioneering the technologies which today might seem unrealistic but tomorrow may be commonplace. However, no matter the specific nature of the role, one factor remains consistent - that medical engineering is fast-moving and multi-disciplinary. Medical engineers therefore need to be people with advanced knowledge and skills, who have a good appreciation of developments in the clinical and biological fields.

Medical engineers may be employed on a wide variety of projects. For example, not only may they specialise in the development of superior artificial joints, they may also develop advanced surgical procedures, which enable surgeons to carry out hip replacement operations more effectively. Other engineers may specialise in medical imaging, developing better ways to see inside the human body without harming patients. Others may focus on the emerging field of tissue engineering, which involves culturing human cells to grow new body parts. Medical engineers therefore need to be flexible and willing to absorb new ideas. In medical engineering, nothing stays still for very long!

A final thought

People working in medical engineering have a great opportunity to influence the lives of many for the better. Hospital doctors can only treat individual patients, but engineers can develop technologies with the potential to save many millions of lives. This can be a great motivator and one tends to find that many medical engineers are extremely dedicated individuals who want their work to benefit mankind.

Suggested Reading

Medical Devices and Systems (Biomedical Engineering Handbook, Fourth Edition) - Joseph D Bronzino and Donald R Peterson, CRC Press, 2015

Biomedical Engineering: Bridging Medicine and Technology - W Mark Saltzman, Cambridge University Press, 2009

Further Information

Institute of Physics and Engineering in Medicine
www.ipem.ac.uk

Engineers Ireland
www.engineersireland.ie

Medicinal Chemistry

Original article by James R Hanson, University of Sussex

Introduction

Medicinal chemistry is the study of the chemistry of compounds that have a beneficial effect on disease states. The aim of the medicinal chemist is to enhance the therapeutic effect of a compound and to diminish unwanted side effects. The medicinal chemist is primarily concerned with the design and synthesis of new therapeutic agents but there must be an interaction with other disciplines such as medicine, biology, biochemistry, pharmacology and pharmacy. A medicinal chemistry course is not an alternative to a pharmacy course, and affords different career opportunities.

Before entering a course on medicinal chemistry, a student will require not only a firm grasp of chemistry, particularly organic chemistry, but also some biology and mathematics. The latter might be replaced by physics.

There are various ways of classifying the drugs that are the topic of medicinal chemistry. Firstly we may consider the chemistry of infectious diseases. Here the object is to design a compound that will target an invading organism without injury to the host. The compound must have an irreversible action on one cell in the presence of another. The development of antibiotics is an example of this. Secondly there is the chemistry of malignant disease in which drugs are designed to injure an aberrant, rapidly proliferating cell in the presence of a normal cell. The third area involves the chemistry of non-infectious diseases in which the compound has a selective action on one type of cell or organ within the host to modify its action. This class may be subdivided into substances which target the central or peripheral nervous system. Another sub-division includes compounds which affect the circulatory system, for example by dilation of blood vessels. A further sub-division involves agents which have a metabolic or endocrine function affecting the hormone balance within the body. Finally there are those agents which target the immune system.

Degree Courses

How are these reflected in a course? Firstly the medicinal chemist requires a knowledge of the organic chemistry of functional groups, stereochemistry, reaction mechanisms and synthesis. The physicochemical aspects of drug design involve a knowledge of bonding, of reaction kinetics and the nature of solutions whilst spectroscopy may shed light on structure. Areas of inorganic chemistry are involved in biological oxidative mechanisms, in the ionic balance in the body. A number of inorganic compounds are drugs in their own right. The first two years of a course must provide that breadth of knowledge without which a medicinal chemist can neither make compounds nor understand how they work In this period, some supporting biology teaching is provided. A good chemical base is constructed and the specialism follows with courses on medicinal targets in the cell, cell signalling and transduction processes, hormone and receptor targets including neurotransmission, antibiotics and antiviral agents, cancer chemotherapy, drug metabolism and the physicochemical aspects of drug design and molecular modelling. A useful aspect giving students an impression of the cutting edge of drug design would involve lectures from the pharmaceutical industry. A research project is an important feature of a medicinal chemistry course, giving the student the chance to make compounds for biological testing. Sometimes, a student spends a sandwich year in industry.

Career Opportunities

The pharmaceutical industry is one of the more buoyant parts of the chemical industry. Medicinal chemists are employed not just in the research laboratory: there are different and obviously challenging opportunities in the development laboratory, drug formulation and in analytical chemistry. Outside the laboratory, there are opportunities for medicinal chemists in drug registration, patent work, information retrieval, and in medical sales and marketing.

Related Degrees

Biological and Medicinal Chemistry; Medicinal Biochemistry; Chemistry, Life Systems and Pharmaceuticals; Chemistry for Drug Discovery; Pharmaceutical Chemistry.

Suggested Reading

Introduction to Medicinal Chemistry
- Graham L Patrick, OUP, 2013

Fundamentals of Medicinal Chemistry
- Gareth Thomas, Wiley, 2003

Instant Notes in Medicinal Chemistry
- Graham L Patrick, Taylor and Francis, 2001

Medicinal Chemistry: a Molecular and Biochemical Approach
- Thomas Nogrady and Donald Weaver, OUP, 2005

Further Information

Medicinal Chemistry Research Group
www.staff.livjm.ac.uk/pacfisma

Royal Society of Chemistry
www.rsc.org

Institute of Chemistry of Ireland
www.chemistryireland.org

Medicine

Original article by Dr David Hughes, formerly Senior Lecturer in Medicine, London Hospital Medical College (now part of Queen Mary, University of London). Additional material supplied by the British Medical Association

Introduction

Learning to be a doctor is one of the longest and most expensive courses of study for any degree (taking 5-6 years), so it is essential that those thinking of medicine as a career are absolutely sure this is what they want to do with their working lives, before taking the first step and applying to enter a medical school. These notes are merely a preliminary guide, and more detailed information can be obtained from the medical schools. Remember, the essential personal qualities for a doctor are compassion, resourcefulness, boundless energy and perseverance.

Degree Courses

There are generally three approaches to the training provided at medical school: the traditional pre-clinical and clinical course, an integrated course or the newer courses specialising in multi- or inter-professional learning. (See Degree Course Descriptions *Medicine Dissected*).

For the traditional courses, students begin their training with two years of 'pre-clinical' work, involving study of the basic medical sciences. This is followed by the 'clinical' course, of approximately three years, during which they work in hospital wards under the supervision of consultants. Throughout the final three years they also attend lectures on all aspects of medical practice. Examples of universities which offer a traditional course include Oxford and Cambridge.

Integrated courses, which the majority of medical schools have now implemented, integrate what is usually learnt at the pre-clinical and clinical stages to provide a seamless course. Teaching methods can include problem-based learning and practical clinical skills. Examples of such universities are Liverpool and Imperial College.

Thirdly, there are now medical schools basing their teaching on or specialising in multi- or inter-professional learning, such as Peninsula and Southampton.

Each course is different and uses different methods of teaching, so it is important that you think carefully about the kind of course that would suit you. You can obtain a copy of the syllabus from each medical school.

Apart from the degree in medicine, most schools offer students the opportunity to take an extra year (sometimes two) in the middle of the medical degree to study a subject of interest, which will lead to an 'intercalated' BSc (Hons) or equivalent. At some schools this opportunity is only available to high achievers, whereas at other schools it is built into the curriculum. For full details on intercalated degrees, you should contact the medical schools directly.

In addition to exceptionally demanding academic entry standards, most schools have adopted the UK Clinical Aptitude Test (UKCAT) to help them select the best candidates. A much smaller group uses the Bio Medical Admissions Test (BMAT). Competition for places to read medicine is very intense. You would need to show that you have a genuine interest in the subject and if possible demonstrate relevant paid or voluntary work experience.

Career Opportunities

Newly qualified graduates from medical school receive provisional registration from the General Medical Council (GMC) and undertake foundation year 1 (F1), which is designed to build on the knowledge and skills gained during undergraduate training. On successful completion of F1, you receive full registration with the GMC and can continue to the second year of foundation training.

Foundation year 2 (F2) training continues the general training in medicine and involves a range of different specialties, which could include general practice. By the end of foundation training, you must demonstrate that you are competent in areas such as managing acutely ill patients, team working and communication skills, to continue training in your chosen specialist area or in general practice.

On successful completion of foundation training, doctors continue training in either a specialist area of medicine or in general practice. The area of medicine you choose will determine the length of training required before you can become a senior doctor. In general practice, the training is of three years' duration; while in general surgery, for example, the training is eight years in duration.

During postgraduate medical training, doctors learn and practise increasingly advanced areas of knowledge and skills in their chosen specialty or general practice in order for them to be able to undertake senior doctor roles once training is completed. Postgraduate training is overseen by the Postgraduate Medical Education and Training Board.

On successful completion of postgraduate training, doctors gain entry to either the GMC specialist register or general practitioner register and are able to apply for a senior post as a consultant or a GP principal. You should note that all doctors are expected to demonstrate continually their fitness to practise medicine, and so learning continues throughout your career as a doctor.

Related Degrees
Complementary Medicine Practice; Medicine (first year entry).

Suggested Reading
Becoming a Doctor: is Medicine really the career for you?
- Matt Green, Tom Nolan, Alex Young and Will Dougal, BPP Learning Media, 2011
Learning Medicine
- Peter Richards et al, Cambridge University Press, 2008
Getting into Medical School
- James Barton and Simon Horner, Trotman Education, 2014
The Essential Guide to Becoming a Doctor
- Adrian Blundell et al, Wiley-Blackwell, 2010
Becoming a Doctor
- downloadable from the BMA website below
So you want to be a Doctor?
- Harveer Dev et al, OUP Oxford, 2013

Further Information
British Medical Association
www.bma.org.uk
Association for the Study of Medical Education
www.asme.org.uk
Irish Medical Organisation
www.imo.ie
Royal College of Physicians of Ireland
www.rcpi.ie
Biomedical Admissions Test
www.admissionstestingservice.org/for-test-takers/bmat/about-bmat
UK Clinical Aptitude Test
www.ukcat.ac.uk

Microbiology

Original article by Professor F G Priest, Heriot-Watt University

Introduction

Microbiology concerns the study of micro-organisms (bacteria, mycelial fungi, yeast and viruses), which affect man in a number of ways, both beneficial and detrimental. Their metabolic activities are responsible for essential (or undesirable) processes which occur in the environment, or can be exploited for the production of compounds (including chemicals, hormones, antibiotics and enzymes) which are of use in the modern world. Micro-organisms are also the causative agents of disease in humans, animals and plants. The combined biochemical and genetic/molecular biological approaches to studying the functions of micro-organisms have led to an understanding of metabolic and disease mechanisms, with the real prospect of effective exploitation and control of microbial activities on a previously unimagined scale.

Degree Courses

Microbiology is a very broad discipline, incorporating aspects of biochemistry, molecular and cell biology, genetics and taxonomy (classification), and a microbiologist may specialise in areas such as food, industrial or clinical microbiology. Training is given in scientific methods and procedures to enable graduates to pursue careers in industry, research laboratories, or to continue with postgraduate training in microbiology or a related discipline. The learning experience involves use of tutorials, seminars, assignments, laboratory work, lectures, fieldwork, industrial visits, and literature and research projects. The particular flavour of a course will depend on the nature of the institution; for example, in a medical school environment there is likely to be more emphasis on clinical aspects of the subject.

At Heriot-Watt University, the Biological Sciences (Microbiology) course provides a thorough general training in the physiology, ecology and biotechnological applications of micro-organisms. It focuses particularly on microbes as producers, as spoilage agents of food, as components of the environment, and as agents of disease, with emphasis on new and emerging diseases. The course aims to provide knowledge and understanding of the microbiological sciences, and sufficient training in scientific methods and procedures to advance to a career in relevant industries, postgraduate training or other spheres of research.

The first and second years of the four-year Honours degree are the same as Biological Sciences. In the third year, the Microbiology course introduces detailed analysis of microbial systems, in particular: Microbiological Aspects of Food and Food Safety; Microbial Pathology and Infectious Diseases; and Molecular Biology, including Genetic Engineering.

Fourth Year students are introduced to advanced topics in microbiology through a choice of modules dealing with: Microbial Interactions with the Human Body During Disease; New and Emerging Diseases; Microbial Growth in the Environment and Molecular Biology; and Genomics. A laboratory-based research project introduces practical techniques at an advanced level.

Other specialisms are available elsewhere.

Career Opportunities

Many graduates enter industries concerned with drugs and agricultural chemicals, biotechnology, food processing, brewing, pest control, sewage and water. Hospitals use graduates in research and analytical diagnostic work. Work in government and private institutions can involve cancer research, entomology, timber technology, plant pathology and conservation. Others take higher degrees and can go on to university teaching. Many also enter the general graduate market for administrative, financial and managerial careers.

Related Degrees

Medical Microbiology; Virology; Environmental Microbiology; Biotechnology.

Suggested Reading

Microbes and Man
- John Postgate, Cambridge University Press, 2000

Molecular Biology of the Cell
- Bruce Alberts et al, Garland, 2008

Brock Biology of Microorganisms
- Michael Madigan, John Martinko, Kelly Bender, Daniel Buckley and David Stahl, Pearson, 2014

Practical Skills in Biomolecular Sciences
- Rob Reed, Jonathan Weyers, Allan Jones, David Holmes, Pearson, 2012

Further Information

Society for General Microbiology
www.sgm.ac.uk

Society for Applied Microbiology
www.sfam.org.uk

Federation of European Microbiological Societies
www.fems-microbiology.org

Microbiology Career Portal, Ireland
http://microbiology.ie

Irish Society of Clinical Microbiologists
www.iscm.ie

Modern Languages

Original article by Professor (Emeritus) Dennis Ager, Aston University

Introduction

Despite the title, no degree courses are limited to the study of a foreign language. They involve the student in learning one or more languages but also in covering a programme of literary studies or studies of linguistics, history, politics or social and economic structure of the relevant country. The reason for this is that learning a language at an advanced level is a matter also of learning to see the world the way others see it, from within their own cultural and historical traditions. Ideally, of course, a graduate in languages would be an expert in the history of the relevant country; in its present-day political, social and economic problems and in its relations with other countries; in its cultural, literary, intellectual and artistic achievements; and be able to assess and compare these with a similar awareness of his own country. In practice, within a three- or four-year degree course, some selection has to be made and a lot of ground left to the initiative of the individual student.

It is possible to start a language course from scratch at most universities and colleges, although rarely in French or German. Success in language learning comes easily to some, who have an ear for the sound patterns of different languages and are able to reproduce particular sounds accurately and to perceive and use the quirks of different grammatical rules very quickly. There are few people who are unable to achieve something approaching perfection in the linguistic skills in a given language; the recipe is a mixture of high motivation, persistence, intelligence and, above all, practice. Modern learning aids can speed up the process, as can carefully designed teaching sequences; but there is no substitute for understanding that a language is a means of communication between human beings, and that the spoken language is more important than the written. In a degree course, however, one is often dealing with more written material than spoken; and the necessity for precision and often finicky accuracy which is a characteristic of some languages in their written form imposes a discipline which is not necessarily characteristic of the spoken language.

Degree Courses

At degree level, mastery of the skills of speaking, writing, reading and listening to a given language itself is often accompanied by practice in such skills as translating and interpreting. Departments vary in the importance they accord to the language skills: some delegate all the learning work to a language centre; others carry out all the work in the language. Many courses now last for four years, with an integrated year abroad - an essential experience for the linguist.

The language may be studied in order to understand its literature. It is usual to provide general survey courses, showing the nature of the literary production of the relevant country over, say, the last 400 years, and in addition to ask students to examine an author, or sometimes even one noteworthy book, in considerable depth. Departments with literary interests may concentrate on one aspect, theme or period.

Alternatively, the 'content' may be oriented towards the specific society - its institutions, politics, economy and international relations. There is usually some history; linguistics may be important. Students often research and write a mini-thesis in the last year.

Universities differ in orientation and course content: there are also differences of course structure to be aware of. You can study one language or two. It is often possible to study one language plus another subject e.g. Popular Music and French, German and History of Science. A popular combination is a language plus business studies or economics. European Studies degrees are popular. Finally, languages often find a place within degrees in other subjects: historians find a knowledge of one or more invaluable, but their requirement is for reading ability; engineers need languages but their prime need is for enough to get the gist of specialist reports plus enough spoken foreign language to understand the main point of a conversation.

Career Opportunities

Modern languages currently enjoy one of the highest employment rates of all degree programmes. Language skills are in scarce supply and can be used in almost any job. Studying a language clearly makes you a communicator, both orally and in writing. Additional skills gained through a language degree include the ability to: gather information, assess and interpret it; lead and participate in discussions and groups; organise workload and work to deadlines; develop opinions and propose ideas; read pages of text and pick out the essential points. On top of this, a year spent abroad during your degree should give you insight into another culture, help you adapt to new and changing surroundings and give you the chance to work both in a team and independently. These skills have value in a job market which is becoming increasingly global and will be appreciated by employers, whatever career you go into.

Related Degrees

French; German; Italian; Spanish; Dutch; Modern Greek; Russian; Scandinavian Languages; Slavonic and Eastern European Languages; Oriental Studies; Chinese; Japanese; Asian Languages; African; Arabic; Persian; Turkish; Hebrew; Arabic/Middle Eastern/Islamic Studies; Latin American Studies.

Suggested Reading

We suggest that, in preparation for a course in modern languages, you should visit a country in which your preferred language is spoken and immerse yourself in its culture and day-to-day life.

Language and Power in the Modern World
- Mary Talbot, Karen Atkinson and David Atkinson, Edinburgh University Press, 2003

Languages and Careers Pack
- produced by CILT with the CfBT Education Trust, available through Central Books:
www.centralbooks.co.uk

The Linguist (magazine)
- published by the Chartered Institute of Linguists. Subscribe via the website below

Further Information

Languages Work
www.languageswork.org.uk .

CILT - National Centre for Languages
www.cilt.org.uk

University Council of Modern Languages
www.ucml.ac.uk

Institute of Translation and Interpreting
www.iti.org.uk

Chartered Institute of Linguists
www.iol.org.uk

Irish Translators' and Interpreters' Association
www.translatorsassociation.ie

Music

Original article by Dr Christopher Mark, Department of Music, University of Surrey

Introduction

Music has undergone a considerable amount of change within the last 10 years or so, reflecting the diverse forms of contemporary music making and the pluralism of post-modern thinking about music and its place in society.

Whereas performance once seemed to be regarded as beneath the dignity of people engaged in lofty musical thought, such is the importance now given to it in university departments that many who intend to become professional performers choose a university rather than a music-college education. The range of subjects that can be studied is wider than ever, too. Western art music from ancient times to the present day still forms the backbone of the historical and analytical studies in most music degree courses, but an increasing number of departments offer units or modules in popular and non-western music. Tuition in composition, which has always been central to the university curriculum, is usually available (several of the country's finest composers hold senior positions in university departments), and performance of student compositions is strongly encouraged. Composition is one area in which computer-based technology has had a big impact, and many departments possess fine electronic-music studios.

Music can be studied either as a single-honours subject or, in some universities, in conjunction with another subject such as English or a European language. Combinations with science subjects are also possible.

Along with A levels or Higher Grades/equivalent, evidence of instrumental or vocal proficiency (Grade 7 or 8 in Associated Board exams) is required. Some departments call candidates to a selection interview, during which they may be auditioned and tested on general musical knowledge and harmony.

Degree Courses

The first year of courses is usually taught as a foundation year, consisting of overview history courses covering most of the Western art-music repertoire (sometimes with particular attention being paid to twentieth-century music), aural training, harmony and counterpoint, analysis, performance (individual and ensemble), and keyboard harmony. The subsequent years normally allow specialisation - typically in performance, composition, or musicology - with a good deal of choice of units/modules in historical, aesthetic, or analytical subjects. Teaching modes differ according to the level and the subject, but include lectures, seminars led by students, and one-to-one tutorials and instrumental lessons. Many departments have resident professional musicians who, in addition to performing and teaching individuals, coach instrumental ensembles. Types of assessment vary from department to department and from module to module, but you can expect a mixture of course work (ranging from short essays and harmony and counterpoint exercises to substantial projects) and examinations.

Opportunities for performance abound: orchestras, chamber orchestras, wind and jazz bands, choral societies, and chamber choirs are run either by departments or student societies. Some of these ensembles are run by student officers, allowing those interested in a career in arts administration to gain useful experience, and some are conducted by (usually more senior) students. But only part of the performing activity of a department is 'official': ad hoc ensembles of various sizes are the lifeblood of many lunchtime concert programmes.

It is important to research each prospectus with great care to ensure your interests and skills will flourish - and in addition to attend open days whenever possible.

Career Opportunities

Music-related posts include music retailing, broadcasting, publishing, musical journalism, librarianship, information services and cathedral organist. Music graduates tend to show considerable resourcefulness in finding jobs in administration, finance, commerce, industry and government.

Competition for careers in music performance can be fierce and the pay is generally below that of other jobs requiring similar levels of skill, training and expertise. To succeed, you must have more than talent alone; you must also have absolute dedication and determination. To get work, you have to be known and this means taking every opportunity - concerts, auditions, awards, bursaries and competitions - to show that you are worth engaging. Even after becoming established, you would find that earning a living as a performer - out of recordings, broadcasts and concerts - is hard work. Many performers combine a performing career with teaching or other work in the community, perhaps as a music therapist. Job prospects for classroom teachers are good, since the demand for music teachers exceeds the supply.

Related Degrees

Music Technology; Music (Performing Arts); Music Production; Creative Music Technology; Electronic Engineering and Music; Popular Music; Jazz Studies; Electronic Music; Music Theatre; Musicianship (Band); Musicology; Music and Sound Recording.

Suggested Reading

How Music Works: a listener's guide to harmony, keys, broken chords, perfect pitch and the secrets of a good tune
- John Powell, Particular Books, 2010

Performing Rites: Evaluating Popular Music
- Simon Frith, Oxford, 1998

Who needs Classical Music?: Cultural Choice and Musical Values
- Julian Johnson, OUP USA, 2011

All You Need to Know about the Music Business
- Donald S Passman, Viking, 2014

New Penguin Dictionary of Music
- Paul Griffiths, Penguin, 2006

Music: A Very Short Introduction
- Nicholas Cook, Oxford, 2000

Preparing for Success: a Practical Guide for Young Musicians
- Susan Hallam and Helena Gaunt, Institute of Education, 2012

How to Make It in the Music Business
- Sian Pattenden, Virgin Books, 2007

Further Information

Incorporated Society of Musicians
www.ism.org

Musicians' Union
www.musiciansunion.org.uk

Conservatoires UK Admissions Service
www.cukas.ac.uk

Royal Irish Academy of Music
www.riam.ie

Neuroscience

Original article by Dr S Barasi, School of Biosciences, Cardiff University

Introduction

The human brain contains about 10^{12} neurones making multiple connections. Our understanding of how this extraordinarily complex arrangement of neurones functions is still rudimentary. Neuroscience is the study of how the nervous system responds to incoming sensory information and organises and executes its response. Study of the human nervous system is further complicated by the need to understand mood, memory and the ageing process, together with the response of the system to infection and accidental damage. Interest in neuroscience has expanded dramatically in the last two decades, and increases in our understanding of how the brain functions in health and disease have been translated into major advances in the treatment of many diseases of the nervous system.

Degree Courses

The discipline of neuroscience includes contributions from a wide range of traditional disciplines such as anatomy, biochemistry, physiology and psychology. Neuroscience courses vary considerably in emphasis and content, so it is vital to study course contents and teaching/laboratory systems in prospectuses and ideally via open day visits.

Cardiff, for example, offers a variety of three- four- and five-year courses in Biomedical Science (Neuroscience). The longest course starts with a preliminary year, offering students who lack the right A levels or equivalent the opportunity to take modules in Biosciences, Chemistry, Maths and Physics. On successful completion of the preliminary year, you would automatically progress into the first year of your chosen degree programme. It also features, like the four-year programme, a professional training year spent in a laboratory in an academic, clinical or a commercial biomedical setting in the UK, Europe or further afield. You would explore a neuroscience-related problem at first hand under the guidance of an experienced neuroscientist. The academic and career benefits of such a year are significant and well-established.

The main three-year programme is a multidisciplinary course, which includes contributions from the Schools of Biosciences, Psychology, Medicine and Optometry. On this course, you would study human physiology, anatomy, pharmacology and neuroscience in Year One before specialising in neuroscience in Years Two and Three. The neuroscience course also offers you the opportunity to follow a psychology or a non-psychology route through the degree during Year Two and the Final Year, depending on your interests. Year One is common to 12 different Bioscience degrees, giving you considerable flexibility of choice. At the end of the first year, you can continue with your original degree choice or change to one of the other programmes served by the common first year.

In your second year, you take modules such as membrane physiology, human neuroanatomy, central nervous system pharmacology, signalling in endocrine systems and experimental synaptic physiology. The Final Year gives you an opportunity to immerse yourself in your chosen field by following a series of advanced research-led modules. These are designed to develop your ability to analyse complex experimental or technical data and to expose you to the central concepts at the cutting-edge of your discipline. You also gain experience of contemporary research through attending a selection of seminars given by international leaders in their fields. The Biology in Society Module equips you both philosophically and ethically for relating your subject to the future challenges of society. You must also produce an original dissertation based either on a laboratory project, an extensive literature analysis or an exercise relating to science teaching/pedagogic research or public engagement.

Career Opportunities

The course provides a good foundation for all, who might want to go on to study Medicine or any of the Healthcare Disciplines.

Other graduates frequently progress to higher degrees (PhD) with a view to becoming professional scientists. Others enter the pharmaceutical or pharmacological industry, the NHS, medical research, teaching or enter the general graduate field for careers in administration, finance, management and so on.

Related Degrees

Cellular Pathology; Neuroscience with Study in Industry; Cognitive Science; Neuroscience with Psychology.

Suggested Reading

Neuroscience: Exploring the Brain
- Mark Bear, Barry Connors and Michael Paradiso, Lippincott Williams and Wilkins, 2015

Thinking Fast and Slow
- Daniel Kahneman, Penguin Books, 2012

Neuroscience - science of the brain: an introduction for young students
- Richard Morris and Marienne Fillenz, BNA, 2003, downloadable from the BNA website below

Neuroscience – unravelling the mysteries of the brain: a career guide for students
- downloadable from the BNA website below

The Brain: A Very Short Introduction
- Michael O'Shea, OUP Oxford, 2006

Further Information

British Neuroscience Association
www.bna.org.uk

Institute of Neuroscience, Trinity College Dublin
www.tcd.ie/Neuroscience

Nursing

Original article by Ken Reynolds, specialist writer on careers and higher education

Introduction

Nurses work in a demanding profession, combining the art of caring with the science of health attainment, maintenance and restoration. To work as a nurse in the UK National Health Service (NHS), you must hold a degree or diploma in nursing (a 'pre-registration programme'), leading to registration with the Nursing and Midwifery Council (NMC). Nursing attracts people from all walks of life and so groups of student nurses are made up of a mixture of ages, sexes and cultures.

Degree Courses

It is important to note that diploma courses have now been phased out, with the effect that new entrants to the nursing profession must take a degree. As we go to press, we await developments regarding a government proposal that would require all would-be nurses to spend up to a year gaining basic healthcare experience before starting their degree.

Nursing degree programmes are normally three years in length (full-time; five to six years part-time) and are offered in four branches - adult, children (paediatric), learning disability and mental health. You normally need to decide before applying which of the four branches you wish to train for, although some Higher Education Institutions (HEIs) offer you the flexibility to select your branch after having started the course. You should note that some degree programmes last four years, while there are accelerated programmes for graduates who already hold a health-related degree. You are therefore strongly recommended to contact the HEI(s) that you are considering before making your application.

You would gain experience in a variety of care settings, including hospitals, nursing homes and the community.

The three-year course is divided into two distinct parts:

- the first year includes core issues and topics, together with experience of a wide variety of care environments. The year focuses upon the concept of health through study of the biological and social sciences, professional studies and communication skills. Placements are based in both hospital and community settings. Depending on the range of courses offered by your chosen HEI, you may share a common foundation programme with, say, medical, physiotherapy, radiography and biomedical science students

- the second part concentrates more on specific branch subjects and practice placements. You will develop skills in, knowledge about and understanding of your chosen branch of nursing. If, for example, you choose to go into mental health nursing, the placements will be mainly concentrated in that environment, and will focus on patients with mental health problems. However, certain aspects of training will be common to all branches

Career Opportunities

Once you have successfully completed your pre-registration programme and registered with the NMC, you can apply for nursing posts.

In the adult branch of nursing, it is possible to work in hospitals or in the community - in patients' homes, attached to a health centre or in nursing homes. Once qualified, many nurses take extra courses to specialise in areas such as cancer care, women's health, accident and emergency, critical care, practice nursing, health visiting or school nursing.

In the children's branch of nursing, you would work with 0 to 18 year-olds in a variety of settings, from specialist baby care units to adolescent services. Children react to illness in a very different way from adults, which is why they need to be cared for and supported by specially trained nurses who understand their particular needs. Children's nurses also support, advise and educate parents and other close relatives. Once qualified, it is possible to specialise in hospital and community settings in areas such as burns and plastics, intensive care, child protection and cancer care.

In the learning disability branch, you would help your patients to live independent and fulfilling lives. This may involve working with people in supported accommodation - typically three to four people with learning disabilities live together in flats or houses with 24-hour support. Some nurses work with individuals who require more intensive support - in hospitals, for example, or in specialist secure units for offenders with learning disabilities. Others specialise in areas such as epilepsy management or working with people with sensory impairment.

Mental health nurses work with GPs, psychiatrists, social workers and others to co-ordinate the care of people suffering from mental illness. The vast majority of people with mental health problems live in the community. Nurses plan and deliver care for people living in their own home, in small residential units or specialist hospital services. Some are based in health centres. It is possible to develop expertise in areas such as rehabilitation, child and adolescent mental health, substance misuse and working with offenders.

Healthcare is constantly developing, the technology is improving, and the needs of the population are changing. Once qualified in any branch, you must keep yourself up to date with healthcare issues and practice. This will be required by the NMC and encouraged by your employer.

Related Degrees
Midwifery education is also available at degree level. You will learn the theory and practical skills required to care for pregnant women, delivering babies, educating and supporting parents. The social, political and cultural issues affecting maternity care are also covered.

Suggested Reading
The Student Nurse Handbook: a Survival Guide
- Bethann Siviter, Bailliere Tindall, 2013

Careers Uncovered: Nursing and Midwifery
- Marie Borrego and Jim Bird, Trotman, 2010

Getting into Nursing and Midwifery Courses
- Wendy Reed, Trotman, 2013

Nursing Practice: Hospital and Home - The Adult
- Margaret Alexander et al, Churchill Livingstone, 2006

Further Information
NHS Nursing Careers
http://nursing.nhscareers.nhs.uk
Nursing and Midwifery Council
www.nmc-uk.org
Royal College of Nursing
www.rcn.org.uk
Nursing and Midwifery Board of Ireland
www.nursingboard.ie/en/careers.aspx

Occupational Safety, Health and Environment

Original article by Dr Adrian Richardson, Faculty of Health and Environment, Leeds Metropolitan University

Introduction

Occupational safety and health is a subject rarely out of the news and there is great demand in industry, commerce and the public sector for individuals to work as health and safety advisers and managers. Understanding and managing risk is at the very core of the profession, from the impact on employees to financial consequences for the organisation. Courses at degree level are still rare at present but the number is growing. Look out for course providers enjoying strong relationships with employers and offering accreditation by the Chartered Institution of Occupational Safety and Health (IOSH). These factors normally combine to mean that graduates are extremely successful at obtaining relevant employment.

Degree Courses

Here are examples of three current degree programmes, featuring different methods of delivery.

The first is a two-year full-time BSc Hons degree, with course modules including: Environmental Control, Organisation and Safety Management; Toxicology, Occupational Health and Safety Surveillance; Health and Safety Regulation Strategies; and Professional Practice.

Our second example is a one-year full-time or two-year part-time degree which recognises the level of experience and practice you may have gained through employment or education. It focuses on operational risk management of workplace hazards and is aimed at professionals who wish to raise their academic and professional standing. It is also suitable for those who wish to transfer from associate professions, who already hold a graduate or postgraduate qualification in engineering or in healthcare, for example, and have an interest in developing competency in this area.

It is important to note that this is a 'top-up' qualification, meaning that you must already be able to demonstrate appropriate learning to access the third year of a degree. You may, for example, have successfully completed a foundation degree or HND, years one and two of a degree course, or have existing health and safety or nursing qualifications

Compulsory modules include: Occupational Safety and Health Management and Law; Occupational Hygiene, Health and Ergonomics; Workplace Health and Safety; Risk Management and Occupational Psychology; Environmental Assessment and Management; and Toxicology and Science Foundation.

Our final example is another 'top-up' qualification but is this time based on distance learning and can take anything from one year to five years to complete. As in the previous example, you should already have a degree or equivalent in an appropriate science- or engineering-related subject, HND/foundation degree or a relevant diploma in an Occupational Safety and Health (OSH) field, with evidence of having gained substantial knowledge, skills and experience.

Course content includes: Introduction to Occupational Safety Practice; Environmental Industrial Pollution; Chemical Hazards; Ergonomics; Physical Agents; Environmental Industrial Management; Management of Risk; and a Dissertation.

All these courses are accredited by IOSH and offer practical hands-on experience alongside your studies in the area of health and safety management. This means that, after a period of individual professional development, you will be able to apply for IOSH Chartered Member status. You may also be eligible for chartered membership of the British Occupational Hygiene Society.

Career Opportunities

Previous graduates are now working as health and safety professionals across a wide range of industries, including road transport and logistics, rail transport and infrastructure, construction, demolition and power generation. Others are working as regulators with the Health and Safety Executive or Local Authorities. If you are already working as a health and safety professional, a degree course offers opportunities for professional and personal development to enhance your career prospects, such as becoming an independent consultant.

Actual job titles include: safety officer, care coordinator, union representative, health and safety manager, and occupational hygienist. Opportunities exist within the private and public sectors, both nationally and internationally.

Related Degrees

Environmental Health; Human Resource Management; Consumer and Trading Standards.

Suggested Reading

Principles of Health and Safety at Work
- Allan St John Holt and Jim Allen, Routledge, 2014

Essentials of Health and Safety at Work
- HSE Books, 2006

Health and Safety in Brief
- John Ridley, Butterworth-Heinemann, 2008

Introduction to Health and Safety at Work
- Phil Hughes and Ed Ferrett, Butterworth-Heinemann, 2011

Further Information

British Safety Council
www.britsafe.org

Chartered Institution of Occupational Safety and Health
www.iosh.co.uk

British Occupational Hygiene Society – Chartered Society for Worker Health Protection
www.bohs.org

Health and Safety Executive
www.hse.gov.uk

Safety and Health Practitioner
www.shponline.co.uk

Health and Safety Authority, Ireland
www.hsa.ie

Occupational Therapy

Original article adapted, with permission, from material supplied by the College of Occupational Therapists

Introduction

Think of the tasks that you do every day, from getting up in the morning, getting washed and dressed and preparing and eating a meal. How, when and where you do these things are unique to you. Think about your likes and dislikes, choosing and wearing your favourite clothes, preparing and eating your favourite meal and going out with friends. Think about how you would feel if you were no longer able to perform everyday activities for yourself. An occupational therapist would look at your lifestyle and help you to live as independently as possible.

As an occupational therapist, you would use your knowledge and skills with people of all ages - from small children to the very elderly - who, for many reasons, are unable to continue with their normal lives and routines. They may have physical or psychological problems. Even people whose difficulties are mostly physical may lack confidence and motivation or they may be depressed by their illness or injury. Occupational therapy covers an extremely wide range of work and career options, and therefore aims to attract a broad cross-section of applicants. The profession is recruiting a larger proportion of men and is currently building a workforce that better reflects Britain's wide cultural diversity.

Degree Courses

You can take a BSc (Hons) in occupational therapy with the following options:

- 3 years full-time (four years in Scotland)

- 2 years accelerated (if you already have a first degree)

- 4 years in-service or part-time for those who have the support of their employer in further training. For part-time programmes applicants do not need to be employed in health or social care

The accelerated postgraduate programmes are for students who already hold a degree, usually in a related field, and have some experience of working in health or social care settings.

The programmes combine both practical and academic study. Academic components include biological sciences (anatomy and physiology), behavioural sciences (psychology and sociology), occupational therapy knowledge and skills, creative and management skills, therapeutic interventions, environmental adaptations and research.

A minimum of 1,000 hours (approximately one third of the course) is spent on practice placements - gaining experience in the main areas of occupational therapy, usually in physical rehabilitation, learning disabilities, mental health or social care and increasingly in new and emerging areas. Students learn how to assess and treat people, normally under the guidance of an occupational therapist, and treat a small caseload of clients under supervision.

All UK programmes are approved by the Health and Care Professions Council (HCPC - the statutory regulatory body for occupational therapists) to meet their minimum standards for education, and are also accredited by the College of Occupational Therapists, meeting its higher standards. Accreditation by the College brings with it automatic approval by the World Federation of Occupational Therapists.

All the programmes are pre-registration, which means that upon successful completion of the programme, you will be able to apply to the HCPC as a registrant to practise as an occupational therapist in the UK.

Career Opportunities

Traditionally, the majority of occupational therapists work in the National Health Service (NHS). Increasingly, however, qualified occupational therapists have found opportunities in other work settings, and this trend seems likely to continue. As a qualified occupational therapist, you can consider working in different job roles, as a practitioner, researcher, manager, lecturer or consultant. You can choose to work in different fields, such as social care, mental health, education, learning disabilities or physical rehabilitation. There are job opportunities in a number of settings including: charities and voluntary agencies; commercial and industrial organisations; disabled living centres; equipment companies; government agencies; housing departments; local community services; NHS and private hospitals; private practice; schools, colleges and universities; social services and social work departments; wheelchair services; hostels for the homeless; and residential care homes.

You also have a wide choice of practice specialisms to choose from, such as eating disorders, hand therapy and substance misuse. You may wish to specialise in working with children, adults or older people. You can also decide whether you want to work for someone else or for yourself, whether you want to work in the community, be based in a hospital, or work in a university educating future occupational therapists.

Related Degrees

Sports Therapy; Sport and Exercise Therapy; Sports Therapy and Rehabilitation.

Suggested Reading

Occupational therapy: new perspectives
- J Creek (Ed), Wiley-Blackwell, 1998

Theoretical basis of occupational therapy
- Mary Ann McColl, Mary Law and Debra Stewart, Slack, 2015

A Journey from Prescription to Self Health: a history of occupational therapy in the United Kingdom during the 20th century and a source book of archival material
- Ann Wilcock, COT, 2002

Occupational Therapy Career Handbook 2015/2016
- downloadable from the COT website below

Further Information

British Association of Occupational Therapists/College of Occupational Therapists
www.cot.co.uk

National Health Service Careers
www.nhscareers.nhs.uk

Health and Care Professions Council
www.hcpc-uk.org

Association of Occupational Therapists of Ireland
www.aoti.ie

Optometry

Original article by Mark Dunne, Aston University

Introduction

Optometrists are primary healthcare specialists, trained to examine the eyes to detect defects in vision, signs of injury, ocular diseases or abnormality and problems with general health. A detailed examination of the eye can reveal conditions such as high blood pressure or diabetes. Optometrists make a diagnosis, offer advice and, when necessary, prescribe, fit and supply contact lenses or glasses. Referrals for specialist advice may be required, patients may require a corrective lens or no further treatment.

It is a good idea to contact local optometrists to see if a practice can offer a period of work experience before you make a full career commitment.

Degree Courses

To become an optometrist you will need to obtain a degree from one of the nine UK universities that run the course; Anglia Ruskin, Aston, Bradford, Cardiff, City, Glasgow Caledonian, Manchester, Plymouth and Ulster. Entry to these courses requires good A levels, higher grades or equivalent, of which at least two are in the sciences. One-year foundation courses are available for those lacking a science background. There is also one course in the Republic of Ireland, at the Dublin Institute of Technology.

Optometry courses are typically three years full time (four at Glasgow Caledonian), after which you are awarded a BSc (Hons) degree. Aston and Manchester also offer the option of a fourth year Master level course, leading to the award of MOptom. Optometry requires a detailed understanding of the functions of the human eye, both as an anatomical structure and as an optical system. The course typically covers three elements: basic studies (such as biochemistry, microbiology, pharmacology, physiology, anatomy, perception and pure and visual optics), optometry and clinical practice. The former are predominant during the early years, with the emphasis moving towards clinical practice in later years.

In the first year you will cover basic studies such as clinical optometry, pure and visual optics, general and ocular anatomy and physiology, physiology of vision and perception, learning and key skills development, ophthalmic lenses and dispensing, and biochemistry.

In your second year you will study further modules in ophthalmic lenses and dispensing, and in physiology of vision and perception, as well as further modules including assessment of binocular vision, low vision and ageing, general and ocular pharmacology, contact lens practice, and clinical methodology and statistics.

The final year is focused towards clinical practice, preparing you for employment. Subjects covered in the final year include general clinical practice, binocular vision and orthoptics, visual ergonomics, abnormal ocular conditions, advanced clinical practice, contact lens practice, law and optometric management, and a research project.

Career Opportunities

After graduation, you complete a Pre-Registration period of training, including work-based assessment and supervision by a registered optometrist, before taking a Final Assessment examination based on the General Optical Council Stage 2 core competencies for optometry. You can then register and practise optometry in your own right.

You may decide to continue your education towards obtaining a higher degree (Masters or Doctorate), which is traditionally research orientated. This, in turn, opens the door to careers in university or industrial research.

Once qualified, you have the opportunity to develop your interests in specialist aspects of practice such as paediatrics, contact lenses, low vision or sports vision. Optometrists can choose to practise in a number of settings, for example in independent or private practice, in a hospital eye department or in research or teaching.

Optometry courses typically claim 100% relevant employment or further study within six months of graduation.

Related Degrees
Ophthalmic Dispensing; Orthoptics.

Suggested Reading
The Professional Qualifying Examinations: A Survival Guide for Optometrists
- Frank Eperjesi et al, Butterworth-Heinemann, 2004

Fast Facts: Ophthalmology
- Anthony Pane and Peter Simcock, Health Press, 2006

Optometry A-Z
- Nathan Efron, Butterworth-Heinemann, 2006

A Career in Optometry
- careers information from the College of Optometrists website below

Further Information
Association of Optometrists
www.aop.org.uk

General Optical Council
www.optical.org

College of Optometrists
www.college-optometrists.org

New Dimensions in Optics
www.newdimensioninoptics.org

Association of Optometrists Ireland
www.optometrists.ie

Opticians Board, Ireland
www.opticiansboard.ie

Pharmacology

Original article by Dr Susan Duty and the late Dr Robin Hoult, King's College London

Introduction

Pharmacology concerns the uses of drugs and the ways in which they and other biologically active chemicals affect the body. Particular emphasis is on the molecular mechanisms by which drugs alter biological processes at the cell and tissue level. Thus the subject is highly relevant to everyday life, not only because of the enormously important health benefits which derive from the intentional therapeutic uses of drugs, but also because it sheds light on topical problems such as drug misuse and addiction. Pharmacology is also very closely related to toxicology - the science of poisons - which seeks to understand how toxicants produce their effects and which is also concerned with drug safety, testing and legislation issues.

The pace of research has accelerated in response to the application of molecular biology techniques: for example, the cloning of many hitherto inaccessible regulatory biomolecules and the use of expression systems to synthesise macromolecules and bioactive proteins that were previously unobtainable. Pharmacology is right at the cutting edge of medical science, playing a very important role not only in new drug development and healthcare but also in the study of disease processes themselves.

Degree Courses

The ever-changing nature of pharmacology has prompted the British Pharmacological Society to develop guidance on core curricula for undergraduate courses that include the subject in the UK. The aims of a typical course will be to develop your understanding of how medicines affect the body, how the body handles medicines and how new medicines are developed, as well as developing many practical and other key skills. The course would involve studying how the body works from the molecular level (e.g. how genes are switched on and off) to the whole body (e.g. what regulates blood pressure) and how diseases occur. You would study the actions of medicines in computer simulations, in cells and tissues from animals, possibly in whole animals, and in student volunteers. You need to understand how the whole body reacts to medicines from the point of view of effectiveness and safety. In addition, you would further your understanding of chemistry as you need to know the relationship between the structure of medicines and their actions.

The second and third years of most pharmacology degrees involve increasing specialisation within pharmacology as well as optional advanced courses in related disciplines. These advanced courses reflect the two different approaches to the study of pharmacology - the systematic one, which concerns the application of drugs to organ systems and disease treatment, and the analytical one, which is concerned with the way drugs work at the molecular level.

In some courses, you would have the valuable opportunity of an extra-mural year spent working in an industrial or academic research laboratory as part of a specialised research team. This is offered between the second and final years, and is an exciting and useful preparation for the final year's study as well as providing valuable perspectives for career opportunities. In many cases, you are placed in organisations abroad, including the EU, North America and the Far East, and language skills as well as technical benefits may accrue.

You can also combine a pharmacology degree with many other subjects, such as biochemistry, chemistry, foreign languages, immunology, management and physiology.

Do be aware that a BSc Pharmacology course is very different from a BSc Pharmacy course. A Pharmacy course aims to train someone so that they can work in a hospital pharmacy or chemist's shop or manufacture medicines in industry. This type of course would include pharmacology but also the formulation of medicines, chemical synthesis, microbiology and the social aspects of medicines.

Career Opportunities

Graduates often enter the pharmaceutical industry, where the degree is a good starting point for several positions such as marketing, medical information and product registration (none of which involve laboratory work) as well as research. Others enter alternative careers such as teaching, the civil service, business and publishing. A BSc in Pharmacology also enables students to gain a place for further study either towards a Masters or PhD (Doctorate) in a related research field, or for graduate entry to study Medicine or Dentistry.

Related Degrees

Pharmacology with Industrial Experience; Pharmacology with year abroad; Toxicology; Pharmacology with a Modern Language; Medical Chemistry.

Suggested Reading

Pharmacology
- Humphrey Rang, Maureen Dale et al, Churchill Livingstone, 2011

Careers with the Pharmaceutical Industry
- Peter Stonier, Wiley-Blackwell, 2003

Pharmacology for Pharmacy and the Health Sciences
- Michael Boarder, Phyllis Navti and David Newby, OUP, 2010

Pharmacology (Fast Track Pharmacy Series)
- Michael Randall, David Kendall and Stephen Alexander, Pharmaceutical Press, 2012

Pharmacology Condensed
- Maureen Dale, and Dennis Haylett, Churchill Livingstone, 2008

Further Information

British Pharmacological Society
www.bps.ac.uk

Careers in Pharmacology
www.careersinpharmacology.org

Department of Pharmacology, Trinity College Dublin
www.medicine.tcd.ie/pharmacology_therapeutics

European Association for Clinical Pharmacology and Therapeutics
www.eacpt.org

Pharmacy

Original article adapted with permission from material supplied by the Royal Pharmaceutical Society

Introduction

An expert in the field of drugs and medicines, the pharmacist may be involved in any aspect of their preparation and use, from the discovery and development of a medicine to its eventual supply to the patient and sometimes beyond, since she/he may well have a role in monitoring its effects.

Degree Courses

Accredited Pharmacy degree courses are currently offered at 25 universities in the United Kingdom (plus three provisionally accredited) and three in the Republic of Ireland. All UK courses last four years, are accredited by the General Pharmaceutical Council and lead to a Master of Pharmacy (MPharm) degree. To register and practise as a pharmacist after the degree, you must follow one year's pre-registration training in a community or hospital pharmacy and pass the General Pharmaceutical Council Examination. University admissions tutors will be looking for evidence that you are equipped to gain from and succeed in such a demanding and highly focused degree course. The surest but not the only indication of this comes from achieved or expected academic qualifications. The course is geared to students who arrive with A level/Higher/IB or equivalent chemistry plus other A level/Higher/IB or equivalent passes, especially useful being biology, physics and mathematics

The primary objective of the course is to provide the necessary theoretical knowledge, understanding and practical skills for the competent and successful practice of pharmacy. During the course, considerable emphasis is placed on the development of a professional attitude and responsibility through links with practising pharmacists.

Much of your learning will be case-based to ensure that the scientific and professional elements are integrated from day one. Within each module, you could expect to study elements of the following areas:

- **Pharmacology and therapeutics** – looking at diseases and their symptoms, therapeutic classes and drug examples
- **Biology and Physiology** – including the anatomy and function of the body and cell biology
- **Pharmaceutics** – the science of making medicines
- **Chemistry** – including physical chemistry and analysis, synthesis and chemical mechanisms, pharmacokinetics and natural products
- **Professionalism and leadership** – including personal development and law and ethics
- **Pharmacy practice** – looking at the key sectors of community, hospital and industrial pharmacy as well as giving you an insight into less known areas of pharmacy practice

You would concentrate in year one on the fundamentals of the main areas of the course: Chemistry, Pharmaceutics, Microbiology and Pharmacology. You would also begin to visit community and hospital pharmacies. Year two would see you consolidating the main areas of pharmacy and starting to explore some of the wider professional and sociological issues. You would begin to develop clinical skills to a much greater extent in year three, and would develop this much further in year four, with a variety of modules in advanced clinical pharmacy, healthcare policy and practice and future medicines.

Although the key areas of pharmacy are covered by all the degree courses, there may be a difference of emphasis depending on the school chosen and further information should be obtained from the schools themselves.

Career Opportunities

Pharmacists are experts in medicines and how they work, which opens up a number of career opportunities. Most pharmacists work in community and hospital pharmacies, but there are several other options available.

The traditional dispensing and advisory role associated with community pharmacy is evolving and pharmacists are playing a greater role in patient care. Some community pharmacists now have prescribing roles and are involved in screening programmes such as weight management counselling. Alongside patient care, there can also be possibilities on the business side of community pharmacy, with the chance to develop different skills such as financial and managerial. Community pharmacists can be self-employed or can work within a larger company.

Hospital pharmacists work as part of a healthcare team alongside doctors and nurses, offering their expertise to help select treatments for managing patient care. The role of hospital pharmacists is also developing, as technological advancements are giving pharmacists more time to work with patients on the wards. Hospital pharmacists have opportunities for career development through management or clinical specialism.

If you are interested in the research and development of new drugs you may consider industrial pharmacy. Industrial pharmacists work with scientists who specialise in other areas to discover safe and effective drugs.

Related Degrees

Pharmaceutical Science; Pharmaceutical Science with Year Abroad; Biopharmaceutical Science; Pharmaceutical Chemistry; Medicinal and Pharmaceutical Chemistry.

Suggested Reading

Careers with the Pharmaceutical Industry
- P D Stonier, Wiley, 2003

Interested in Pharmacy?
- careers leaflet downloadable from the RPS website at:
www.rpharms.com/careers-in-pharmacy/careers-materials.asp

Hospital Pre-registration Pharmacist Training
- Aamer Safdar and Shirley Ip, Pharmaceutical Press, 2009

The Pre-registration Interview
- Nadia Bukhari, Pharmaceutical Press, 2007

Further Information

Royal Pharmaceutical Society
www.rpharms.com
General Pharmaceutical Council
www.pharmacyregulation.org
Association of the British Pharmaceutical Industry Careers Site
http://careers.abpi.org.uk
National Pharmacy Association
www.npa.co.uk
Pharmaceutical Society of Ireland
www.thepsi.ie
Irish Pharmacy Union
www.ipu.ie

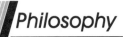

Philosophy

Original article by Antony Flew, formerly Professor of Philosophy, University of Reading

Introduction

It is difficult to explain to people who have never done any what, in this present sense, philosophy is. (Would you care to try to explain what mathematics would involve to someone who had been to a school in which no one had learnt any at all?) This difficulty is one of several good reasons why anyone considering this as a degree subject is well advised to try for one of the institutions - Keele, for instance, or Reading - giving students opportunities of sampling one or two new things before they have finally to commit themselves on what subject or subjects they will read for honours.

The distinguished Cambridge professor, G E Moore, always replied to the question, 'What is philosophy?' by pointing towards his bookshelves: 'It is what all those are about.' So let me too start by saying that philosophy is the main subject of most of the writings of Plato; of Aristotle's *Metaphysics* and *Nicomachean Ethics*; of large parts of the works of St Thomas Aquinas, Duns Scotus and William of Ockham; of the *Discourse* and *Meditations* of Descartes: of Berkeley's *Three Dialogues* and *Principles of Human Knowledge*; of Hume's *Inquiry concerning Human Understanding*; of Kant's *Critique of Pure Reason*; and finally, in more recent times, of Moore's own books, of Bertrand Russell's *Our Knowledge of the External World* and *Mysticism and Logic*, and of Wittgenstein's *Tractatus Logico-Philosophicus* and his posthumous *Philosophical Investigations*.

If you do decide to do philosophy you will certainly be introduced to many of these classics. However, unless and until you have been thus properly introduced, you had perhaps best stick to books written fairly recently, and books written as introductions. Try, for instance, Bertrand Russell The *Problems of Philosophy* (an OUP paperback); and/ or either Anthony O'Hear *What Philosophy Is* or Brenda Almond *Exploring Philosophy* (Blackwell). And, whatever you do, don't set out for an interview without readying yourself to say something lively about some philosophy book which you have recently worked through. They probably want to sign you up. But you do need to give them some help!

You will not find many facts in any philosophy book, and those which you do find will be mainly facts about what particular philosophers have said. What you should find is arguments, and the more the better. So one good test for telling whether you are a person who could become fascinated by philosophy is to ask yourself whether you care about the validity or invalidity of arguments, and the sufficiency or insufficiency of evidence offered, as well as about the truth or falsity of conclusions reached, and the acceptability or otherwise of cases presented. If you do not, then certainly philosophy is not for you.

Consider, for example, the much disputed issues of 'free will or predestination' and 'free will or determinism'. The strictly philosophical questions here are not the questions of theological or scientific fact. They are not, that is, the questions: whether on the first day of creation God wrote what the last day of reckoning shall read; nor whether everything that happens, including everything which people do, could on the basis of a full knowledge of the laws of nature and the past condition of the whole universe, in principle be predicted. They are, rather, the questions: whether the idea of a creator God - not only all foreseeing, but also the sustaining cause of our every action and our very existence - is logically compatible with the ideas of human responsibility and human choice; and whether the sciences, and in particular the human sciences, logically presuppose or imply some form of determinism. If so, is this a sort of determinism logically compatible with our everyday talk and assumptions about human choice and action?

The philosophical questions about free will and determinism and predestination, therefore, like other philosophical questions, though they may arise out of suggestions or discoveries about what is as a matter of fact the case, are themselves not questions of this factual sort, but questions about what does or does not follow from what, and what is or is not logically incompatible with what else. It is this fact which makes philosophy excellent pure mental training. Certainly it is not career-linked in the way in which law, say, and medicine both are. Certainly too it is not, unlike the usual school subjects, something from which graduates can hope to earn their livings by teaching. But when you are competing for any of the other jobs done by arts graduates there is no call whatever to be shy about admitting that you read philosophy.

Career Opportunities

Philosophy graduates seem to do well in finding employment in a wide range of careers. Their intellectual training is greatly valued.

Related Degrees

European Philosophy and Literature; Mental Philosophy; Ethics; Moral and Religious Studies; History and Philosophy of Science; Philosophy, Politics and Economics; Intellectual Ideas.

Suggested Reading

See paragraphs two and three opposite. You might also consider:

Reading Philosophy: Selected Texts with a Method for Beginners
- Samuel Guttenplan et al, Wiley-Blackwell, 2002

Philosophical Writing: An Introduction
- Aloysius P Martinich, Wiley-Blackwell, 2005

Philosophy in Practice: An Introduction to the Main Questions
- Adam Morton, Wiley-Blackwell, 2004

Philosophy: the Essential Study Guide
- Nigel Warburton, Routledge, 2004

Think: A Compelling Introduction to Philosophy
- Simon Blackburn, Oxford Paperbacks, 2001

Further Information

Philosophical Society of England
www.philsoceng.uk

Philosophy by Topic
http://users.ox.ac.uk/~worc0337/phil_topics.html

Irish Philosophical Society
www.irishphilosophicalsociety.ie

Limerick Philosophical Society
http://sites.google.com/site/limerickphilosophy

Physics

Professor Jim Al-Khalili OBE, Department of Physics, University of Surrey

Introduction

If you were asked to name three great scientists, whom would you choose? Einstein? Newton? Hawking? All three are physicists. Physics is regarded by many as the most fundamental of all the sciences; it deals with the deepest and most profound questions we can ask, whether they are about the nature of space and time, the search for the fundamental building blocks of matter, or the origins of the Universe at the Big Bang (or, possibly, even before). More broadly, physics provides the foundations for engineering, chemistry, computing, material science and biology. Even medicine would not be where it is today without physicists' discovery of x-rays, lasers and MRI scanners.

Many choose to study a physics degree because they are curious about the Universe. But physics is not only about finding answers to the most fundamental questions of existence. It also underpins so much of the technology we take for granted in the modern world; the principles of quantum physics are behind modern electronics, computers, mobile phones and iPods; physics put man on the moon and made the internet possible. Most importantly, physics will without doubt transform and shape tomorrow's world, from nuclear fusion to quantum computers.

Degree Courses

Wherever you choose to study physics, you will find you cover broadly similar core material; topics that any physics degree worth its salt must contain, such as electromagnetism, quantum mechanics, optics, thermodynamics, solid state physics, atomic, nuclear and particle physics and relativity theory. In addition to these there will be modules covering mathematics, computing, lab classes and data handling skills. Thereafter, many degree courses will have their own unique flavour. This will often reflect the research carried out at the university and will allow you to take optional modules, from biophysics to astrophysics, from philosophy to finance. Such options may be available for the beginning of the course if you enrol on a 'Physics with..' course. Many students will wish to keep their options open, however, by taking a 'straight' physics degree, but will then typically have a wide range of optional choices available to them by the time they reach their final year of study.

Most physics departments offer two types of undergraduate physics degrees, usually known as BSc and MPhys. BSc degrees provide ideal training for a wide range of career options. They traditionally involve three taught years of study, but often include an additional (optional) professional training year, usually between the second and third years of study, involving paid work in a company, organisation or research lab that gives students a taste of the 'real world' and the way their physics training can be applied. Such 'years out' significantly enhance the student's employability after graduation.

MPhys degrees take four years and are ideal for those students considering following a research career, possibly going on to a postgraduate degree. MPhys (sometimes called MSci) programmes differ from one university to the next. Some have four taught years, covering material in the final year that goes beyond a BSc. Others also offer periods of research away from lectures, either at the university or at an external organisation, often overseas. Such research placements can be crucial in helping the student decide whether a research career is right for them.

Career Opportunities

Physicists play a vital role in many technology-based industries, such as optoelectronics, nanotechnology, computing and renewable energy. Others work on investigating the universe; searching for extra-solar planets or looking for the remnants of the big bang. Many go on to apply their knowledge in healthcare (medical physics), or study the processes of the Earth (geophysics) and the climate (meteorology).

The knowledge and skills that studying physics develops are important in other areas as well. Predicting future market behaviour is vital in finance, and so a physicist's ability to model complex systems is particularly valued in this sector, while a logical approach and ability to understand new technology is useful in law, for example, when patenting new inventions.

Physics provides a broad training in skills that are valued by all employers; an ability to grasp concepts quickly, a determination to find coherent answers, along with problem solving, analytical, mathematical and IT skills. Work in any physics-related industry after your degree, and you will find that the skills and knowledge you gain from a physics degree will always help you whatever your chosen career path. Indeed, studying physics at degree level is a good way of keeping your options open.

Related Degrees

Physics with Astronomy; Physics with Astrophysics; Applied Physics; Experimental Physics; Theoretical Physics; Physics with Maths; Biophysics; Chemical Physics; Physics with Chemistry; Physics with Medical Physics; Physics with Optoelectronics; Physics with Photonics; Physics with Computing; Physics with Acoustics; Engineering Physics; Atmospheric Physics; Physics with Space Science; Physics with Satellite Technology; Environmental Physics; Physics with Languages; Physics with Education; Physics with Cosmology; Physics with Nuclear Astrophysics; Physics with Philosophy; Physics with Management; Physics with Finance.

Suggested Reading

Physics, Penguin Dictionary of
- Valerie Illingworth, Penguin, 2009

A Brief History of Time/The Universe in a Nutshell
- Stephen Hawking, Random House, 2013

University Physics with Modern Physics
- Hugh D Young and Roger A Freedman, Pearson Education, 2013

Further Information

Institute of Physics
www.iop.org

My Physics Course
www.myphysicscourse.org

Student Room, Physics Degree
www.thestudentroom.co.uk/wiki/Physics_Degree

Institute of Physics in Ireland
www.iopireland.org

Physiology

Original article by Dr D J Begley, King's College London

Introduction

"General physiology is the basic biological science toward which all others converge. Its problem is to determine the elementary conditions of vital phenomena." (Claude Bernard, 1865)

Physiology is undoubtedly the most open-ended of the biological sciences and for this reason is also probably the most challenging. A physiologist is constantly attempting to explain, by a careful and critical analysis of well-planned research and experiment, how organisms work. A physiologist can work at any number of levels within the organisation of a species. At the cellular level they can study how cells function or move, or how the nervous impulse is transmitted and how messages are received and interpreted by the cell. Alternatively, they may focus on individual organs or tissues of the body (eg the brain or the liver) or on complete systems (eg the nervous or endocrine), studying how they control and regulate function. Or their interest can be in how several organs and systems interact (eg to maintain the constancy of the composition of the blood) or in the important area of developmental physiology (ie how the fertilised egg interprets and unfolds its genetic potential and develops into the mature adult). Or they may study the organism as a whole and its responses to external stimuli and environmental change.

In recent years, interest has been concentrated on cellular physiology as powerful new research tools have increasingly miniaturised the scales at which living systems can be experimentally manipulated. Of course, there is still much to be discovered in other areas but studies into these must be built on firm foundations at cellular levels. Recent advances in cellular physiology have revolutionised the ways in which we examine and interpret higher function (eg in the working of the brain).

Because physiology forms the meeting point for a number of biological sciences, the physiologist utilises experimental methods and tools derived from related disciplines - for example the electron microscope from anatomy, radioactively labelled molecules from biochemistry, x-ray analysis from biophysics, and from pharmacology new substances which mimic or modify the action of natural molecules in the body. New applications of genetics such as transgenic animals are also becoming increasingly important. It also means that the physiologist's armoury of experimental techniques is constantly expanding.

Degree Courses

The content and structure of an undergraduate physiology or physiological science degree is very much dependent upon the university. The following outline gives an idea of typical course content and structure but you should look at individual university websites for more detailed information.

Physiology modules in the first year usually remain broad, ensuring that you gather a sound basic understanding of all aspects of the subject. Topics may include an introduction to the principles of cellular physiology and the functions of the major systems of the body (such as cardiovascular, respiratory, alimentary and the central nervous system).

In the second year, students begin to take a more in-depth look at specific areas of physiology, and consider recent advances within the field.

Physiology is very much a 'hands-on' subject, meaning that you would spend time in practical classes studying physiology in action. This might involve studying how the body reacts to different levels of exercise, measuring how quickly you can respond to a visual or auditory stimulus, or how your kidneys react when you drink different amounts and types of fluid.

During the first and second year of study, students are often required to choose from a selection of modules to study alongside and support their learning in physiology. Modules may include anatomy, molecular biology, psychology and pharmacology, amongst others; this provides an opportunity for you to tailor your degree to your career aspirations.

The final year of study focuses entirely on physiology, with an emphasis on in-depth training in specialist modules. Topics covered in year three usually reflect the research interests of the university. There is greater opportunity for private study in year three and students are expected to become familiar with reading and interpreting scientific literature; you would also be encouraged to attend seminars given by academics at the top of their field of physiology research.

A substantial research project usually forms a major component of the final year of study. At most universities this project is written up as a dissertation and presented orally to examiners.

In addition to the academic content, physiology courses develop IT knowledge and introduce students to new software packages. You should develop independent and team working skills, together with communication, analytical and time management skills.

A couple of universities now run a four-year programme in physiology, in which students can work towards gaining an MBiol integrated Master level degree. In the third year, you may undertake a one-year work placement, usually in paid employment in research (either in industry or another organisation).

Career Opportunities

Physiology forms an excellent platform to gain a further qualification such as an MSc or PhD, and for postgraduate entry into many courses including Medicine.

There is great demand for graduates in the biomedical and biomolecular sciences within the health services and in industry, particularly leading or working as part of research teams, and many students choose this career path. Industries employ bioscientists for research and development into pharmaceuticals, biotechnology, chemicals, cosmetics and toiletries, food and drink.

Apart from laboratory work, some physiology graduates choose to enter legal careers, using their scientific knowledge to provide patenting advice, others opt for such areas as scientific journalism or teaching biology at school/college level.

There are also diverse career opportunities away from science, all of which will call on the broad analytical and scientific skills developed as an undergraduate; graduates might, for example, embark on careers in management, consultancy, investment banking, accountancy, political research or IT.

Related Degrees

Human Physiology; Clinical Physiology; Cancer Research; Physiological Health; Animal Physiology; Sports Science; Psychology, Philosophy and Physiology.

Suggested Reading

Principles of Anatomy and Physiology
- Gerald Tortora and Bryan Derrickson, Wiley, 2011

Further Information

Physiological Society
www.physoc.org
Understanding Life
www.understanding-life.org
Federation of European Physiological Societies
www.feps.org

Physiotherapy

Original article written with the help of material supplied by the Chartered Society of Physiotherapy and the Admissions Tutor, School of Health Sciences, Faculty of Medicine and Dentistry, University of Birmingham

Introduction

Physiotherapists use physical means to help patients recover from injury or sickness, and assist them in rehabilitation after operations by restoring their muscle and other functions. Their main techniques involve therapeutic movement, electrotherapy, massage, manipulation, the use of vibration and certain types of radiation, e.g. infra-red. They also frequently work with sports persons, e.g. footballers or cricketers, to build up their strength, and thus avoid potential injury.

Physiotherapists are found almost everywhere in hospitals and the community. They are located in: *Outpatients*: treating spinal problems, arthritis, accidents, sports injuries; *Intensive care*: keeping limbs mobile, chests clear for unconscious patients; *Maternity*: ante-natal classes, exercise, posture.

Physiotherapy is a physically demanding profession. You would usually need to be generally fit and capable of moving and handling both equipment and patients. Offers made by universities may be subject to your passing a health screening medical examination, although applicants with a physical disability are advised to contact the admissions tutor at the relevant university. Sympathetic consideration will be given, with careful assessment of the disability to ensure that you can meet the demands of the course. Students with a visual impairment can train for physiotherapy with support from the Royal National Institute for the Blind.

Degree Courses

Qualifying physiotherapy degree programmes now exist in 33 schools/universities across the UK, with several other providers offering veterinary physiotherapy. The physiotherapy degree involves the study of clinical sciences such as anatomy, physiology and pathology while developing analytical and practical skills that will enable students to identify and resolve their clients' problems of movement and function following injury or disease. Most courses are of three and sometimes four years duration. Courses vary and it is essential to consult prospectuses to find out what each one covers.

A typical course is a three-year modular course (or four-year in Scotland) in which the emphasis is on small groups. The *First Year* is largely pre-clinical and includes studying anatomy and biomechanics in the human movement module, whilst physiology is studied with electrotherapy in the biomedical science module. A study of injury and disease is included alongside research method and behavioural science. (Later on, students are seconded to placements where they assess and treat patients under guidance.)

Students are later introduced to new areas of pathology, when disease processes are investigated and practical skills developed. The year is divided equally between the university and clinical work. In the *Third or Fourth Year* more specialist academic and practical work is introduced; students meet more complex clinical situations. This allows them to evaluate and modify treatment programmes in order to improve the standard of care. To develop research skills, each student completes a research dissertation.

Assessment for the final degree classification is by course work on both practical and theoretical components with occasional unseen examinations. Assessment of clinical work plays an important role in the final degree.

There is also a two-year postgraduate course if you already have a relevant first degree.

Career Opportunities

More than four million patients a year receive physiotherapy through the National Health Service (NHS), particularly those with a musculo-skeletal disorder such as arthritis or long-term conditions such as cystic fibrosis, or those who have had a stroke. Treatment plays an important role in keeping some people well enough to be able to continue working. There is, however, some concern that the continuing effect of the economic downturn since 2008, combined with the provisions of the Health and Social Care Act 2012, could affect employment prospects and bring about a reduction in the number of training places.

Having completed a period of junior rotations in the NHS, physiotherapists might stay in the service and progress to the senior grades, move into private practice or specialise in the private sector in areas such as health farms, occupational health or sport.

Suggested Reading

Interested in a career in physiotherapy?
- resources for a careers talk, downloadable by registered members from the CSP website below

Getting into Physiotherapy Courses
- James Barton, Trotman, 2014

Tidy's Physiotherapy
- Stuart Porter, Churchill Livingstone, 2013

The Physiotherapist's Pocketbook: Essential Facts at your Fingertips
- Karen Kenyon and Jonathan Kenyon, Churchill Livingstone, 2009

Further Information

Chartered Society of Physiotherapy
www.csp.org.uk

National Health Service Careers
www.nhscareers.nhs.uk

Health and Care Professions Council
www.hcpc-uk.org

Irish Society of Chartered Physiotherapists
www.iscp.ie

Podiatry (Chiropody)

Original article adapted with permission from material supplied by the Institute of Chiropodists and Podiatrists

Introduction

Podiatry is a healthcare profession involving the assessment, treatment and management of patients with foot and lower-limb abnormalities. Podiatrists give professional advice on the prevention of foot problems and proper care of the foot. As a podiatrist, you would become an autonomous professional with a caseload of patients from all walks of life and age groups and would become part of a highly skilled multidisciplinary team.

There are five main areas of work:

- General clinics, the starting point for all newly qualified podiatrists. The job involves assessing, evaluating and advising on foot care for a wide range of patients. You listen to a history of the patient's health and hear about any foot problems; you then examine the foot, possibly using specialised equipment, and discuss possible treatments with the patient.

- Biomechanics, concerning the very complex structure and function of the foot. Podiatrists working in this area are concerned to preserve this mechanism, restore it when it is damaged and ensure that it is capable of working at its maximum capacity. One of the main areas is orthotics or specially designed insoles, fitted inside shoes to help solve structural problems such as fallen arches or to correct problems with children's feet.

- Podopaediatrics or working with children. Many children present with developmental biomechanical problems, leading some podiatrists to develop an in-depth understanding of this area of practice.

- High Risk, concerned with patients who have an underlying illness or condition that puts their lower limbs and/or feet at high risk of damage. Examples include problems with circulation or people who have lost the feeling in their feet or lower limbs.

- Surgery, involving routine surgical procedures such as treating in-growing toenails or cutting away soft tissue problems. This may involve the use of local anaesthetics, ultrasonics or freezing techniques. Some podiatrists opt for further study to enable them to work on more invasive surgery.

Graduate podiatrists are eligible for state registration in the UK, which means you can work within the NHS or privately. You will also learn the business skills needed to run your own clinic.

Degree Courses

You can choose from 13 accredited degree courses in the UK. Until 2008, there was no relevant degree in the Republic of Ireland, so would-be podiatrists usually studied in the UK - especially in Belfast - before returning home to develop their career. This remains an option but there is now a course offered by the National University of Ireland, Galway.

In the first year of a typical course you would study the key concepts and theories of podiatric practice, with topics including anatomy, biomechanics, physiology and podiatric medicine. You would also undertake shared learning to give you a broad perspective of multidisciplinary work and gain practice skills through supervised placements in local NHS Trusts.

The second year would see you increasing your podiatric knowledge and contributing to practice in the care of children/older people. You would take on more responsibility in placements, developing confidence and personal skills required to work in this field, and would learn about treating lower-limb disorders, applying physical/mechanical therapies, pharmacology and surgery.

In your final year, clinical practice and theory is patient-focused and addresses contemporary health issues. You would undertake an in-depth supervised project in an area of your choice and would learn essential management skills (including how to write a business plan) to prepare you for running your own practice.

Some courses takes four years to complete, depending on where you choose to study. The part-time course is usually completed over four and a half years.

Career Opportunities

Employment rates are very high for state registered podiatrists, providing opportunities to work in the public, voluntary or business sectors. You can gain employment with the NHS or with private health services, or after gaining experience, can opt to work as a self-employed podiatrist running your own clinic. Self-employment means that your career path and the hours you work can be extremely flexible.

The Society of Chiropodists and Podiatrists claims that 83% of students seeking employment secure a job within six months of graduation and 100% within the first year. This compares very favourably with many other graduate employment rates.

Suggested Reading

Clinical Skills in Treating the Foot
- Warren Turner and Linda M Merriman, Churchill Livingstone, 2005

McMinn's Colour Atlas of Foot and Ankle Anatomy
- Bari M Logan et al, Saunders, 2011

Illustrated Dictionary of Podiatry and Foot Science
- Jean Mooney, Churchill Livingstone, 2009

Further Information

National Health Service Careers
www.nhscareers.nhs.uk

Institute of Chiropodists and Podiatrists
www.iocp.org.uk

Society of Chiropodists and Podiatrists
www.scpod.org

Alliance of Private Sector Practitioners
www.thealliancepsp.com

British Chiropody and Podiatry Association
www.bcha-uk.org

Society of Chiropodists and Podiatrists of Ireland
www.podiatryireland.com

Podiatry at NUI Galway
www.nuigalway.ie/podiatry

Politics and Government

Original article by Peter Dawson, London School of Economics

Introduction

Politics, political science, political theory and institutions, government - these are some of the names by which university departments teaching in this field are known and, although the specific subjects which they teach may differ, their broad concern is the same. The simplest way of describing this concern is to say that it is with the exercise of governmental power within and between nation states. Beyond that it is a concern with the processes by which power is acquired and used, and the restraints, both material and ethical, which may be placed upon it.

Degree Courses

The oldest and most persistent strand of political studies is political philosophy, with an ancestry going back at least as far as Aristotle and Plato. Political philosophy involves a concern - or 'engagement' - with the basic concepts of the discipline (eg politics, government, power, authority) and with the rights and obligations of both rulers and ruled, and much else. It cannot be assigned however to a separate and remote compartment. Philosophical considerations underlie all aspects of the study of politics and most enquiries tend to lead back to such concerns.

Some people distinguish political thought as a separate field from political philosophy. It entails an examination of the ideas of certain prominent thinkers and of their significance in their own and in subsequent times. Plato, Aquinas, Machiavelli, Rousseau and Marx would be just a few of the names which fall within this category.

Next there is a large area of empirical studies and theorising about them, which may, for convenience, be divided into three parts. The first is the study of individuals and their motivation and behaviour in different political roles (eg voters or leaders). The second is the study of groups from the organised and articulate (eg political parties or pressure groups) to those with a possibly more diffuse voice who are less organised (eg racial or religious groups). Third is the study of governmental institutions - parliamentary assemblies, courts, cabinets, civil services - and constitutionally defined offices of leadership or direction (eg those of presidents, prime ministers and ministers). Public administration as an academic study is principally concerned with this third part.

Comparative politics - the methodical and simultaneous study of several political systems - has been one of the major developments of political science in recent years. The study has been aided by an accompanying elaboration of the concept of political systems. A primary concern in comparative politics is to show by examination of a number of countries how apparently similar institutions and structures may perform different functions or, conversely, how the same function may be performed by different structures. It becomes possible, for example, to analyse in some detail how political parties or the mass media perform widely varying roles in different countries, or how the functions attributed in the UK to Members of Parliament may elsewhere be performed by civil servants or influential, non-elected intermediaries.

Another aspect of comparative politics is the attempt to classify political societies and order them in generic groups. It tends to lead to an examination of such terms as totalitarianism, pluralism and participation. Closely related to this approach is the examination of political ideas or bodies of widely held beliefs like nationalism, socialism or conservatism. But by now the circle is almost closed, since this sort of concern brings one into close proximity again with political philosophy.

A final area of concern is international politics or international relations, which in some universities is taught within a separate department but elsewhere is covered under politics or government. Essentially it is the study of politics between states and of such institutions as the United Nations and the European Union, which constitute forms of international government. The various approaches outlined above are equally appropriate in this field.

What are the principal methods of studying politics as an undergraduate? It remains above all a 'book' subject, pursued by reading the works of other scholars, but there also exist opportunities, which vary from topic to topic, to use primary sources such as official publications and newspapers both contemporary and historical. Novels, plays, poetry and other artistic works may have their relevance and there is an increasing use of survey data (eg public opinion samples), in some instances prepared by students themselves.

Career Opportunities
Graduates are often in demand for their understanding of the influences of government on industry, trade, export and import. Approximately 50% enter central and local government, Armed Services, rail, water, gas, electricity, banking, insurance, financial services and 25% enter Higher Education or train to be teachers, solicitors or barristers. Management, administration, sales and marketing are popular areas.

Related Degrees
International Politics; International Relations; European Politics; Parliamentary Studies; Public Administration; Public Sector Management; Government and European Politics; Politics, Philosophy and Economics; Political Science; Public and Social Policy.

Suggested Reading
Plato to NATO: Studies in Political Thought
- Brian Redhead (intro), Penguin, 1995

Modern Political Thought: Readings from Machiavelli to Nietzsche
- David Wootton, Hackett, 2009

Principles of Political Economy and Chapters on Socialism
- John Suart Mill, Oxford Paperbacks, 2008

The Politics
- Aristotle, introduction and notes by Richard Stalley, Oxford World Classics, 2009

The Globalisation of World Politics: an Introduction to International Relations
- John Baylis, Steve Smith and Patricia Owens, OUP Oxford, 2013

Political Studies
- journal available to members of the Political Studies Association at: **www.psa.ac.uk**

Study Politics
- guide to university courses, downloadable from the Political Studies Association at: **www.psa.ac.uk**

Further Information
How Government Works
www.gov.uk/government/how-government-works

Foreign and Commonwealth Office
www.gov.uk/government/organisations/foreign-commonwealth-office

Political Studies Association
www.psa.ac.uk

UK Civil Service
www.gov.uk/government/organisations/civil-service

Political Studies Association of Ireland
www.psai.ie

Prosthetics and Orthotics

Original article by John Head, University of Salford

Introduction

Prosthetics is the science of body part replacement with artificial alternatives. Many people rely on prosthetic limbs to attain independence in their lives and work, and it is a tribute to the skill of prosthetists and their support staff, and a credit to today's technology, that many would appear to have no discernible loss of function or ability. Orthotics is similar to prosthetics, except that the body part is not replaced but is assisted by an artificial device. Such devices can be simple, such as an insole, or they can be intricate and complex, such as devices to assist in the walking of people who have total paralysis of both legs. The work of a prosthetist/orthotist is clinically based, usually within a hospital setting, and involves the prescription and assessment of the patient's needs, and ultimately the production of 3-D models of the body part or residual limb in what is known as the casting process. Traditionally, this is achieved using plaster of Paris, but more recently laser-pens and computer-aided design and manufacturing have been employed to complete the models required. It is from these that teams of technicians produce the prosthesis/orthosis to the specifications laid down by the clinician and which will then be fitted by the latter when it is complete.

Degree Courses

Training is centred at just two UK universities: Salford and Strathclyde. There are at present no degree courses in Prosthetics and Orthotics offered in Ireland. Prosthetic/orthotic education is currently a four-year honours degree course, which contains a final year of clinical experience. Although the courses vary, they both consist of three years of academic learning mixed with clinical tuition. The final stage involves two six-month clinical placements, one orthotic and one prosthetic. The Strathclyde course also offers the possibility of a fifth year to obtain a Master level qualification.

Subjects within the course include anatomy - the structure of the body; physiology - the functions of the body; pathology - causes and nature of disease; biomechanics - forces in/on the body; materials science - how materials perform; and orthotic/prosthetic science - practical solutions to problems.

For further information on courses, you should contact the universities directly.

The work is of a practical nature and is most suited to people who are keen on using their hands, looking after and dealing with people. It is also important that the prosthetist/orthotist has an eye for problem solving and 'thinking on their feet'.

Career Opportunities

With an international shortage of prosthetists and orthotists, career prospects throughout the UK and the rest of the world, particularly the USA, are excellent. Most prosthetic and orthotic graduates start their careers working for commercial companies. However, an increasing number of opportunities are arising within the health service. As you develop skills and experience, you will be able to assume positions with increased responsibility. Eventually this may lead to a managerial role or you may become an acknowledged specialist in a particular area of clinical work. Teaching is another option and these posts offer opportunities for research. The UK training programme is recognised to be of an exceptionally high standard and many opportunities exist for graduates to work abroad. Prosthetic and orthotic work is especially important in areas of the world where development programmes are working with communities traumatised by war.

Suggested Reading

Prosthetics and Orthotics
- Donald Shurr and John Michael, Prentice-Hall, 2001

Orthotics: A Comprehensive Clinical Approach
- Joan Edelstein and Jan Bruckner, Slack Inc, 2002

Orthotics and Prosthetics in Rehabilitation
- Michelle M. Lusardi, Milagros Jorge and Caroline C. Nielsen, Saunders, 2012

Further Information

British Association of Prosthetists and Orthotists
www.bapo.com

University of Salford
http://www.salford.ac.uk/ug-courses/prosthetics-and-orthotics

University of Strathclyde
**www.strath.ac.uk/undergraduatecourses/engineering/
bschonsprostheticsandorthotics**

NHS Careers
www.nhscareers.nhs.uk

International Society for Prosthetics and Orthotics
www.ispo.org.uk

Psychology

Original article by Dr Marie Falahee, Psychology Department, Aston University, with additional material supplied by the British Psychological Society

Introduction

Psychology is the scientific study of people: how they think; how they act, react and interact. Psychology is concerned with all aspects of behaviour and the thoughts, feelings and motivations underlying such behaviour.

To study psychology you have to learn scientific methods - observing, measuring, testing, using statistics - to show that what you find is reliable evidence and not just down to chance. But psychologists do not simply collect evidence to explain people's behaviour; they use their understanding to help people with difficulties and bring about change for the better.

There are several main types of psychologists, depending on their specialist qualifications or training: Clinical, Counselling, Educational, Forensic, Health, Occupational, Neuro, Sport and Exercise and Academic Teaching and Research.

Degree Courses

If you intend to pursue a career in psychology, it is important that you choose a degree course accredited by the British Psychological Society for the Graduate Basis for Chartered Membership (GBC, formerly known as GBR). University courses (whether single, joint or combined honours degrees) typically cover all of the main areas of psychological knowledge necessary to go into further training. However, more and more degrees are becoming modular and it is often necessary to choose particular modules to qualify for the GBC. Check with the individual course organisers the status of the course you are interested in and ensure that you follow an accredited pathway of modules within your degree.

A typical course would cover all of the basic areas of psychology, such as cognitive, developmental, biological, social, and abnormal psychology. The first year modules would provide short introductions to these areas, while the second year modules would investigate them in greater depth. In the third year, you would choose options from modules which reflect the research interests of members of staff, and you would be given the opportunity to design empirical studies of your own. There is usually considerable emphasis on practical work, and you would be given a thorough grounding in research methods (including methods of statistical data analysis).

For students on a four-year programme, the third year may sometimes be spent in work experience which can provide insight into the application of psychological principles in the outside world and allows students to see what a career in a particular branch of psychology or business might be like.

Career Opportunities

Psychology degrees develop many of the transferable skills which all graduate employers require, for example: communication; numeracy; information technology; independent learning; and the ability to work in teams.

Psychology courses accredited by the British Psychological Society contain substantial teaching on statistics and research methodology, as well as scientific methods. Because of these areas of study, psychology students are able to understand and manipulate both quantitative and qualitative data, use computers and problem-solve effectively. Consequently, psychology graduates are well placed to move into research or numeracy-based careers such as market research, academia and accounting. Psychology students also develop many of the skills of humanities graduates, such as critical thinking and essay writing.

Only 15 to 20 per cent of psychology graduates progress to be chartered psychologists. If you want to move into this area of work, it is vital to undertake as much work experience as possible whilst on your undergraduate degree. Placements in clinical psychology can be notoriously difficult to access but any relevant paid or voluntary work can be beneficial, e.g. working with children or adults with learning difficulties; mentoring; befriending; working in care homes or with those who are mentally distressed.

Related Degrees
Psychology with Neuropsychology; Business Administration with Psychology; Applied Psychology; Sport and Exercise Psychology; Health Psychology; Social Psychology; Psychosocial Studies; Forensic Psychology; Human Psychology; Behavioural Science; Clinical Psychology; Psycholinguistics; Psychology, Philosophy and Physiology

Suggested Reading
The Psychologist
- official magazine of the British Psychological Society and an essential introduction to the main issues in psychology today. For full details, go to:
www.thepsychologist.org.uk

Your journey into Psychology
- official careers portal at: **http://careers.bps.org.uk**

Getting into Psychology Courses
- Joel Rickard and John Cooter, Trotman, 2014

Atkinson and Hilgard's Introduction to Psychology
- Susan Nolen-Hoeksema et al, Cengage Learning, 2014

Approaches to Psychology
- William Glassman and Marilyn Hadad, McGraw-Hill Higher Education, 2013

The Presentation of Self in Everyday Life
- Erving Goffman, Penguin, 1990

How to Think Straight about Psychology
- Keith Stanovich, Pearson Education, 2013

Psychology: The Science of Mind and Behaviour
- Nigel Holt et al, McGraw-Hill Higher Education, 2012

Further Information
British Psychological Society
www.bps.org.uk

Psychological Society of Ireland
www.psihq.ie

European Federation of Psychologists' Associations
www.efpa.eu

Radiography

Original article adapted with permission from material supplied by the College of Radiographers

Introduction

To be a radiographer, you need an interest in science and you should be a caring and compassionate person, sufficiently level headed not to get upset when dealing with the sick. You should be calm when faced with people who may be frightened or difficult. Your health must be good and you have to be reasonably strong, because you may have to help lift people and move heavy equipment.

A Diagnostic Radiographer works with advanced technology to produce high quality images to help in diagnosis. Radiography equipment is becoming increasingly complex and much of it is computerised. For example, computerised tomography (CT) and magnetic resonance imaging (MRI) scanners can give information about the body not possible with conventional radiographs. The information obtained from this equipment can differentiate between the different organs without the need for the patient to undergo surgical procedures or injections. Radiographers who operate CT scanners have to be familiar with keyboards and computer language. As they learn to operate many different types of equipment, radiographers may specialise and train in different areas, including ultrasound.

Therapeutic Radiographers treat people with cancer and non-malignant diseases. The aim is to determine the correct dose of radiation, decide where the beam should enter and exit, and which structures should be treated and which avoided. The location of a tumour and its size are discovered with the aid of CT or magnetic resonance scans or other diagnostic procedures. Conventional X-ray and cobalt units are being phased out and being replaced by a new generation of treatment equipment. These include linear accelerators, which can treat either deep-seated or superficial tumours. Therapy radiographers are likely to work more regular hours than diagnostic radiographers, though it is necessary to have some out-of-hours cover for specific treatments.

Degree Courses

A typical Diagnostic Radiography course will be composed of time spent in the lecture theatre and tutorials and an approximately equal time spent working with patients in the actual department. Since radiography is a clinically orientated profession with a considerable degree of patient contact, students need a detailed knowledge of the human body - its structure, pathology and function. A diagnostic radiographer deals with potentially very dangerous equipment and has to acquire a knowledge of how to use this both confidently and safely.

In a typical course, you would study anatomy and physiology, physics, the science of imaging, pathology, pathophysiology, psychology and sociology. In your last year, you would extend your knowledge and experience of the practice and science of imaging, and probably also study sociology, ethics and management. In this year, and possibly earlier, you are likely to carry out some independent supervised research.

You would also, at some stage of the course, deal with the principles and practice of radiography and of complementary imaging, health and safety, principles of patient care and health education.

In a Therapeutic Radiography course, you will acquire the skills needed to be able to work in a department of clinical oncology. Modules might include health studies, radiation sciences, oncology, anatomy and physiology. There could be further modules such as psychosocial studies, oncology and radiotherapy, and radiation science, as well as further modules in anatomy and physiology. The final year would include further modules, often extensions of earlier ones and a research project.

Career Opportunities

There is currently a worldwide shortage of both diagnostic and therapy radiographers, which should mean excellent career prospects for anyone holding the highly regarded UK qualification. State registration is a key factor in developing your career, indicating that you meet the high ethical standards required, have achieved educational and professional excellence and are committed to duty of care.

Suggested Reading

A Career in Radiography
- information and career profiles at the Society of Radiographers website at:
www.sor.org/about-radiography/career-radiography

Radiographic Techniques and Image Evaluation
- Amanda Royle and Elizabeth Unett, Nelson Thornes, 1996

Clark's Pocket Handbook for Radiographers
- Charles Sloane, A Stewart Whitley, Craig Anderson and Ken Holmes, Hodder Arnold, 2010

Ball and Moore's Essential Physics for Radiographers
- John Ball and Adrian Moore, Wiley-Blackwell, 2008

A Guide to Radiological Procedures
- Nick Watson, Saunders, 2013

Further Information

Radiography Careers
www.radiographycareers.co.uk

Society and College of Radiographers
www.sor.org

National Health Service Careers
www.nhscareers.nhs.uk

British Institute of Radiology
www.bir.org.uk

British Medical Ultrasound Society
www.bmus.org

Health and Care Professions Council
www.hcpc-uk.org

Irish Institute of Radiography and Radiation Therapy
www.iirrt.ie

Religious Studies and Theology

Original article by Professor John R Hinnells, School of Oriental and African Studies, London

Introduction

Religion is a driving force both in contemporary society and in past history. It has inspired some of the most noble, creative and generous actions. Equally, it has been associated with the most savage cruelty, oppression and degradation. A balanced understanding of many major events commonly involves an appreciation of the religious factors at work. Whether it is in the Middle East, Latin America, Africa, Afghanistan or remote parts of China - religion and politics are commonly interwoven. Religion may inspire people, or it may be used by people, but it is commonly a significant dimension for the study of human life.

Many describe British society as secular and wrongly say that religion is declining. Membership of the established churches may be dropping, but that is not a measure of the state of religion in the country. This ignores the growth of new religious movements, the ecstatic movements, the 'cults', and the central importance of religion in Asian and Afro-Caribbean communities. People who have migrated, or feel victims of prejudice, commonly reassert their identity in and through religious traditions. Much of contemporary British law, custom, values etc., are the product of a particular religious tradition.

Religion is crucial not only in the understanding of politics and society but also of the arts. Until recently, the Church was the main patron of the arts - painting, music, architecture, and drama. The Church commissioned works of art and dictated the form, content and style of much of that art. The Church often repressed the artist - not only through the mass destruction following the Reformation, but also in more recent times when its stance on the depiction of the nude and the condemnation of some aspects of drama or literature has been narrow-minded. It is hardly possible to understand many of the art forms of other cultures without the religion of which they are an essential part - whether it is the great civilisations of China and India, or of the small-scale societies in Africa or the North American Indians. A failing of so many art histories is that they study the arts as though they were merely produced for the 'antiseptic' atmosphere of most art galleries, whereas often artefacts are produced to be used to inspire devotion or to teach the illiterate.

Degree Courses

Many students who are religious wish to study religion, and in Britain that often means Christian. But some people study religion in order to find a faith and some because they believe it will confirm or develop their faith. A few study religion because they want to enter the ministry. A university is a secular institution and not a priestly seminary. Within a department of religious studies there will be people of various faiths, and many of none. In theory, a student's own religious position should make no difference to their studies. That is an ideal situation - and neither students nor staff are ever ideal. It is a self-delusion for people to think they have no prejudices. The danger time is when we are not aware of them. At least one major benefit of the study of religion is that it compels people to recognise their prejudices and to analyse them.

How should one study religion? In some departments, religious studies means basically studying the Christian Bible. One argument for this is that it, more than any other document, has affected the course of western civilisation. The methods used to study that text are intellectually demanding and diverse (e.g. languages, archaeology, literary studies, Roman history etc.), but if you are interested in studying Asians in Britain then, frankly, it is not relevant. If you want both, make sure both are available.

I believe that religion has to be studied from many points of view. The study must necessarily bring together a range of disciplines - anthropology, sociology, languages, history, art, archaeology and philosophy. I accept the old dictum 'he who knows one knows none', i.e. that the study of any one religion is not the study of religion and such a focus precludes a balanced view of even that one phenomenon. It is only by a study of several that you see what is distinctive of each.

Religious studies more than any other subject wrestles with some of the ultimate issues: the concept of God; life after death; the nature of good and evil and ethical issues - what are the arguments for and against euthanasia, surrogate motherhood, nuclear power? If anyone thinks any of these are simple clear-cut issues they have evidently not thought them through.

Career Opportunities
Theology and religious studies graduates develop skills in communication, analysis, logic and argument, which can be valuable in many careers. A few theology graduates enter the ordained ministry but are often more attracted to 'caring' professions, such as social and community work, charity administration and nursing. Approximately 25% enter teacher training or train as solicitors, barristers, librarians, social workers etc. Others enter commerce, the Civil Service, careers in management services, computing, finance, sales and marketing.

Related Degrees
Religious Education; Divinity; Biblical Studies; Christian Ministry; Religion Ethics and Western Society.

Suggested Reading
The New Penguin Handbook of Living Religions
- John R Hinnells, Penguin, 2000

Religion Today: A Reader
- Susan Mumm, Ashgate, 2002

The Concise Oxford Dictionary of World Religions
- John Bowker, OUP, 2006

The World's Religions
- Huston Smith, HarperOne, 2009

The Compact Guide to World Religions
- Sean O'Callaghan, Lion Hudson, 2010

Further Information
Ethics Updates
http://ethics.sandiego.edu

Sociology of Religion Study Group
www.socrel.org.uk

Irish Theological Association
http://irishtheologicalassociation.wordpress.com

Retail Management

Original article by Jacqui Gush, Bournemouth University

Introduction

The definition of retailing is widening as more and more commercial activities participate in selling goods and services to the final consumer. This makes retailing an increasingly exciting area of study and employment. The retailing business is about people: our rapidly changing tastes and demand patterns; what influences us to buy and understanding where, how and when it happens. Some of the current challenges in retailing include the threat or opportunity of electronic shopping, the increasing merger between retailing and the leisure industry, meeting customer needs through the increasing use of technology and the internationalisation of retailing activities.

Students on a retail management degree course benefit from all the knowledge and skills gained as part of a more general business studies course. However, significant added value is gained by specialising in retailing, as the student develops a sound, in-depth knowledge of the sector. There is strong encouragement and support from leading retailers in the development, review and provision of specific courses.

Degree Courses

A typical course is a four-year sandwich, which includes a 40-week industrial placement.

Year one is a stimulating introduction to retailing at the sharp end, focusing on the role and responsibilities of the store manager.

Strong emphasis is placed on the development of commercial and personal skills. These are learnt from theory as well as practical retail work experience. Skills such as group working, writing business reports and making effective presentations are an important aspect of generic business skills learnt in year one.

In *year two*, retailing is studied from a head office perspective, concentrating on corporate functions and operations, e.g. marketing, finance, buying and human resource management. At the beginning of this year, students are offered the opportunity to study on an exchange programme with a retailing school in mainland Europe.

The experience of the year out in industry during *year three* allows students to develop their personal skills and gives them the opportunity to put theory into practice by applying the knowledge and skills gained during their first two years on the degree programme. While on placement, students are able to qualify for the City and Guilds Licentiate award.

The *final year* concentrates on subjects which support top management decision-making for companies in an international as well as a national market. It reflects the dynamic nature of the retail industry and students analyse how companies seek to achieve advantage in an intensely competitive environment. The focus is strongly on student-centred learning and includes two major group projects, which are commercially and academically challenging. Students work in the live business environment, and the project outcomes are presented to retailers and investment companies.

Career Opportunities

Opportunities are available in the major national retail organisations - but with competition from other graduate disciplines. The basic training, however, should open up many management, marketing, financial and commercial careers in business generally.

Ethically driven trends such as recycling, animal welfare, human rights and environmental issues such as climate change or the carbon footprint of a product look likely to play a much greater role in people's buying choices in the future. Retail companies will, therefore, need to pay much more attention to these issues in terms of how they manufacture their products and how ethically sound they are. Given that such issues will drive customers towards certain retailers and away from others, it could be worth focusing on them as you plan your own career development.

Related Degrees
Marketing, Retail and Distribution; Fashion Buying for Retail; Supply Chain Management; Food Management.

Suggested Reading
Retailing: an Introduction
- Roger Cox and Paul Brittain, Financial Times/ Prentice Hall, 2004

Principles of Retailing
- John Fernie Suzanne Fernie and Christopher Moore, Routledge, 2003

Retail Marketing
- Peter McGoldrick, McGraw-Hill Higher Education, 2002

Retail Desire: Design, Display and the Art of the Visual Merchandiser
- Johnny Tucker, RotoVision, 2004

Fashion Brands: Branding Style from Armani to Zara
- Mark Tungate, Kogan Page, 2012

Further Information
British Retail Consortium
www.brc.org.uk

A Career in Retail
www.acareerinretail.co.uk

Chartered Institute of Marketing
www.cim.co.uk

Retail on the Web
www.retailontheweb.co.uk

Chartered Institute of Purchasing and Supply
www.cips.org

Retail Excellence Ireland
www.retailexcellence.ie

Irish Management Institute
www.imi.ie

Enterprise Ireland
www.enterprise-ireland.com

Marketing Institute of Ireland
www.mii.ie

Rural Resource Management

Original article by Ken Reynolds, specialist writer on careers and higher education

Introduction

What is rural resource management? It is about using the rural environment for such purposes as:

- farming - crops and animals for food and fibres

- natural resources - timber, energy, water and minerals

- housing

- employment

- recreation and leisure

Rural resource management tries to balance all these demands to protect the long-term future of the rural environment. This means taking into account everything from animal welfare to environmental and socio-economic needs. Attitudes are changing and sustainable land use is becoming a key phrase.

Degree Courses

You will find that institutions offering degrees in rural resource management structure the course in different ways. At one university, for example, a common core for the first two years of study (Stages 1 and 2) is shared with all other agriculture programmes. This means that you could specialise in any of the Honours options (Agronomy; Farm Business Management; Animal Production Science; Organic Food Production) in your final year (Stage 3). In Stage 1 you would cover: soil and crop science; animal physiology, biochemistry, genetics and nutrition; economics and computing; current agricultural issues.

In Stage 2 you would apply these skills to both animal and crop production, and to farm management. The range of modules includes: agronomy and improvement of arable, grass and forage crops; farm management, agricultural economics and marketing; ruminant livestock, pigs and poultry; animal breeding, nutrition and health; agriculture and the environment.

You would not specialise in rural resource management until your final year, taking modules in: sustainable land management; rural enterprise diversification; estate management; countryside management; law and land use; options - including alternative agriculture, forage utilisation or land reclamation.

An important feature of the programme at another university is the wide range of visits to, and projects and exercises conducted with, rural enterprises and organisations. The visits programme enables you to explore management issues at first hand, and provides insights into a variety of career opportunities. You may elect to spend a year in between Parts 2 and 3 of the programme obtaining work experience and you can also spend one term studying in another European country.

In a third institution, a common first year lays the foundations for the sustainable management of the environmental, social and economic contexts of rural life and explores the interactions between these, conservation issues and future management policies.

All first year students have a timetabled opportunity to learn and hone practical countryside skills such as hedge laying and tractor driving.

Specialist areas of study or interest can be individually developed as part of the final year dissertation and consultancy modules.

It is clearly important to research course content and structure very carefully before you apply.

Career Opportunities

The realisation that wildlife and landscape conservation need to be considered to achieve the sustainable use of land for agricultural and forest production has created the need for rural resource managers who can work across traditional disciplinary boundaries.

People with such interdisciplinary skills are in demand as: managers of rural businesses, including farm and woodland enterprises which are diversifying to meet market needs; planners, who are increasingly required to integrate knowledge of the social and management sciences with an appreciation of the ecological problems and opportunities of the rural environment; ecological scientists and countryside managers, who are increasingly required to understand economic, social and cultural issues along with the scientific basis of conservation and sustainable land management.

Past rural resource graduates have found employment in sectors as diverse as local authorities, wildlife trusts, National Parks and forestry, as well as in educational and consultancy positions.

Related Degrees

You might also be interested in a degree in: Agricultural Business Management; Agriculture; Animal Science; Countryside Management; Countryside Conservation; Landscape Management; Wildlife Management; Environmental Biology or Environmental Science.

Suggested Reading

Visit the Routledge Environment and Sustainability website for an extensive reading list at: **www.routledge.com/sustainability**

Further Information

Chartered Institute of Ecology and Environmental Management
www.cieem.net

Natural England
www.gov.uk/government/organisations/natural-england

Scottish Natural Heritage
www.snh.gov.uk

Natural Resources Wales
http://naturalresourceswales.gov.uk

Northern Ireland Environment Agency
www.doeni.gov.uk/niea

Heritage Council, Ireland
www.heritagecouncil.ie

Social Policy

Original article by Dr Tony Maltby, University of Birmingham

Introduction

Social policy is about the welfare of people. It is concerned with social needs and social problems. The study of social policy is largely concerned with those aspects of people's lives that are affected by government action or inaction. Recently, social policy has widened its scope to consider the family, the environment, penal policy and the role of the market in delivering welfare. We consider the contribution of non-government groups and agencies in the field of voluntary organisations, employer-provided services, self-help groups, family and neighbour support networks.

Degree Courses

In a typical **Social Policy** degree course (allow for an additional year in Scotland), through a series of lectures, classes and workshops, you would initially gain a broad understanding of the main disciplines involved: sociology, political science, social history, economics and research methods. You would also investigate and debate social policy issues (i.e. unemployment, poverty, the family, health, housing, education, citizenship and equal opportunities).

In the subsequent years, you would develop and refine what you have learned earlier. Thus students are able to choose combinations of specialist modules according to their particular interests. You would learn more of the ideas of different schools of political and social thought and about the way in which societies can be organised. You would consider different principles, such as those concerned with equity, citizenship, democracy and social justice. Students also begin to examine more closely the problems and issues involved in the removal of social, economic and political disadvantage in modern Britain.

Standing alongside the above example, the **Public and Social Policy Management** course is designed for people who feel they might be interested in pursuing a managerial career in the public or voluntary sectors - dealing with services such as education, health care, leisure and recreation, social services, consumer advice and housing. You would learn about government policies, and the institutions which currently provide services for the public. Within this context, the degree aims to give students an understanding of, and expertise in, areas of management which are relevant to the provision and delivery of services.

There are five streams, or sets of modules, which run in parallel through the programme.

- The *contextual stream* deals with the institutions and legislation which structure public and voluntary organisations.
- The *options stream* enables students to look in more depth at particular areas of social policy - such as education, housing, health care - and to examine the organisations which have been set up to produce these services
- The *management stream* focuses on the role and work of managers in the public and voluntary sectors. It analyses how organisations work, how co-operation between and within organisations can be hindered or achieved and what is meant by public accountability.
- The *techniques* and *economics streams* add to these skills by providing training in the information needs of managers, and the ways of analysing situations and problems.

Part of the degree requirement involves a part-time fieldwork placement within a public or voluntary organisation. This takes place during the third year and forms an important, and assessed, element of the degree programme. For, as well as providing relevant work experience, it gives you a glimpse of some of the real-world practicalities of public policy management.

Joint honours degrees are suitable for students who, while interested in studying Social Policy, also wish to pursue a companion subject in depth. The first year of all the degrees is very similar, while in the later years the equivalent of five single Social Policy modules and five single modules in the second discipline are studied.

Career Opportunities

Social policy graduates enter a wide range of careers, and national surveys show that there is a very good record of finding work in both the public and private sector. In general, a social policy degree is useful for any career that involves working with people. Typical careers for which social policy is particularly relevant include management or policy work in central or local government; human resource management; leisure and sports management; health service management and health education; law; the police; penal institutions; work in voluntary agencies.

In addition, social policy affords a good general grounding for those wishing to pursue careers in media or journalism, social research, nursing, librarianship, computing, retail management, marketing, teaching or work in developing countries.

These days, many careers require professional training as well as a first degree, and many social policy graduates continue their education either on postgraduate courses or when they begin employment.

Related Degrees

Public and Social Policy; Social Administration and Policy; Public Policy and Community; Housing Studies.

Suggested Reading

Social Policy in Britain
- Pete Alcock with Margaret May, Palgrave Macmillan, 2014

Changing Welfare, Changing States: New Directions in Social Policy
- John Clarke, Sage, 2004

Social Policy: an Introduction
- Ken Blakemore and Louise Warwick-Booth, Open University Press, 2013

The Classic Slum: Salford Life in the First Quarter of the Century
- Robert Roberts, Penguin, 1990

The Student's Companion to Social Policy
- Pete Alcock et al, Wiley-Blackwell, 2012

Social Policy
- John Baldock et al, OUP Oxford, 2011

Further Information

UK Social Policy Association
www.social-policy.org.uk

Irish Social Policy Association
www.ispa.ie

Institute of Public Administration, Ireland
www.ipa.ie

Social Work

Original article by Professor Ralph Firth, University of Northumbria

Introduction

A degree in Social Work will enable you to develop the skills for pursuing a career in social work by integrating academic study and professional practice. The overall aim of the course is to equip you with the skills to become a competent social work practitioner.

At some universities, you will study units alongside other students in health and social care, such as nurses, midwives, community workers, and occupational therapists. This inter-professional learning reflects the reality of the healthcare environment, where communication between professions is crucial to ensuring correct and appropriate care of clients.

Degree Courses

On a typical course, you will develop core academic skills and explore the key disciplines informing social work, studying five modules that will introduce you to the social and organisational context of social work: *Social Welfare and Social Inequalities*; *Psychology and Human Development*; *Social Work Contexts*; *Social Work Skills, Values and Approaches*; and *Research for Evidence-based Learning*. The social work regulatory body, the Health and Care Professions Council (HCPC) and the College of Social Work also require that, before you go out into your practice placements, you demonstrate the basic skills needed to work with a variety of people and to communicate with service users with understanding and respect.

During the second year you will complete 70 days of professional practice learning, in addition to five academic modules designed to help you develop and apply the knowledge, values and skills required in social work practice. These include Social Work Theory, Methods and Practice, Law for Professional Practice, Research for Evidence Informed Practice, and Social Identity and Citizenship. You will also complete an Enhancing Skills module, working closely with service user and carer colleagues and practitioners. Placements, which can be challenging but also very rewarding, may be in:

- Family support and prevention
- Domestic violence
- Refugee and asylum work
- Special educational needs
- Fostering
- Child protection
- Disabilities
- Substance misuse

In your final year you will complete a further 100 day professional practice learning placement, together with two academic modules designed to support you in consolidating and extending your ability to become a competent practitioner. You will also complete a dissertation on a social work topic of your own choice.

If you have an undergraduate degree in a different discipline, you can convert to social work via a postgraduate programme endorsed by the HCPC and the College of Social Work. There are also fast-track programmes for entry to social work with children and families, such as Frontline or Step Up to Social Work.

Before applying for a qualifying programme, you will be expected to have some experience of working with service users in a voluntary or paid capacity, to determine if social work is the right career path for you. A number of organisations recruit volunteers to work with a range of social care service user groups. 'Do it' and 'A Question of Care' are good online resources. If you prefer paid work, it may be possible to carry out temporary work as a social care assistant with a local authority or residential unit.

Career Opportunities

There is normally a very clear progression from the social work programme to professional practice. Once your training is complete, you must register with the HCPC. You will need to renew your registration every two years to continue to practise. As a newly-qualified social worker, you will continue your development with support from your employer through the Assessed and Supported Year in Employment (ASYE).

This is a 12-month programme available to social workers in the statutory, private and voluntary sectors. You would be given a caseload to develop your skills and confidence and receive ongoing support from your line manager or social work supervisor. You would be continually assessed in your work and, on completion, you would gain certification from the College of Social Work.

Related Degrees

Applied Social Work; Youth Studies; Community Studies; Counselling Studies and Society; Family and Child Care Studies; Women's Studies; Human/Community Care.

Suggested Reading

Social Work Practice
- Jonathan Parker and Greta Bradley, Learning Matters, 2014

A Brief Introduction to Social Work Theory
- David Howe, Palgrave Macmillan, 2009

The Blackwell Companion to Social Work
- Martin Davies (Ed), Wiley-Blackwell, 2013

Further Information

College of Social Work
www.tcsw.org.uk

Community Care
www.communitycare.co.uk

Frontline
www.thefrontline.org.uk

Step up to Social Work
www.gov.uk/step-up-to-social-work-information-for-applicants

Do-it – Volunteering Made Easy
www.do-it.org.uk

A Question of Care
www.aquestionofcare.org.uk

Health and Care Professions Council
www.hcpc-uk.org

Scottish Social Services Council
www.sssc.uk.com

Institute for Research and Innovation in Social Services, Scotland
www.iriss.org.uk

CORU Health and Social Care Professionals Council, Ireland
www.coru.ie

Sociology

Original article by Dr Jane Pilcher, University of Leicester

Introduction

A complex society surrounds us and shapes every aspect of our lives. In order to understand ourselves, we have to understand how that society works. Sociology attempts to do this through studying the relationship between people and social groups, the role of social institutions (like the family, paid employment, or education) and how all of these are related to the wider society. Students are encouraged to think and work in original and critical ways.

One way in which sociology tries to answer questions about contemporary society is through comparing it with earlier periods of history and with other societies around the world. Through encouraging students to think comparatively, sociology helps to increase our understanding of processes of social change and the distinctiveness or otherwise of current social arrangements. Sociological ideas or concepts and theories about how social groups, institutions and societies work are also tested through carrying out research, and in this way, we can see whether our ideas and theories match the way that society is organised.

Sociology isn't new. Most basic social theory, particularly the work of Karl Marx, Max Weber and Emile Durkheim has a pedigree dating from the nineteenth century. If you want a taste of timeless social theory, read the Communist Manifesto by Karl Marx and Frederick Engels (Bookmarks Publications).

You won't get much of a chance to research real live people actively and personally on a typical three-year course, although you will get a chance to study sociological analyses and descriptions of what life is like for other people. A brilliant example of what your and other people's life is like as seen through the eyes of a sociologist is Erving Goffman's *The Presentation of Self in Everyday Life* (Penguin).

A common but erroneous idea is that sociology analyses those bits of society which are left after economics, psychology and anthropology have carved off their bits. In fact the reverse is true. Sociology can be distinguished from all other disciplines through its ability not only to analyse society without the use of other disciplines (which is its chief function) but also to analyse competently the operations of all other disciplines. Natural science itself has become a target for some sociologists. They enquire: How do scientists make discoveries? Is it some sort of magical process? How is it that, occasionally, several scientists simultaneously but individually discover the same thing? Coincidence? If you want to know how it actually happens, take a look at Thomas Kuhn's *The Structure of Scientific Revolutions* (University of Chicago Press).

Degree Courses

Here is an example of sociology provision at one university. The BSc degree allows full-time study of sociology throughout three years, while the BA degree has a first year consisting of sociology and two supplementary social science subjects. Both courses, like most sociology degrees, are designed to introduce the subject, cover its central areas and enable considerable choice of specialised areas of study through optional modules.

All BA and BSc sociology students take modules in theory (Sociological Analysis modules, Sociological Texts modules), methods (Research Sources and Methods modules) and the comparative study of societies (Contemporary Societies modules). Although these modules are compulsory, a range of optional modules provides students with opportunities to construct large parts of their degree according to their own interests. Optional modules offered by the Sociology Department include Health,

Illness and the Body, Popular Music and Society, Crime and the City, Research Project Option, Popular Culture and the Mass Media, Sociology of Education, Schools and Society, Childhood and Society, the Rise of Japan, Consumer Society, Race and Identity Politics and Football and Society.

Career Opportunities

Many sociology graduates are attracted to careers that centre on the challenges and demands that members of a society face. This leads to work in social services, education, criminal justice, welfare services, government, counselling, charities and the voluntary sector. Possible jobs include charity fundraiser, community development worker, counsellor, lecturer, housing officer, teacher, probation officer, social researcher, social worker and welfare rights adviser. There are a range of specific abilities and skills associated with a degree in sociology but there are also wider transferable skills, such as the ability to judge and evaluate evidence; understanding the complexity and diversity of situations; collecting information; and making reasoned and logical arguments. Sociology students also develop a wider set of transferable skills including team-working; verbal communication skills; showing initiative; and being able to work in a way that is supportive of equality and diversity in the workplace.

Related Degrees

Social Policy; Social Research; Social Sciences; Social Studies; Cultural Studies; Women's Studies.

Suggested Reading

See suggestions in paragraphs 3, 4 and 5 opposite

The Student's Companion to Sociology
- Jon Gubbay, Chris Middleton & Chet Ballard (Eds), Blackwell, 1997

Thinking Sociologically
- Zygmunt Bauman and Tim May, Blackwell, 2001

Foundations of Sociology: Towards a Better Understanding of the Human World
- Richard Jenkins, Palgrave Macmillan, 2002

Sociology
- Anthony Giddens and Philip Sutton, Polity Press, 2013

Oxford Dictionary of Sociology
- John Scott, OUP Oxford, 2014

Further Information

British Sociological Association
www.britsoc.co.uk

Sociological Association of Ireland
www.sociology.ie

Speech Sciences

Original article by Dr Jane Maxim and Dr Janet A Wright, Department of Human Communication Science, University College, London

Introduction

When people talk to each other, a complex series of messages is sent out, received, understood and then responded to. The processes involved in human communication require the interaction of several brain functions, neuromuscular mechanisms, sight and hearing. Listening, for most people, involves paying attention to what is being said, to facial expression and body posture. Such complex processes may break down or not develop along normal patterns. Speech sciences is the study of these processes in both normal and abnormal human communication. There are several degree courses in this area, which usually appeal to students interested in speech therapy, audiology or the education of children with special needs. Not surprisingly, this science requires students to look at a range of widely differing subjects in order to acquire the integrated knowledge necessary to understand human communication. Speech sciences cross the boundaries between science and the arts, including anatomy, physiology, psychology, phonetics, linguistics, sociology, education, medical sciences and speech pathology and therapeutics.

It may seem incredible that we still know so little about human communication but it is certainly the most complex of human functions and, perhaps because of this complexity, we are still only at the start of solving this particular jigsaw puzzle. Let us consider how we understand just one word. We know that when it is heard, the acoustic and phonetic or speech sound properties have to be decoded. The brain then has to decide whether it has heard that particular word before. If it has then the word is processed to the semantic system, where its meaning is retrieved. But, even within this simple process, we still know very little about where words are stored in the brain and how they are stored in the semantic system.

For the student who is academically adventurous and sees research as a possible future goal, this field still holds many possibilities. For that same reason, this is not a field for those seeking ready-made solutions. Clients with communication disorders may have the same diagnosis but the severity of the problem and the way in which it affects that particular client mean that an individual programme of therapy has to be worked out for each client. Many students wishing to enter the field feel that they want to help such individuals but such a desire to help must be coupled with a real curiosity about human behaviour and what can motivate the individual to change that behaviour. The child with cerebral palsy or the adult with multiple sclerosis both have problems with neuromuscular co-ordination but the treatment needed may vary from a programme to help mildly unintelligible speech to the provision of a complex computer system through which the client may communicate.

In common with other science degrees, speech sciences require practical work. This component has two different strands: work in the laboratory concerned with speech and audiological sciences, and clinical work which takes place in a variety of settings. The practical work therefore has a dual purpose: to enable the student to understand normal and abnormal speech processes and to help the student apply that knowledge in a clinical setting. Knowledge used in a clinical environment also needs to be applied in a way which is appropriate for the client-therapist relationship; in other words, the student learns how to apply personal and communication skills in a professional and effective way. The application of these skills also has to be implemented with a compassionate understanding for that particular individual. In some client groups the cause of the disorder may be a psychological disturbance, manifesting as, for example, a voice disorder. In such a case, the student learns how to differentiate a voice disorder resulting from vocal abuse and poor vocal production

214

from a voice disorder which requires counselling or referral to the psychiatric or psychology service.

Degree Courses

Most courses in speech sciences begin with study of foundation subjects, which usually include human anatomy and physiology, psychology, phonetics, linguistics and research design and statistics. In any science degree, the last subject is usually a basic component without which the student is unable to understand research methodology and critically evaluate research.

Students are introduced to clinical work first by structured observation of normal communication - observing the development of children as babies, in nursery schools and at primary schools; maybe also observing elderly people so as to gain perspective of development across the whole life span. Students then go on to acquire their clinical skills in a variety of settings, such as community clinics, mainstream and special schools, hospitals and rehabilitation centres. Some may have clinical placements in homes for the elderly, centres for adults with severe learning disabilities and psychiatric units. The timing and length of these clinical placements tends to vary between courses. Most courses mix weekly clinical placements with longer periods in a particular setting, while others use a sandwich course model.

Career Opportunities

The majority of openings occur in the NHS, where speech and language therapists use their clinical skills with a wide range of patients. However, although employed by the NHS, many work in schools with children.

Related Degrees

Human Communication Sciences; Speech Science; Speech Pathology and Therapy; Linguistics and Language Pathology; Clinical Language Sciences.

Suggested Reading

These are not necessarily about speech sciences and speech and language therapy directly. Some are explorations of the issues of language development or of communication breakdown. But if you find them interesting and thought provoking, this may be the study area for you:

The Articulate Mammal: Introduction to Psycholinguistics
- Jean Aitchison, Routledge, 2011

How to Manage Communication Problems in Young Children
- Myra Kersner and Jannet Wright (Eds), David Fulton, 2002

A Career in Speech and Language Therapy
- downloadable from the Royal College of Speech and Language Therapists website below

Further Information

Royal College of Speech and Language Therapists
www.rcslt.org

UK Speech
www.ukspeech.org.uk

National Health Service Careers
www.nhscareers.nhs.uk

Irish Association of Speech and Language Therapists
www.iaslt.ie

Sport and Exercise Science

British Association of Sport and Exercise Sciences (BASES), the recognised professional body for promoting sport and exercise sciences in the UK

Introduction

Sport and Exercise Science is the application of scientific principles to the promotion, maintenance and enhancement of sport and exercise related behaviour. It is fast becoming one of the most popular subjects to study at both undergraduate and postgraduate level.

Most undergraduate sport and exercise science degrees tend to be based around three aspects of science - physiology, biomechanics and psychology. A graduate would, therefore, be expected to have a broad knowledge base covering all three aspects, together with interdisciplinary approaches:

- Biomechanics: an examination of the causes and consequences of human movement and the interaction of the body with apparatus or equipment through the application of mechanical principles
- Physiology: the branch of the biological sciences concerned with the way the body responds to exercise and training
- Psychology: the branch of sport and exercise science that seeks to provide answers to questions about human behaviour and mental processes in sport and exercise settings
- Interdisciplinary: seeking to contribute to the body of knowledge or solve a real-world problem in sport or exercise using two or more disciplines in an integrated fashion from the outset

Degree Courses

With so many courses available, it is important that you consider which would be the best for you. To help you with this decision, use the following questions as a guide to the key characteristics to look for in a sport and exercise science degree:

- Are all three aspects of science covered, as well as interdisciplinary approaches?
- Are there good laboratory facilities to which you will have access? Check that there is a strong practical skills element to the course.
- How many of the staff are accredited by BASES?
- What active research and community projects exist? Involvement in these projects will allow you the opportunity to gain experience and skills beyond the formal curriculum. Universities with high-ranking research groups will generally publicise this.
- Does the course provide you with information on the career pathways of its graduates? Look for institutions that are successful in placing graduates in sport and exercise related occupations.

It is important that you obtain detailed information about the actual content of the courses for which you are thinking of applying. Courses with the same name often have very different content; equally, courses with different names may in fact cover the same material.

Some universities offer discipline-specific programmes of study, for example in the psychology of sport and exercise. These courses tend to provide less breadth of study than traditional sport and exercise science courses, although they may appeal to applicants with a very clear idea of their disciplinary interests and potential career progression. Generally, however, a broad understanding of sport and exercise science is best achieved through multidisciplinary study at undergraduate level. A specialism can then be developed through relevant postgraduate study.

Career Opportunities

The career opportunities available to sport and exercise scientists are expanding all the time and this expansion appears likely to continue for the foreseeable future. Most sports now recognise sports science as an integral part of their sport's development and success, and most athletes consider the application of sport science as an important part of everyday training and competition. In relation to exercise, many hospitals are starting to appoint specialists with exercise backgrounds to work in areas such as cardiac rehabilitation and health promotion.

Despite the increasing number of job opportunities in sport and exercise science, the number of sport and exercise science graduates is also growing, making competition for jobs intense. You should, therefore, take every opportunity to develop yourself whilst at university, by getting involved in activities that will enhance your career prospects.

Recent data suggest that 60% to 75% of sport and exercise science graduates find immediate employment after completing their first degree, while 15% to 20% go on to further study.

Around 50% to 60% of sport and exercise graduates enter jobs directly related to their area of study. The remainder use the skills and knowledge they have acquired during their degree to enter the wider job market as graduates with a strong and applied background in human science.

Related Degrees

Sports Studies; Sport and Management; Sport Development; Coaching Science; Physical Education; Sports Therapy; Fitness and Health.

Suggested Reading

Guide to careers in Sport and Exercise Sciences
- downloadable from the BASES website below

Sport and Exercise Science: an Introduction
- Dean Sewell, Murray Griffin and Philip Watkins, Routledge, 2013

Physiology of Sport and Exercise
- Larry Kenney, Jack Wilmore and David Costill, Human Kinetics, 2011

Further Information

British Association of Sport and Exercise Sciences
www.bases.org.uk

Careers in Sport
www.careers-in-sport.co.uk

International Society of Biomechanics
http://isbweb.org

English Institute of Sport
www.eis2win.co.uk

Sport Scotland Institute of Sport
www.sportscotland.org.uk/sisport

Sports Institute Northern Ireland
www.sini.co.uk

Chartered Institute for the Management of Sport and Physical Activity
www.cimspa.co.uk

UK Sport
www.uksport.gov.uk

Irish Sports Council
www.irishsportscouncil.ie

Town and Country Planning

Original article by Huw Thomas, Department of City and Regional Planning, University of Cardiff

Introduction

The Royal Town Planning Institute (RTPI) defines its basic discipline as 'spatial planning' and says that planning education should seek to "promote critical thinking about space and place as the basis for action or intervention." Spatial planning is regarded as much more than the operation of any statutory land-use system, or the broader historical concepts of town and country, or urban and regional planning, although it certainly embraces all of these.

Initial planning education is made up of three elements, two of which require academic study: 'spatial planning education' and 'specialist planning education'. The third element, known as the 'Assessment of Professional Competence' (APC), requires a period of structured experience in the workplace, culminating in a formal process of assessment.

Spatial planning education should be designed to provide a broad understanding of the main principles relevant to the making of place and the mediation of space, in particular sustainability, and of alternative ways in which such principles can be applied in practice. Emphasis should be placed on the integration of relevant knowledge, skills and values so as to produce rounded appreciation of how spatial planning can significantly enhance people's lives by improving the quality of place and organisation of space.

Specialist planning education should be designed to explore ideas, perspectives and debates to a considerable degree of depth in one distinct area of planning. The purpose of this is both to ensure that the breadth offered by a spatial planning programme is complemented by a period of in-depth study, and also to provide an opportunity to begin the process of specialisation. For some, this initial opportunity to specialise may subsequently be developed to a much higher level through professional experience, further in-depth study or lifelong learning. Although the RTPI does not seek to restrict what might qualify as a specialism, 'regeneration', 'environmental management', 'urban design', 'transport planning' and 'planning research' are examples of the scale expected.

Programmes that provide both the spatial and specialist element of planning education are now known as 'combined planning programmes'. The RTPI believes that a healthy planning educational sector will be characterised over the next few years by a rich diversity of provision, with a range of spatial, specialist and combined programmes on offer to potential students.

Degree Courses

Students wishing to fulfil the RTPI's requirements for initial planning education must complete both its spatial and specialist elements. A four-year combined planning programme is required at undergraduate level to cover both these elements together. Students may alternatively choose to take an accredited three-year undergraduate programme covering only the spatial element of initial planning education but, in order to become Chartered Town Planners, they must subsequently complete an accredited specialist planning programme at graduate level which, if desired, could be taken at another planning school.

As an example, one school is now offering a brand new, restructured, fully accredited, four-year BSc in City and Regional Planning, which includes a placement in year three. The school also provides a choice of five areas of specialist study in the form of a one-year Masters Degree.

Career Opportunities

Planners work in a wide range of places and for a wide range of employers. Many follow careers in the private sector for consultancies; others choose the public sector, advising government or working for agencies providing specialist advice on the environment.

Like the construction industry generally, planning has highs and lows reflecting the state of the national economy. In the downturn that started in 2008, the building sector shrank considerably and with it opportunities for town planners. However, the UK construction industry has turned around in 2014 to become one of the fastest-growing sectors in the economy, offering new hope for planners in the years to come. The government's new National Planning Policy Framework, intended to make the planning system less complex and more accessible, has prompted fierce debate between traditionalists and reformers. Insiders fear that the new proposals could lead to both job cuts in the industry and shortcuts in working practice.

The environmental field is a growing area of work, offering increasing opportunities for professionals to become involved in the planning process for environmentally sensitive development schemes.

Planners have the opportunity to become involved in a wide range of disciplines, from traditional statutory planning through transport, regeneration, urban design and beyond. Planning's engagement with key national and international issues, such as climate change, housing supply and building sustainable communities, means that its profile is increasingly significant.

Related Degrees

Urban Planning; City and Regional Planning; Urban Regeneration; Planning and Development; Design Development and Regeneration.

Suggested Reading

Urban and Regional Planning
- Peter Hall and Mark Tewdwr-Jones, Routledge, 2010

Urban and Environmental Planning in the UK
- Yvonne Rydin, Palgrave Macmillan, 2003

Planning and Urban Change
- Stephen Ward, Sage Publications, 2004

Town & Country Planning in the UK
- Barry Cullingworth and Vincent Nadin, Routledge, 2014

Further Information

Royal Town Planning Institute
www.rtpi.org.uk

Planning Officers Society
www.planningofficers.org.uk

Planning Portal
www.planningportal.gov.uk

Irish Planning Institute
http://ipi.ie

Veterinary Medicine

Original article adapted from material supplied by the Royal College of Veterinary Surgeons

Introduction

There are eight universities in the United Kingdom and one in Ireland offering undergraduate Veterinary Medicine degree courses: Bristol, Cambridge, Edinburgh, Glasgow, Liverpool, London (Royal Veterinary College), Nottingham, Surrey and University College Dublin. The length of the course is five years (six years at Cambridge).

The number of applications for entry to the Veterinary Schools far exceeds the number of places available. It is important to remember therefore that applicants who satisfy general entrance and course requirements are not necessarily guaranteed a place. Students applying for places on the veterinary degrees at either Cambridge or the Royal Veterinary College must also register for the BioMedical Admissions Test (BMAT) as it is a requirement for each of these universities.

As well as the academic requirements, all of the university Veterinary Schools require candidates to show evidence of their interest and commitment by having gained experience of working in a veterinary practice and working with and handling animals, including livestock.

Degree Courses

The first two years are traditionally pre-clinical, involving lectures, practicals and tutorials, with a focus on the healthy animal, although the newer courses in the UK, at Surrey and Nottingham, offer a more integrated programme throughout the five years. While the title of the modules may vary, a typical university course will include anatomy, embryology, histology and physiology. You would also spend some time studying biochemistry, genetics, immunology and animal husbandry. You will learn about agriculture and will also study the nutrition and housing of animals.

Disease processes are studied in pathology, while courses on infectious disease and parasitology deal with the organisms that cause disease. You will become familiar with drugs used to combat disease and a course in pharmacology helps in this direction. Later in the degree course, in the clinical or final stage over your last two years, you will spend time on various aspects of veterinary clinical science.

You are likely to be away from university, spending much of your time at the school's veterinary field station. When animals are diseased, their use for food is affected; you therefore study Veterinary Public Health (VPH), which encompasses issues relating to animals and the environment and food production methods as well as exposure to practical matters related to VPH e.g. community health.

In the earlier vacations during the course, you will normally be expected to spend time working on farms, in stables and in kennels, on what are known as extra-mural rotations. Later in the course, you will be expected to work in an abattoir and with veterinary surgeons in practice (possibly abroad).

The veterinary degree awarded by the universities listed above confers on the holders the right to register and become a member of the Royal College of Veterinary Surgeons (MRCVS), and have your name listed within the RCVS Register of Members. The Surrey course has not yet produced any graduates but the University is currently liaising with the RCVS to ensure that a Recognition Order will be made in 2019. Every veterinary surgeon has an obligation to deal with emergencies in any species at any time. Anyone contemplating a career in veterinary practice should remember this. A veterinary surgeon is a veterinary surgeon 24 hours a day, 365 days a year.

Career Opportunities

There are career opportunities in a number of areas including:

- **General Practice** - The veterinary surgeon is responsible for the maintenance of health and production of farm or domestic animals, for the prevention of disease and for the medical and surgical treatment of animals.

- **Veterinary Teaching and Research** - Teaching and research is undertaken at the Veterinary Schools and at research institutes, departments financed by the Government, in laboratories and by private enterprise. Many careers in research span the interface between human and veterinary medicine.

- **The Department for Environment, Food and Rural Affairs (DEFRA)** - A large staff, including veterinary surgeons, is maintained to control major epidemics. Other opportunities exist in commerce and industry, in the public health service and in countries overseas.

There is a growing trend towards specialisation in the veterinary profession within animal groups, such as farm animals, small animals and horses, or within disciplines, such as cardiology or anaesthesia. Any specialisation can only take place after first obtaining a veterinary science degree. There is a wide range of further postgraduate qualifications available, many of which can be taken by those working in practice.

Related Degrees

Bioveterinary Science; Equine Science; Veterinary Nursing; Animal Science; Veterinary Conservation Medicine; Pre-Veterinary Science; Animal Nutrition and Physiology; Animal Science, Care and Management.

Suggested Reading

Getting into Veterinary School
- James Barton, Trotman, 2013

Vet on Call: my First Year as an Out-of-Hours Vet
- Marc Abraham, Ebury Press, 2011

Small Animal Surgery Secrets
- Joseph Harari, Hanley and Belfus, 2004

Veterinary Science...for all walks of life
- series of short films viewable on the VetCareers channel on YouTube

Further Information

Royal College of Veterinary Surgeons
www.rcvs.org.uk

VetCareers Channel on YouTube
www.youtube.com/vetcareers

BMAT
www.admissionstestingservice.org/for-test-takers/bmat/about-bmat

Department for Environment, Food and Rural Affairs
www.gov.uk/government/organisations/department-for-environment-food-rural-affairs

The Nerdy Vet's Vet School Success
http://vetschoolsuccess.com

Veterinary Ireland
www.veterinary-ireland.org

Veterinary Council of Ireland
www.vci.ie

Zoology

Original article by Professor R McNeill Alexander, Leeds University

Introduction

Zoology is about animals, including the whole range from protozoans (although these are no longer formally included in the animal kingdom) to humans. It is about corals, beetles, dinosaurs, lions and all the rest. Zoology is also about all aspects of the structure and lives of animals. It includes the biochemistry of animals, not so much the universal processes of the tricarboxylic acid cycle and suchlike, which are studied mainly in biochemistry courses, but more special processes such as the metabolic tricks that enable tapeworms to live in the anaerobic environment of our guts. It includes the structure of animals, of their cells, their organs and their whole bodies, the amazing diversity of form in the animal kingdom and the ways in which structure is adapted to different ways of life. It is about how animal bodies work, dealing with all aspects of physiology but taking special notice of differences between animal groups. If you study physiology at university you will learn how 'typical' muscles (in practice that means frog muscles) work, but if you study zoology you will learn also about many other kinds of muscle: the muscles of insect wings with their built-in resonance, the special muscles that lock clams shut, and so on. Zoology includes the behaviour of animals, how their nervous systems control their behaviour and why particular behaviour patterns have evolved.

Zoology includes animal ecology, the study of the interactions of animal populations with each other, with plants and with the physical environment. Behavioural ecology asks what are the best ways to behave that will be favoured by natural selection. Should a redshank eat every worm it finds or just the big juicy ones, should a stag fight a rival and risk injury, and so on? Finally, zoology includes evolutionary theory, both the basic theory of how evolution works, and the evolutionary history of animals.

Degree Courses

Zoology is not all like the natural history programmes on television. It is about gorillas and whales and strange animals in exotic places, but there is a lot more to it than that. It involves painstaking work in laboratories with advanced, complex equipment. It involves difficult concepts, some of them mathematical. It involves muddy fieldwork and messy, sometimes smelly, dissections.

You should be prepared for dissection (that means cutting up dead animals). Some schools now do little or no dissection, and zoologists on degree courses do much less than in the past, but a limited amount of dissection is generally regarded as an essential (and very rewarding) part of a degree course in zoology. You cannot really appreciate how an animal is built until you yourself have taken it apart, and zoologists need dissecting skills for many kinds of research. Nearly all the zoologists I know have a profound respect for life and are careful not to cause pain to animals, but feel that it is justifiable to kill a few members of common species both for research and for teaching, and also of course to use animals that have died naturally. If you feel otherwise you probably ought to avoid zoology (and most other biological subjects).

Zoology is not an easy option for students who have trouble with physics and mathematics. Zoologists use physics to explain how nerves, muscles and cilia work; to sort out the osmotic problems of life in fresh water; to understand the heat balance of desert animals; and for many other purposes. The mathematics we use is not just statistics (though that is important). We use mechanics to explain how people and other animals run, how fish swim and how birds fly; we use computer models to develop ecological theories; and we use calculus to work out optimum strategies for behaviour and reproduction. We also use chemistry, as is well known. Most zoology lecturers assume that their students have a good basic knowledge of biology but may know less about some of the other sciences and teach accordingly.

Many people study zoology simply because they are interested in animals (an excellent reason). Others have more practical motives. Zoology is the essential basis for conservation work, and for understanding the effects of pollution. It deals with agricultural pests, with parasites that cause disease in humans and farm animals and with vectors (such as mosquitoes) that transmit diseases. It is important for commercial fisheries and for aquaculture. Finally, much of our understanding of humans comes from research done by zoologists on other species.

Career Opportunities

Graduates enter posts in the medical/veterinary industries and professions, the Civil Service, agricultural industries, pharmacy, teaching and also financial and general administrative/management careers

Related Degrees

Animal Biology; Applied Zoology; Zoology with Industrial Experience; Parasitology; Marine Zoology; Biological Sciences (Zoology); Animal Ecology.

Suggested Reading

How Animals Work
- Knut Schmidt-Nielsen, Cambridge University Press, 2003

The Blind Watchmaker
- Richard Dawkins, Penguin, 2006

Oxford Dictionary of Zoology
- Michael Allaby, OUP Oxford, 2014

Integrated Principles of Zoology
- Cleveland P Hickman et al, McGraw-Hill Higher Education, 2013

The Naked Ape
- Desmond Morris, Vintage, 2005

Further Information

Zoological Society of London
www.zsl.org

Edinburgh Zoo
www.edinburghzoo.org.uk

British and Irish Association of Zoos and Aquariums
www.biaza.org.uk

The Electronic Zoo
http://netvet.wustl.edu/ssi.htm

Dublin Zoo
www.dublinzoo.ie

Sport and Exercise Therapy - Zoology